BRISBANE BURNS

HOW THE GREAT FIRES OF 1864 SHAPED A CITY AND ITS PEOPLE

SHARYN MERKLEY

First published 2017
Australian Academic Press Group Pty. Ltd.
18 Victor Russell Drive
Samford Valley QLD 4520
Australia
www.australianacademicpress.com.au

Copyright © 2017 Sharyn Merkley.

Copying for educational purposes
The Australian Copyright Act 1968 (Cwlth) allows a maximum of one chapter or 10% of this book, whichever is the greater, to be reproduced and/or communicated by any educational
institution for its educational purposes provided that the educational institution
(or the body that administers it) has given a remuneration notice to Copyright Agency Limited (CAL) under the Act.
For details of the CAL licence for educational institutions contact:
Copyright Agency Limited, 19/157 Liverpool Street, Sydney, NSW 2000.
E-mail info@copyright.com.au

Production and communication for other purposes
Except as permitted under the Act, for example a fair dealing for the purposes
of study, research, criticism or review, no part of this book may be reproduced,
stored in a retrieval system, or transmitted in any form or by any means electronic,
mechanical, photocopying, recording or otherwise without prior written permission
of the copyright holder.

ISBN: 9781925644005 (paperback)
         9781925644012 (ebook)

Front cover main picture: Queen Street December 2 1864.

Publisher: Stephen May
Cover design: Luke Harris, Working Type Studio
Typesetting: Australian Academic Press
Printing: Lightning Source

Contents

Acknowledgments	v
About the Author	vii
Map of the Fires	ix
Introduction	x
Photograph of Queen Street 1864	xii
1 Queen Street 1864	1

The Fire of April 11

2 Edward William Fegan – The grocer who made history	7
3 Rowland Illidge – The gentleman hairdresser	11
4 Richard Ash Kingsford – Grandfather of 'Smithy'	15
5 Simon Fraser and John Francis Buckland – A formidable duo	21
6 North Brisbane Hotel – A treasure trove of tales	25
7 The Brisbane Volunteer Fire Brigade – 'Useless', said the Press	39
8 The 12th Regiment – Unruly Redcoats	45
9 John Phillip Jost – A pesky pork sausage maker	53
10 Robert Bulcock – A shrewd politician	59
11 William Keith – Dented but not defeated	63
12 John Markwell – The ironmongering tailor	67
13 John Alexander McDonald – An indefatigable quite achiever	73
14 The smoke clears … for now	81
15 Refuge Row	85
16 Set for disaster	89

The Fire of December 1

17	Alexander Stewart – the 'Royal' Scot	97
18	William Hemmant – A purveyor of ladies and gentlemen's apparel	103
19	Emile Gaujard – The flamboyant Frenchman	109
20	George Cutbush – A rocky road to success	117
21	Donald Dallas – Dogged by disaster	123
22	James Collins – A starry-eyed butcher	127
23	Isaac Lenneberg – The Café De Paris	137
24	Albert John Hockings – A legacy of plants, trees, parks and gardens	143
25	George Edmondstone – Pragmatic Scot and honest politician	155
26	Augustus John Kosvitz – Scoundrel or Saint	163
27	The Victoria Hotel – A chequered history	173
28	The Sovereign Hotel – Dispensing utmost civility and attention	183
29	Benjamin Henry Palmer – Shadowed by misfortune	189
30	Nathaniel Lade – A tragic tale	199
31	James Robert Dickson – A most extraordinary citizen	205
32	The curious case of Mr. Pillow's Humpy	215
33	Dawn breaks	223

Postscript

Thinking Like A Surveyor:
How Brisbane CBD Got Its Shape   227

Endnotes   **231**

Cast of Characters   **239**

Bibliography   **245**

Acknowledgments

Compiling family histories requires a lot of research. This book was no exception. My sincere thanks goes to the well resourced and friendly staffed John Oxley Library from which all of the pictures in this book stem, except for the images for AJ Hockings sourced from the Brisbane City Council. The advertisements and notices featured throughout are drawn from Pugh's Almanac, a fascinating resource available online via the Text Queensland website. The Australian National Library's Trove website continues to provide a growing wealth of historical digitised print resources, making the research task of all historians just that little bit easier.

Thanks also to my publisher Stephen May who helped wrangle my manuscript into a publishable form and contributed to the opening text of each chapter explaining the progression of the fires. Thanks also go to other family members for valuable comments, feedback and editing suggestions. Their support is greatly appreciated. My son Erik however gets a special mention as his helpful enthusiasm in tracing down the information required for the map of the fires resulted in the addition of his Postscript to this book.

About the Author

Sharyn Merkley was born in Brisbane and is a family historian with a lifelong passion for the lost stories of the city and its people. She is a researcher for the Genealogical Society of Queensland, which involves undertaking a range of specialist research projects primarily focussed on early Queensland settlers. She has worked on the Annie Wheeler Project looking at the lives of over 2500 World War I soldiers and is currently working on an index of Battle of Waterloo veterans who settled in Australia after the conflict. She regularly volunteers as a library research assistant and is currently completing further studies on family history through the University of Tasmania.

With a specific interest in the local and social history of Brisbane, Sharyn was inspired to write the story of the 1864 fires by a chance discovery of a newspaper article about the personal impacts of the fire on the citizens of the young city. She was determined to bring to light the stories of both ordinary and well-known personalities whose lives were touched by the fires – people who contributed to the early commerce of Brisbane and helped shape its growth.

MAP KEY

A	John Markwell & Co
B	Bulcock Buildings
C	R A & J Kingsford
D	Fraser & Buckland
E	North Brisbane Hotel
F	Jost's Butchery
G	Parliamentary Buildings (Old Convict Barracks)
H	Cafe De Paris
I	Albert J Hockings
J	Edmonstone's Butchery
K	Victoria Hotel
L	Mason's Concert Hall
M	Sovereign Hotel
N	Ben Palmer's
O	New Town Hall
P	Bank of New South Wales
Q	Mr Pillow's Humpy
R	Flavelle's Jewellers

Map of the Fires

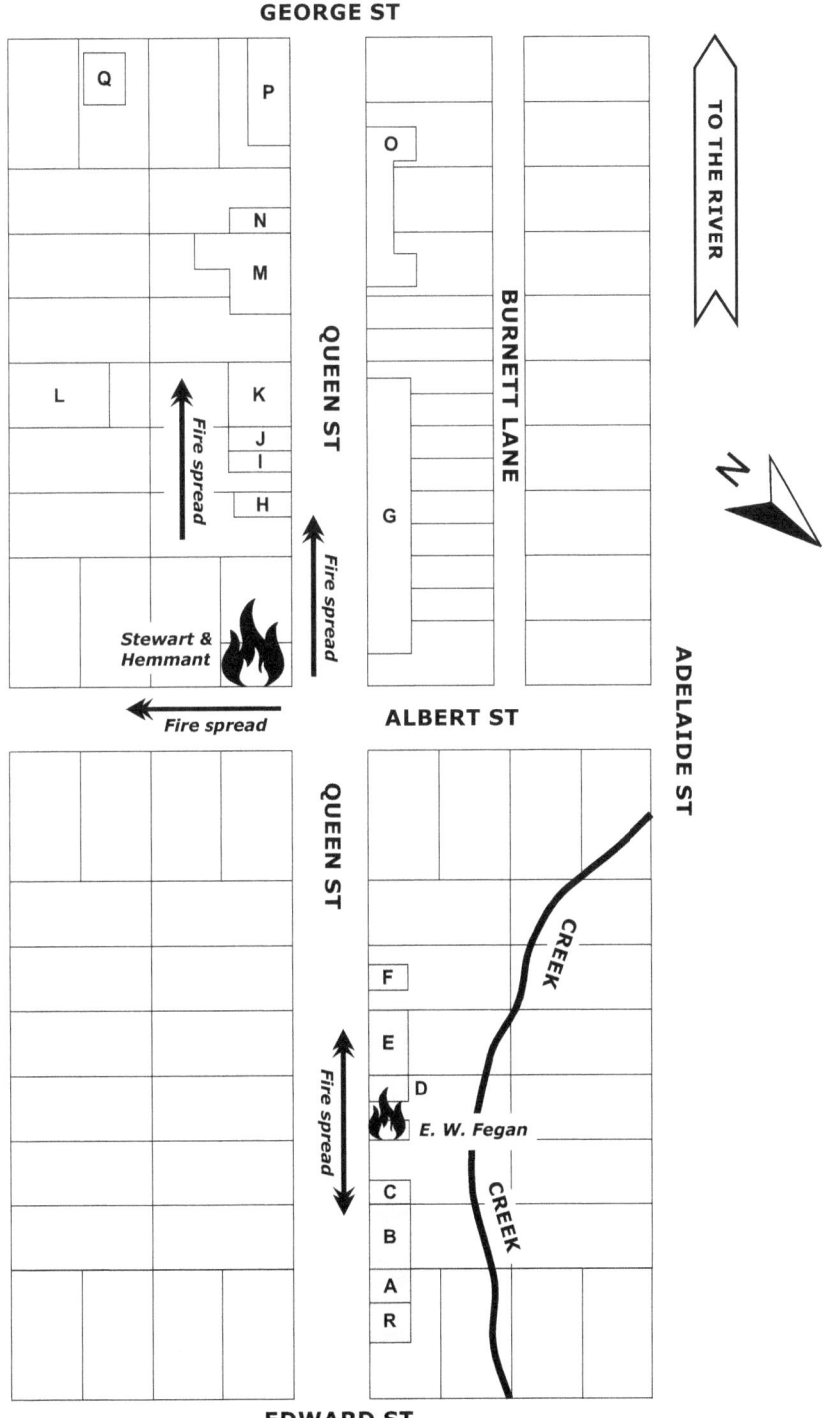

Introduction

In 1864, as Brisbane struggled to throw off the shackles of a harsh penal settlement, two devastating fires, one in April and the second, and worst, in December, swept through the commercial hub of the post-convict era colony. Nearly 70 shops, offices and homes in Queen, George, Elizabeth and Albert Streets were destroyed, a terrible blow to the growing community.

This book is the dramatic, uplifting, at times heart-wrenching, historical record of those who saw their dreams and hopes reduced to ashes, yet survived to lay the foundations of the booming sub-tropical metropolis that today is Australia's third biggest city.

To help the reader better navigate their way through the story of the fire and the people affected by it, and perhaps for those interested in their own family links to early Brisbane, several important reference tools are included within this text. The map on page ix helps place the events of 1864 in today's city blocks. The photograph on page xii not only provides a rare image of Queen Street in 1864, it includes evidence of the already changing nature of the street as substantial new buildings can be seen under construction after the April fire. Highlighted in italics through the book the reader will also find the names of local houses and estates, the ships upon which so many of the inhabitants arrived, and the newspapers and journals of the time that recorded events and laid judgement upon the city's citizens and their activities. Finally, at the back of the book on page 239 is a list of names and basic family information of the key people featured in the stories told here.

There were drapers, butchers, grocers, nurserymen, restaurant owners, jewellers, saddlers, auctioneers, members of Parliament, City Councillors, policemen, volunteer firemen, hairdressers, ironmongers, tinsmiths, publicans and ex-convicts.

On the night of both fires thousands of souls were out on the streets as flames took hold of buildings housing both businesses and homes, a frenzied scene of confusion and terror as it became clear that with no available water and little organised authoritative support, it was up to the citizens to save themselves. It was their response, the aftermath and recovery in the face of great odds that created history from Brisbane's darkest hours.

An observer listening to the frightful cacophony of noise from disintegrating buildings, barked orders and screams of fear would have had trouble untangling the vast array of accents as Irish, Scottish, Prussian (German and Polish) English and the newly-formed drawl of first and second generation Australians competed for attention.

After the fires, the rough wooden shanties built as the town grew, were replaced with splendid brick and stone structures, many of which would endure for another century and longer. The city fathers finally regulated the building industry, ensured piped water to the city and created the fire brigade, thus ensuring that even though fires remained a risk, never again would the city be threatened with such a disaster.

The legacy of the Great Fires of Brisbane are enshrined in the stories of the people, weaving through significant events in Brisbane and Australia's history from the convict era, through the gold rushes, riots and depressions to the advent of the motor car and the First World War.

Extensive research through newspapers, libraries, memoirs and other historical sources reveal, often for the first time, a rich and varied tapestry both tragic and triumphant.

Fact, indeed, is often stranger than fiction.

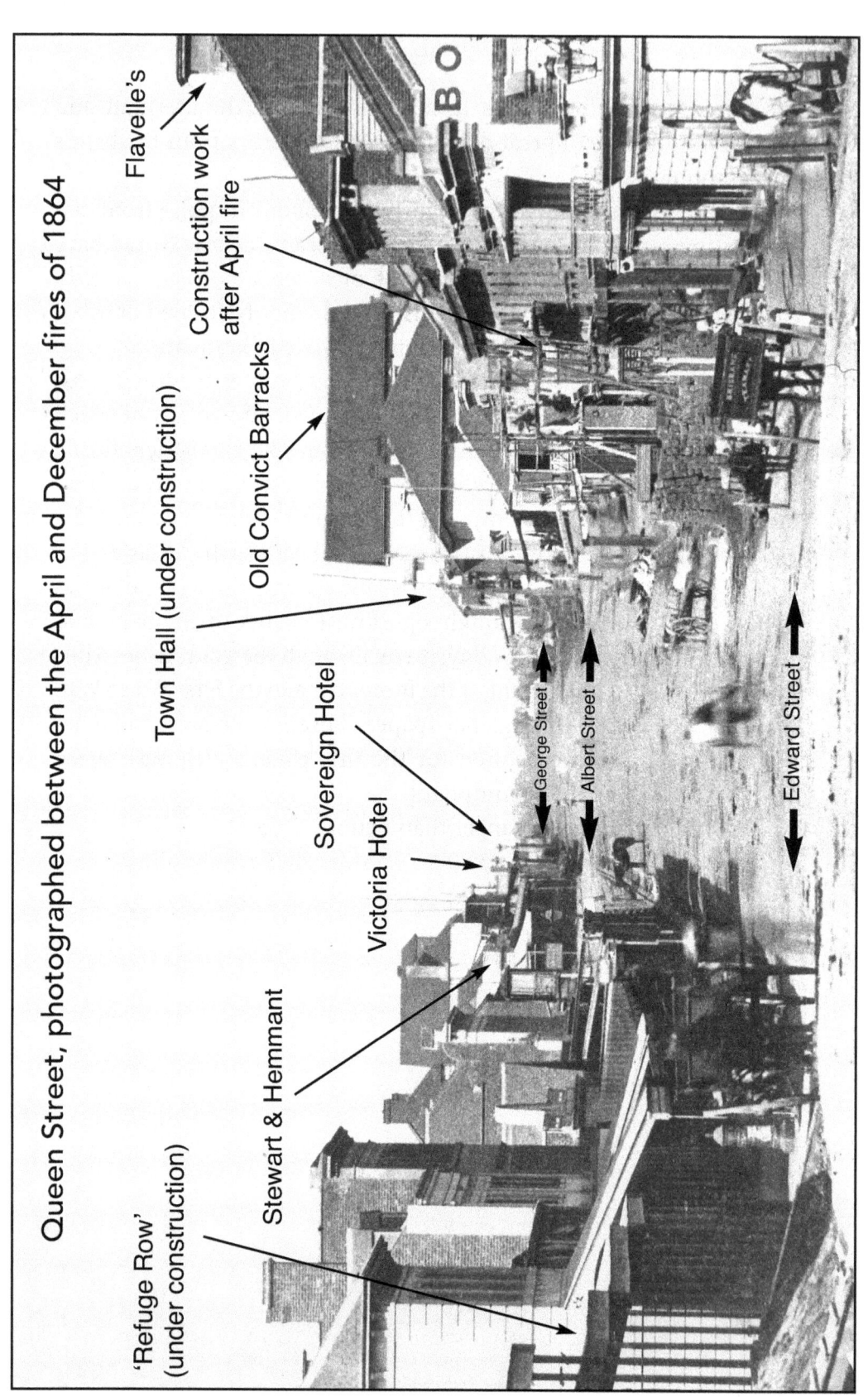

Chapter 1

Queen Street 1864

From Edward to George Street towards the river, the roadway rose sharply, the skyline dominated on the western side by the Old Convict Barracks and former Gaol, at this time serving as the Parliamentary Buildings and Court House. The building was constructed in 1828, extended in 1829 and stretched almost the length of the block from George to Albert Street – a reminder of the harsher days of Brisbane. Its dour face had witnessed the evolution of Queen Street. Most of the convict stone and brick building was two storeys with a central three storey tower. After the convicts left, the building was leased to new immigrants before being used for offices and shops.

Beyond these buildings and out of sight in the view accorded by the photographer's lens stood the new Town Hall, (a soaring edifice of brick and stone with a shaded arched colonnade along the footpath) still having its finishing touches applied. On the opposite side of the road at the corner of George and Queen Street, the new elegant two-storey Bank of New South Wales building flanked by wrap-around verandahs was nearing completion. On the eastern side of the street, the bank's temporary house of business had a large garden growing fruits, vegetables and bunches of bananas which hung over the fence and fed hungry passersby.

A few small shops were strung between the garden and the Sovereign Hotel which was built in 1843, serving the first free settlers in Brisbane. The block defined by Queen, George, Elizabeth and Albert Streets was the first portion of land sold to free settlers in 1842. The Sovereign's frontage was to Queen Street, featuring a large lantern post out front as required by law for all such establishments but its ancillary yards and out buildings occupied a plot through to Elizabeth Street. Largely built of timber, the long, low single story building had a shingle roof and brick sides. A verandah ran the full length of the front shaded by the overhanging roof.

Next door was the solid double storey brick and stone building housing a bank. George Mason's Victoria Hotel occupied the next plot of land, it also featuring a large lantern post out front, and having been there since the earliest days of free settlement. Its spacious billiard room was always in high demand. Another brick and stone building came next and then a stretch of largely wooden buildings housing a butcher, cafes, saddlers and drapers stretching to Stewart and Hemmant's wooden shop anchoring the Albert Street corner.

An assortment of wooden buildings stretched down the steep slope on the western side of Queen Street between Albert and Edward Streets. Some had brick walls and most were shingle-roofed. The double-storeyed North Brisbane Hotel and R A Kingsford's drapery store were the most substantial structures.

The street itself was a rough dirt track, surveyed at 121 links wide (24.4m). Its contours were more varied than today, the hills higher and the troughs deeper. Along the edge of road were deep, open drains, more likely created by the constant run of rainwater and effluent than intent. At intervals, rough timber planks bridged the gully allowing access to the rough unpaved footpath bordering the shops and businesses.

Wood was cheap and plentiful, construction quick, and the result cool and efficient. There were no building regulations and the majority of the population of Brisbane still lived within

Bank of NSW cnr Queen and George Streets

Chapter 1 — Queen Street 1864

the North Brisbane municipal boundary.

Many of the buildings fronting Queen Street had dwellings above or behind and every hotel was required to stable at least six horses. Merchants and traders kept horses to pull drays and vans. The blocks adjoining Queen Street were therefore a jumble of poorly-constructed flimsy outbuildings, interspersed with a few more substantial wooden structures and some stone and brick buildings.

Town Hall, Queen Street

Even in the early 1860s overcrowding in town was becoming a problem. The influx of immigrants on top of a high birth rate meant many more people lived within a small area. Cooking and heating was by wood or coal, often on semi-open fires. Gas lighting didn't arrive until 1865; candles, kerosene lamps, lanterns and even chandeliers were the order of the day.

Despite these conditions, shop displays in town were excellent as many builders favoured the newly-arrived plate glass. Retail premises were well-lit with an abundance of kerosene lamps. New goods arrived constantly by ship, and traders competed fiercely to attract customers. Two creeks flowed through the centre of town and during rainy weather these had to be waded. For the more adventurous, a flimsy plank of wood or a tree trunk provided an alternative. In dry weather the creeks became a string of stagnant pools.

There was no sanitation system, and nightsoil and rubbish was dumped along the edge of the river. The intersection of Elizabeth and Albert Streets, known as Frog's Hollow, was a swamp. The Botanical Gardens, the only park, had been allowed to deteriorate. A new cemetery was urgently needed as development encroached upon the Milton cemetery.

There was no articulated water to the town. Residents and businesses relied on their own galvanised iron tanks to collect rainwater from roofs or sometimes risked bucketing from the rank, slow-moving, muddy creek that ran between Adelaide and Queen Street to Creek Street. Where extra water was needed it was hauled across from an open reservoir near Roma Street about a kilometre west of Queen Street. The reservoir was little more than a dammed murky waterhole and prone to drying out. There were no fences to stop stock wandering into, and even dying in, the pond.

Roma Street reservoir

Queen Street might have been its bustling heart but the Brisbane of 1864 remained very much a harsh frontier settlement, its peoples of many and varied backgrounds, united by the day-to-day concerns of survival and the dreams of a better life.

The Fire of April 11

Brisbane Burns

Chapter 2

The grocer who made history

Edward William Fegan 1829–1895

> *From the middle of the city dense volumes of smoke rose and obscured the sky, while a lurid glow overspread all beneath. Presently the surrounding heights were brilliantly illuminated as flames shot upwards with startling fierceness, informing all observers that fire had gained the mastery in our very midst.*[1]

Around three-thirty on the morning of 11 April 1864, Brisbane's first big fire of the year crackled into life. Sergeant Lang, a police constable on his rounds in Queen Street, spotted a light burning in the window of Fegan's Grocery Store on the western side of the street midway between Albert and Edward Street. He soon heard a crash, saw flames, and began rapping on nearby doors. He enlisted the help of Francis Marriott a bookseller who lived behind his own small shop situated down a laneway which ran beside Fegan's, shouting 'Up you get Marriott, Mr Fegan's place is on fire.'[2] Pulling on a shirt and trousers, Marriott grabbed an axe and two buckets of water and raced to the main entrance of Fegan's store in Queen Street. He could clearly see flames through the shop's closed timber shutters and decided the best course of action was to break in so he could dowse the flames. As he began chopping at the shutters a horrified Thomas Holborn, an assistant from the adjoining shop who lived on the premises, came racing out. He had seen through gaps in the brick partition between the stores how strong a hold the fire already had inside Fegan's shop and feared that demolishing the front of Fegan's would ensure the fire's quick passage to his own employer's shop. He shouted to Marriott to stop. Marriott's wife had by now joined Francis on the street and was also trying to persuade her husband to cease his attack on the shopfront for fear of having to pay for the damage.

Hounded from both sides, but undeterred in his quest to extinguish the blaze Francis Marriott dropped the axe, threw two buckets of water through the shutters and then raced back down the laneway to get more water, rousing John Dowling, Fegan's porter, who lived in a shack in the yard behind the shop and had just begun to get up to see what all the commotion was about. The frantic barking of a large Newfoundland dog kept chained a couple of feet inside the store's side door into the laneway added to the din. The two men hastily exchanged thoughts on whether to use Marriott's axe on this door or another around the back that opened into a storeroom without a wildly excited guard dog chained inside.

Dowling took Marriott's axe and unsuccessfully attempted to break down the rear storeroom door while Marriott stayed at the side door with two more buckets of water. Returning the axe to Marriott in the laneway Dowling told him to have a go at breaking the side door down and he would deal with the dog.

Marriott was successful after a single blow. Both men scrambled inside, Dowling quickly seizing the dog by its collar. Another locked door inside blocked Marriot's progress. With the help of the axe and an onlooker who had followed them into the store, William Edwards, they finally managed to reach the main shop floor, only to find that the fire had by now ignited the roof. The heat was too intense. Marriott threw his two buckets of water randomly and they all fled the building. Dowling took the dog and ran to the rear stables to rescue the horses. Nothing could stop the flames now as they began to consume the adjoining store on one side and leap across the narrow laneway on the other.

Edward William Fegan had established his grocery, wine and spirit business in Queen Street in 1861 after bringing his family from Sofala in New South Wales, a gold mining area near where Edward Hargreaves famously discovered gold in 1851. He married Marie Claire Meillon, who was 18, at St. Michael's Church Bathurst on 6 November 1855. Marie Meillon was the sister of the great grandfather of John Meillon, the iconic Australian actor.

Chapter 2 — Edward William Fegan

Edward Fegan ran a grocery store in Sofala accepting gold as payment. In one consignment alone he sent 85 ounces of gold to Sydney, worth £300. When he advertised the business for sale in November 1856 he noted that the average takings were £600 to £700 per month.³

> **E. W. FEGAN,**
> GROCER, WINE AND SPIRIT
> **MERCHANT,**
> QUEEN STREET,
> BRISBANE.
>
> Goods supplied at Sydney prices with freight and expenses added.

The following year he was admitted as a partner to Meillon and Son (run by his father-in-law) a profitable firm dealing in general merchandise operating both in Sofala and Bathurst and eventually opening a branch in Sydney. As the alluvial gold petered out, Fegan consolidated his investments with a view to trying his luck elsewhere, left the partnership, and moved to Brisbane to become a merchant.

Following the fire that destroyed his store a lengthy inquest was held into its cause. After extensive questioning of Fegan's staff, neighbours and himself, during which time he must have felt a great degree of blame given the devastating outcome (the eventual loss of 14 buildings) it was decided that the fire was an accident. Fegan himself had arrived about half an hour after the fire had started to find his shop well alight. The next day he managed to salvage the company's books and papers after breaking open his fire scarred but intact solid iron safe. His horses had been saved by the quick actions of Dowling, his porter. Little else remained. His shop had been full of newly imported stock, much of it heavy and cumbersome in crates, sacks and boxes. Most was lost at a cost of about £4000. Insurance only covered half that amount and by the next month he was urgently requesting that outstanding debts be paid.

Luckily, he and his family did not reside on the premises. On the night of the fire he had raced across from his home in Margaret Street once alerted, leaving his heavily-pregnant wife and family behind, as they watched the towering flames visible four streets away. Edward and Marie Fegan had six children – John, Joseph, Edward and Clair born in New South Wales and James and Mary born in Brisbane.

Fegan had leased the old building belonging to David Pettie who lost other buildings in the same fire. The week following the disaster, popular architect James Cowlishaw advertised for tenders to erect a lowset brick shop for Fegan on the same site, but it is unclear who paid the building costs. Edward Fegan managed to continue trading, although in 1866 his business with Hugo Peitzeker (his former shopman and now partner) was assigned to trustees and dissolved by a dividend payment to creditors.

Mid 1866 brought financial meltdown to Brisbane. The London based Agra and Masterman's bank had collapsed and its customer, the Bank of Queensland, had closed its doors. There was rioting in the streets as hundreds of recently arrived immigrants employed on government infrastructure programs suddenly found themselves unemployed. Businesses, many already in precarious positions after the fires, had debts recalled and went bankrupt.

The last advertisement for Edward Fegan's store in Brisbane appears on 29 October 1869. The next mention of him is in an article about Brisbanites seen walking the streets of San Francisco, then the 10th largest city in the United States, which was in the midst of the Comstock Lode silver boom. Having experienced Australia's gold rush, perhaps Edward Fegan thought a new fortune awaited him in the silver city.

By 1872 he was back in Sydney, without a fortune, where he continued to operate as a grocer with a shop at 659 Elizabeth St in 1880. He died in Redfern in 1881 aged just 52. His wife, Marie Claire died 22 May 1892 aged 55 in North Sydney.

Chapter 3

The gentleman hairdresser

Rowland Illidge 1826–1907

The single storey brick hairdressers and perfumery shop belonging to Rowland Illidge was alight. Timber verandahs, shutters and interiors hastened the progress of the flames. The fire's intensity was growing, such that painted shopfronts on the opposite side of the street were beginning to blister and crack[1]. Yet Illidge, his assistant Thomas Holborn, and the older members of Illidge's family, having run out via the rear entrance, were now furiously removing what possessions they could before the entire building went up. Chairs, glass cases, an expensive cheval mirror, mattresses and an assortment of hairdressing implements were hauled out on to the street. Other residents and merchants in the line of the fire were doing the same.

> *A long high ridge stretched down the street – a hillock composed of all sorts of merchandise, piled up in rude disorder.*[2]

Rowland Illidge, 'Haircutter, Perfumer, Wig and Ornamental Hair Manufacturer'[3] and his family had arrived in Brisbane in 1859 just before Queensland became a separate colony. Originally from London, Rowland joined his brothers Thomas and Josiah in Sydney, arriving with his wife, Lucy, and four of his children in 1857. Thomas ran a grocery store in George Street Sydney which he had started 20 years earlier. Josiah also had a store in the same street having arrived in 1843. Rowland Illidge had operated a small perfumery business in Newtown, Sydney, before moving to Brisbane.

Under the heading 'The Toilet Saloon', Rowland Illidge described his business in Queen Street Brisbane as providing haircutting and headwashing 'at a very moderate charge, by the single visit, or annual subscription'. According to Illidge, such luxury services could 'not be obtained at any other establishment in Queensland.' He carried combs, brushes, mirrors perfumery and 'gentleman's superior leather travelling dressing cases with first class fittings'[4] as well as razors, strops, shaving soaps, lavender water, cosmetics, hair oils and dyes.

> **R. ILLIDGE'S DUGONG POMADE;**
>
> ACKNOWLEDGED to be the most efficacious preparation for strengthening the Hair ever offered to the Public.
>
> Ladies and Gentlemen are strongly recommended to make trial of its powerful restorative qualities, which have been attested by persons of high respectability. In numerous cases where the Hair had fallen off from illness, change of climate, or other causes, the continued use of R. ILLIDGE'S Dugong Pomade has been found a sure remedy.
>
> For Children's Hair it is both stimulant and nutritive, and entirely prevents the accumulation of dandriff, and is greatly admired for its fragrant perfume.
>
> Price 3s. 6d. and 4s. 6d. per bottle, and in 1lb. tins, for the convenience of travelling, 10s.
>
> Sold by R. ILLIDGE, Haircutter, Perfumer, Wig and Ornamental Hair Manufacturer, Queen Street, Brisbane.

Such was the confusion during the fire, many of the rescued contents of the shop disappeared. In the days following, Illidge advertised for the return of the missing items including the expensive cheval mirror – not hard to miss if it had been lying in the street. Claiming to be 'a great sufferer' of the inferno, he was 'compelled to relinquish business'[5] for three weeks until he set up premises in Refuge Row (temporary buildings on the vacant land on the Edward and Queen Street corner) aided by friends and customers who helped fund the construction. By August 1865 he was back in business in Queen Street, once again dispensing 'Dugong Pomade' with its 'powerful restorative qualities'.

Illidge was not the only merchant to make such use of the shy and docile mammal that grazed on sea grass in the shallow bays and estuaries of Moreton Bay. Dugongs or 'sea cows' were hunted and trapped for their meat, oil, bone and hides. As early as the 1850s the curative properties of dugong oil were promoted by physicians and others, with Dr. William Hobbs of Brisbane claiming that 150 gallons (680 litres) were exported from Moreton Bay in 1858. Nets 120 metres long and 8 metres deep were strung along river mouths and bays entangling and drowning the animals. During the 1850s there was a small boiling-down factory on St Helena Island and many hunters camped there between trips. Dugong oil was considered useful for stomach complaints, tuberculosis and hair restoration. As late as 1881 Dugong Pomade was still promoted as a hair restorer.

> A nutritious Pomade for promoting the growth of hair, and keeping the head clear from dandruff.[7]

Illidge's return was short-lived. In December 1865 the business was in receivership and the contents of his shop were sold at public auction. In March the following year a final dividend of two shillings in the pound was paid to his creditors. It would be another 13 years before he returned to hairdressing in Queen Street. By late 1884 he was working as a Ladies Hairdresser from his son Rowland Junior's home at North Quay.

Although he and his wife Lucy had 11 children, they lost five of them at very young ages. One of the terrified children who ran from the fire in 1864, Mr Illidge's 14-year-old son Rowland, would become a respected amateur entomologist and ornithologist and founder of the Entomology Society Queensland and the Queensland Naturalist Society. In 1934 his collection of beetles given to the Department of Entomology at the University of Queensland by his sons was acknowledged as one of the best in Australia, containing no fewer than 20,000 specimens – the result of nearly 40 years of collecting, minus his boyhood collection, lost in the fire.

Rowland Illidge Senior died at his home in Paddington Brisbane on 16 January 1907 aged 83. His wife Lucy died on 9 September 1913 aged 81.

Brisbane Burns

Chapter 4

Grandfather of 'Smithy'

Richard Ash Kingsford 1818–1905

Racing both north toward Edward Street and south toward Albert Street the fire began consuming more premises. R A and J Kingsford's cloth and haberdashery business was spread over two establishments – a small single storey store adjoining a more substantial two-story brick building with a fine front verandah. The main store had entrances onto both Queen Street and at the back to Adelaide Street. The smaller timber construction quickly began burning fiercely, communicating itself in short time to the timber verandah beside it.

Mr Kingsford himself, alerted to the fire early on by his neighbour Thomas Holborn as well as the growing din outside his windows, had gathered most of his staff to remove his stock out to Adelaide Street while he tried to restrain the growing crowd of 'helpers' out the front of his store hellbent on using whatever tools they had to help 'save' the buildings. Already he had witnessed their misguided zeal in attempting to rescue an expensive plate glass shop window by chopping it out with an axe. He refused them entry to the front of his store as his staff continued to race against time.

While much stock was quickly hauled out as the building's roof and upper storey burned, most of his household furniture and personal belongings were consumed. Efforts continued until the upper storey began to give way.

The fire was always going to win.

> *He invited forbearance for a few minutes, and when it was certain that the place must burn, he called upon those zealous persons to raze the edifice.*[1]

Richard Ash Kingsford was born in Kent, England in 1821, the son of a maltster (one who made malt from grain for brewing beer). Aged 30 he married Sarah Southerden. Arriving in Brisbane in 1853, Richard and Sarah Kingsford bought a drapery business in Queen Street. A popular and prosperous businessman, he was well educated and deeply religious with an immense interest in the municipal and parliamentary life of the colony. He was Mayor of both Brisbane and Cairns and a member of the Legislative Assembly for South Brisbane, but he will always be better known as the grandfather of Sir Charles Kingsford Smith 'Smithy' pioneering aviator and Queensland hero.

When R A Kingsford bought Benjamin Cribb's business in 1855, he shared his business experience with his new customers declaring that

> with an experience of 12 years in the English Markets, and a connexion with one of the leading Mercantile Firms in Sydney for upwards of 3 years, combined with a well selected and extensive stock, and close attention to business, he will be enabled to offer such Inducements that must secure him a liberal share of support.[2]

He opened his new business on 21 April 1855 selling shawls, dresses, mantles, ribbons, millinery, hosiery, shoes and gentlemen's clothing. He had chosen one of the most competitive trades in Brisbane, where half a dozen such stores would be in one block. When he relocated in 1859 to the site on the western side of Queen Street, he virtually faced Southerden Drapers run by Sarah's brother, Edward, one block south from the Edward Street corner and a prominent landmark in many early photographs of Queen Street.[3]

The Kingsford's first child, Catherine Mary (mother of Sir Charles Kingsford Smith) was born in July 1857, followed by Emily Jane in 1859 and Caroline Elizabeth in June 1861.

Richard's brother, John Kingsford, a Baptist pastor, arrived in 1861 and immediately after he joined the business, Richard, Sarah and the children returned to England on the *Cairngorm*. Initially only intending to be away about 18 months, tragedy struck in November 1862 during his visit when four-year-old Emily died after accidently falling into boiling water. Three months later, while still in England, Richard Arthur, was born.

Back in Brisbane, John Kingsford was struggling to keep the business going. After an intense rainstorm in March 1863, the sewer running between Adelaide and Queen Streets which in earlier years was called Wheat Creek, was blocked with rubbish and as water rushed down the hill from Petrie Terrace and joined the run-off from Adelaide and Queen Streets, it quickly backed up, flooding the shops and businesses from the western side of Queen Street through Adelaide Street to the reservoir (now the site of Roma Street railway station). Water invaded the lower floors and cellars on the western side of Queen Street to a height of about a metre and a half within minutes, forcing the Kingsfords from their dining room and inundating the attached warehouse containing bales of the latest arrivals of drapery, blankets and linen. For days afterwards, blankets and linen were draped over fences to dry in the sun, finally being disposed of at discount prices.

John was also the new Pastor of Jireh Particular Baptist Church in Gipps Street, Fortitude Valley, a 200-seat chapel designed by Benjamin Backhouse and opened in March 1862. John was so busy as part-time minister and drapery business owner that marriages were held at the Kingsford's home and shop in Queen Street rather than at the chapel. He looked forward to the return of his brother.

Richard Ash Kingsford returned to Brisbane in February 1864 alone, spending just four months attending to business and allaying the fears of brother John who had thought his management of R A and J Kingsford was only temporary. Just six weeks into the visit, Richard, John and John's family escaped from the Queen Street shop where they lived as the 11 April fire destroyed their premises and much of their stores. Stock valued at between £8,000 and £10,000, household goods, furniture and personal affects were lost, insurance covering less than half.

Any stock that had been saved from the fire was stored temporarily in local churches until they recommenced business in early May in hastily erected buildings on Gaol Hill (now Brisbane's General Post Office, and formerly the Women's Prison). Come June the same year Richard was off again back to England, leaving John to deal with the aftermath of the fire and the construction of a new shop. This time he travelled via Marseille, France, and in the following years Kingsford's advertised a large assortment of French products, Richard making a shrewd investment in up-to-date popular French fashions on his way home.

R A & J Kingsford rebuilt on the devastated site. The old double storey brick and timber, verandah fronted, shingle roofed store was replaced by a double storey brick and stone structure with plate glass windows in front flanked by columns of stone. The second storey was decorated with tall windows topped by arches. Kingsford's shop, offices and storerooms occupied the ground and lower floors while the offices above were let to professional tenants. Many telegraph messages and letters must have crisscrossed the world between John and Richard before the new store was opened on 18 August 1865.

It would be three more years before Richard Kingsford returned, still without his family. This time he attempted to sell some of the business and terminate the partnership with his brother who was still juggling work, home, and church commitments. Brisbane was in the grip of a financial crisis during 1867, so rather than lose money the business remained unsold and continued trading. Once again Richard returned to England via Marseille. Finally, in October 1871, he and his family came back to Brisbane. John left the partnership and pursued his career with the Baptist church becoming a full time minister. He remained as Pastor of the Jireh Particular Baptist Church until 1899.

Now back for good, Kingsford threw himself into public affairs selling his business in anticipation of a career in government. 'For Sale, the oldest established Drapery Business in Brisbane, with a first-class family and ready money connection'[4], the sale advertisement read.

He stood for election in November 1873 for the seat of Enoggera in the Legislative Assembly but was disappointed, losing to fellow Queen Street trader James Robert Dickson. Undeterred, he tried again two years later and was successful in being elected for the seat of South Brisbane campaigning for the release of large parcels of land to be subdivided into smaller farms for immigrants, cheap well-run railways, the 'expenditure of money in the districts where it was raised', free trade, 'a pure, free and national education', and a university.[5]

The rebuilt RA & J Kingsford building, 1870.

Kingsford was elected Mayor of Brisbane in February 1876. A full-time politician by now without business ties in central Brisbane the Kingsford family was able to move further out to *The Springs*, Tingalpa, purchased in February 1877, an already established 108 acre (44 ha) farm. The house was a small four-roomed cottage with 270 orange trees of various types, lemon, peach, guava, mango and apple trees, trellised vines, five acres (2.02 ha) of sugar cane and three grazing paddocks. A well-organised fowl house with attached yards facilitated the breeding of different types of chickens. Extensive gardens and a fully equipped aviary together with a collection of unusual birds completed the estate.

The following year, eldest daughter Catherine Mary married William Charles Smith and by 1884 they and their five children were living in Cairns where William was a bank manager. Richard, his wife, and daughter Caroline moved to Cairns to be near them. Son Richard remained in Brisbane in partnership in another drapery company.

Unable to remain out of politics, Kingsford, aged 64, was elected Mayor of Cairns in 1885. The same year, Caroline Elizabeth married William Henry Swallow, son of Thomas Swallow of the Hambledon Sugar Estate. Eventually Kingsford purchased the sugar company which he left to son-in-law William Swallow to run.

After five years in Cairns, perhaps concerned about his wife's health, or looking for a complete change of climate, Richard and Sarah moved to Launceston Tasmania purchasing *Fairview*, a large double storey house on 2 acres (0.81 ha). Despite the change – or because of it – Sarah died the following year in September aged 72. Richard stayed on and at the age of 71 married 23 year-old Emma Jane Dexter on 31 August, 1892 who bore him another daughter, Dorothy, in 1893.

Returning to Cairns two years later, the new Kingsford family settled at *Invicta* on the Esplanade. Age and ill health finally forced Kingsford to retire from public life. He was nursed by his young devoted wife until his death, aged 81, on January 2 1902. After his death she was 'very much prostrated'[7] and needed nursing herself. The following year she and Dorothy returned to Brisbane and ultimately settled in Toowoomba where Dorothy was Dux of Spreydon Girl's College in 1909. In 1916 Dorothy moved to Sydney where she studied music at the conservatorium. Emma Jane Kingsford died in 1932 in Buenos Aires, Argentina.

When Richard Ash Kingsford died in 1902, his grandson Charles was only five. He would never know that 'Kingsford' would live on in Queensland's history through his own and the achievements of his family and the famous aviator 'Smithy'.

Chapter 5

A formidable duo

Simon Fraser 1824–1889 and John Francis Buckland 1825–1910

To the south the fire had now jumped the narrow laneway beside Fegan's store and quickly began consuming the old single storey wooden shop which housed *Fraser and Buckland,* auctioneers, land and commission agents. The partners had barely been in business a year. Their stock was minimal – a few odds and ends from the previous auction. It was quickly cleared out on to the street along with some sparse office furniture and they watched as the building burnt to the ground.

Born in Inverness, Scotland, in 1824, Simon Fraser, his wife Lucy Anne and three children Alexander, Eliza, and Hugh left Liverpool for Brisbane in 1862. Simon was an ironmonger in Liverpool but keen to start a new career in Brisbane. They settled in Margaret Street, naming their house *Inverness Cottage* as a reminder of home, where they took in boarders in the early years to supplement their income. Lucy Anne was an accomplished seamstress and offered her skills on the new-fangled sewing machines to the women of Brisbane.

John Francis Buckland, a year younger than Simon Fraser, was born in Runnymede, Surrey, England in a hunting lodge that had once belonged to King John of Magna Carta fame. He joined the gold rush to Victoria in the early 1850s, married Ellen Gertrude Ashton and moved to Queensland in 1862.

Simon Fraser wasted no time enmeshing himself in the hierarchy of Brisbane, becoming a foundation member of the Grey St Congregational Church in 1866 and being elected to Parliament for the seat of North Brisbane two years later. Lucy Anne Fraser was able to give up sewing and devote herself to their growing family with four more children born in Brisbane from 1863 to 1870. John and Ellen Buckland never had children.

When gold was discovered at Gympie in 1867, Fraser and Buckland opened a branch office in Gympie, and Buckland became a director of the Lady Mary Gold Mining and Quartz Crushing Company. He served on various committees lobbying government for the treatment of Gympie as a thriving new settlement not just 'a straggling place with men starving on it'[1]. By the end of 1868 Buckland was a trustee of the new cemetery set aside for Gympie and continued his involvement in the settlement's affairs before leaving for Brisbane early the following year. Fraser and Buckland bought, sold and auctioned land, dealt in land orders, loaned money, and had interests in gold mining and ore crushing companies.

Privately they used their local knowledge to invest in land, John Francis Buckland acquiring a prize hilltop location in the current suburb of Hamilton where in the early 1860s, he built his residence *Balmoral Cottage*, later known as *Runnymede* and today called *Lochiel*. Simon Fraser preferred the breezy hilltops of South Brisbane and in 1876 built his home in Dornoch Terrace, naming it *Torbreck*, a Gaelic word meaning 'the brow of a hill'[2]. In 1932 Florence Lord, in an article in The Queenslander, noted that *Torbreck* was 'a quaint old place inside; with its angles and short passages' and it was 'more roomy than one might imagine' with 'uninterrupted views of the city from the back windows.'³ *Torbreck* remained in the family until Fraser's death in 1889 when it was sold to Mr and Mrs Praeger. In 1958 it was demolished and construction began on Brisbane's first multi storey residential block also named *Torbreck* and still a landmark on the South Brisbane skyline.

Today described as a fine example of a suburban estate, *Lochiel*'s masonry core originates from the 1860s. It was owned by John F Buckland for over 30 years until he lost it in bankruptcy in 1893.

Fraser and Buckland continued until 1873. Their 10 year partnership was dissolved when Buckland and his wife returned to England for a visit. At this time Simon Fraser also became MLA for Bundamba but continued an independent auctioneering career until his son joined the business a few years later. A measure of their success until this point is reflected in John Buckland's return to Brisbane with a pack of imported greyhounds. Buckland also continued an independent career as a commission agent and in 1876 began lending money. As the result of a by election Buckland also became MLA for Bulimba in 1882 which he held for 10 years.

From 1880 for eight years Simon Fraser represented Brisbane South. Both families continued to prosper. On Christmas Eve 1888 Simon Fraser fell ill with peritonitis and although he rallied for a short time over Christmas, died on 8 January aged 64 and is buried at South Brisbane Cemetery. For many years a member of the Congregational Church at South Brisbane, he was described in a memorial service at the church as:

> a good citizen, a good statesman, a Christian, a man; one who had done good service, the memory of whom was fragrant, and who had left his footprints behind.⁴

The boom years of the 1880s ended in 1890 with a crash in the real estate market and a rise in unemployment. Land values dropped and houses remained empty and unsold. The ensuing depression in Brisbane claimed many high profile victims. In March 1892, after being declared insolvent, John Francis Buckland was forced to resign his seat of Bulimba to concentrate on his financial affairs. With debts of over £20000 (almost $2 million today) he blamed depreciation in land value and losses in mining investments for his woes. His Parliamentary salary ceased, he owed rent on his vacated Queen Street shop and the following year the contents of *Runnymede* were sold. His landlord, John Cameron, eventually purchased *Runnymede* and, after Buckland's death on 21 September 1910 aged 85, set up a fund to assist Mrs Buckland.

Within days £27 ($2500) was collected with George Randall adding this opinion of John Francis Buckland (along with a guinea which was £1 1s as his donation):

> Unselfish, unobtrusive, uncomplaining of the straitened position in which he found himself through the reverse of fortune by which he was overtaken, after he had passed his prime, this eminently independent minded, high-principled, fine type of Englishman and colonist had gone to his rest.[5]

His wife, Ellen died a year later on 8 October 1911.

Chapter 6

A treasure trove of tales

North Brisbane Hotel 1851–1864

The North Brisbane Hotel was an establishment of some bulk. Standing beside Fraser and Buckland, it was built in brick and two storeys high. Yet it too had a large front verandah of timber and a flammable shingle roof. As the flames of the fire had by now grown in considerable height they were reaching the timber eves of the Hotel. It was soon ablaze, 'lighting up the scene with terrible distinctness, and filling the space around with a hot and withering air.'[1]

The residents of the hotel, having been roused from their slumber by the dreadful commotion outside, hastily gathered their belongings and fled into the street. Honora Thomas, a widow of one week and the latest in a long line of licensees worked desperately beside soldiers who had now joined the throng in Queen Street to rescue the furniture and household effects of both her business and home. Its demolition – the only defence now left to the fire at its southern front – then began in earnest under the calm direction of the city's 12th Regiment.

At the North Brisbane Hotel, babies were born, marriages celebrated and mothers and fathers died before their time. Budding musicians came to call, and new immigrants set up home. Convicts found a living, ex-soldiers discovered peace, and Brisbane had acquired a thriving drinking establishment. As well as Honora Thomas losing her home, Brisbane was denied a slice of its early history with the destruction of the Hotel, the first two-storey hotel in Queen

Street, built in 1851. An early sketch and a photograph show a shingle-roofed, brick building with a chimney at each end, and a shady timber verandah across the second storey.

The story of the North Brisbane Hotel has its origins in the final days of convict transportation to the Moreton Bay Penal Settlement. Brisbane was a place of secondary punishment (1825–1842) for prisoners transported to New South Wales who had committed new offences within the colony. By the mid 1830s the colony at Moreton Bay was proving to be quite expensive and already there were suggestions that it be closed. With parliamentary recommendations from London disapproving of transportation as a punishment, and promoting work on roads in chains as an alternative, the population of prisoners at Brisbane waned. Later that decade the colonial government in Sydney recognised the usefulness of the colony as an outpost of New South Wales and began exploring its possibilities for free settlement. In 1839, the remaining prisoners under Colonial Sentence in Brisbane (committed secondary offences) were returned to Sydney and replaced by 55 Ordinary Prisoners of the Crown, among them Matthew Stewart and his brother Thomas who arrived in Brisbane on the *Curlew* in July 1839.

Convicted of stealing a cow in Londonderry, Ireland, the brothers, both weavers, were sentenced to ten years transportation and had arrived in Sydney aboard the *Waverley* earlier in 1839. Londonderry was a centre for the weaving of linen from flax. Prior to 1820 much of the weaving was carried out on handlooms by family groups. After this time industrialisation destroyed the livelihoods of many home weavers and by 1839 Matthew and Thomas would have worked in a mill. Long hours, dangerous conditions and meagre wages were powerful incentives for supplementing income with a little cattle rustling on the side.

Surveyors had arrived in Brisbane by 1839 to explore and map the district and generally plan for future land sales. Twenty-one of the prisoners from the *Curlew* were assigned to assist the surveyors. A further three went to the Hospital Department, one to the Pilots Boat crew, four to the Settlement Boats Crew and the rest were assigned to general tasks. These prisoners were sent to Brisbane to assist the expansion of the colony and to prepare for free settlement, not merely for the sake of punishment.

Where Matthew and Thomas ended up is unclear, but they probably settled into the colony quietly as there were no newspaper reports of any exploits. Matthew received a Ticket of Leave in 1846 allowing him to take up paid employment or run a business within the Brisbane district. Earlier that year he had married Honora Minogue (no relation to Honora Thomas) on 29 January 1846. Together they would have 12 children, the first, Alexander, born in 1847. His new life of freedom nearly ended in disaster when, in the same year his canoe, laden with wood, tipped over into the river. Clutching the canoe, Matthew spent an anxious hour floating in the swift current of the river until rescued by David Pattie, master of the *Nelson*. No doubt he reflected how ironic it would be that just as his life was turning around it might end in this muddy swirling, unforgiving foreign river.

A sketch of the North Brisbane Hotel, circa 1854.

It seems a convict record did not prevent anyone from holding a publican's license and by 1849 Matthew Stewart was the publican of St. Patrick's Tavern situated on the eastern side of Queen Street between Edward Street and Albert Street close to the Albert Street corner. With the arrival of immigrant ships *Artemisia, Fortitude, Chasely* and *Lima*, the colony was booming and Matthew saw a chance to leave his mark. With the profits from the healthy trade at St. Patrick's Tavern, he purchased two properties, one in Queen Street almost opposite St. Patrick's Tavern, between Edward Street and Albert Street, and the other directly behind fronting Adelaide Street. On the Queen Street site, three blocks from the Albert Street corner he built the Donnybrook Hotel, for which his license was granted in September 1851.

In a Letter to the Editor in 1922 in The Brisbane Courier Mr. F. W. S. Cumbrae Stewart of the Historical Society of Queensland, discussing the history of the Donnybrook, stated that when the builder asked Stewart for the name of the hotel he replied he was a Scot but his wife was Irish and she chose Donnybrook as a reminder of home. Matthew Stewart was a convict from Ireland not Scotland, specifically from Londonderry, an area of which is called Donnybrook. Perhaps he was just carefully hiding his real origins. Once a convict had received their Ticket of Leave or Pardon, their past was seldom mentioned. By the 1850s up to 20% of the population of Brisbane were freed convicts and their families – too many people for the new colony to be fussy about their origins. Many of the residents were already successful and hard-working contributors to the new society. Although continuing to own the property, Matthew Stewart relinquished the license of the Donnybrook in 1853 and it was taken over by Edward Bond who re-named it the North Brisbane Hotel.

The hotel trade must have been profitable as Stewart purchased two more blocks of land in 1854 and, a year later, he bought a small boat suitable for river trade. Now settled at Holman Street Kangaroo Point, the family continued to grow – not a bad outcome for a man who started life in Brisbane as a convicted criminal. His brother Thomas only enjoyed freedom for a short time, dying at Matthew's home in 1857.

Like many publicans of his time, too many nights (and days) were spent as genial hosts, and drunkenness became a way of life. Even though Matthew Stewart was no longer the licensee, he no doubt spent many evenings at the North Brisbane Hotel amongst his friends. On one occasion in 1858, Stewart was so drunk he was taken from his home and jailed for his own protection and probably that of Honora and the children. He died of chronic bronchitis in 1873 aged 63, leaving his wife Honora and children Alexander 26, Mary Ellen 23, Thomas Henry 20, Michael 15, Annie 10 and Andrew 8. Sadly his death certificate also revealed the previous loss of six sons.

Edward Bond's time as licensee of the North Brisbane Hotel was just under 18 months, from April 1854 to September 1855. Little evidence remains of his time in Brisbane, except for the renaming of the hotel and the one remaining sketch he commissioned.

After briefly passing through the hands of John Campbell, the license of the hotel went to Matthew Walker. Thanks to the fascinating reminiscences from Letters to the Editor of his grand-daughter Pauline Seal in the 1920s, we have a unique glimpse into two years of the life of the hotel.

Sergeant Major Matthew Walker arrived into Moreton Bay from Norfolk Island in 1855 having spent over 20 years as a guard on the brutal Norfolk Island Penal Settlement. Pauline Seal recalled in her letters that Matthew Walker was the successor to Commandant John Giles Price on Norfolk Island. Just prior to the recall of Price, Walker was an Assistant Superintendent. After Price left, Walker became a Superintendent but appeared to be part of the Convict Police Force, not the military, and was never in charge of the settlement.

Born in Scotland in about 1809, Matthew Walker joined the 4th Regiment Royal Lancaster (King's Own) in 1829 and two years later was with the regiment on Norfolk Island. When the 4th Regiment on Norfolk was disbanded he returned to Sydney where, in 1837, he married an 18-year-old Irish girl, Jane Holliday. Their first daughter Mary Anne was born in Sydney the following year at the Carter Barracks (at that time a debtor's prison).

By the time their second daughter Margaret Victoria was born in 1840, they were back living on Norfolk Island and Matthew Walker was a Sergeant Major in the Convict Police Force. Matthew may have returned to Norfolk with Alexander Maconochie, the new Commandant. Maconochie, in his brief term of four years, instituted radical reforms to the prison system on Norfolk. He was a generous and compassionate man who believed that reform instead of punishment, rewards instead of cruelty, and respect for human decency would have more effect on the prisoners than the previous decades of harsh brutality. Unfortunately his reforms were often seen as leniency. Worried that Norfolk Island punishment was no longer a deterrent, he was recalled and replaced in 1844. Norfolk descended once again into a hell-hole of floggings, hangings and suicides.

Orders to wind up the settlement had arrived on Norfolk in July 1854. The previous year the notorious penal administrator, Commandant John Giles Price, had been recalled at his own request after investigations into his irrational and excessive punishment of prisoners. It was such a brutal period in the history of Norfolk Island that Matthew Walker chose to send his family on the perilous voyage to Hobart in 1851. The two eldest girls, Mary and Margaret, then 13 and 11, were to attend boarding school. Jane, his wife and the younger children returned to Norfolk where their youngest daughter Ella was born in 1853.

Walker, a 46-year-old veteran of the British Army, eventually left the prison service after Norfolk Island and resettled in Brisbane. The family was reunited when his daughters returned from Hobart. They left behind the two tiny graves of their daughters Matilda and Elizabeth in the Norfolk Island cemetery guarded by enormous pine trees and edged by the rolling Pacific Ocean. Walker and his family were warmly greeted by the large ex-soldier community. Chief Constable Sam Sneyd, a former military man, hosted the family until they could find a house. Quietly adjusting to being a family again, without military or policing responsibilities and living in a new community, Matthew Walker wondered what to do next.

Military veterans were always in demand in government service, respected for their organisational ability, leadership and discipline. Old soldiers also loved a drink and a chat and Sam Sneyd's cottage behind the old prisoners' barracks in Queen Street was the favoured venue. Perhaps, on one such occasion, the idea of being a publican was raised.

In April 1856 Walker took over the Prince of Wales Hotel in Edward Street. Ten months later John Campbell wanted to leave the North Brisbane Hotel. Sam Sneyd and Matthew Walker were already drinking mates and Sam Sneyd's local was the North Brisbane. Not long after that, Matthew Walker and his family moved house to the North Brisbane Hotel.

In addition to the hotel, Matthew Stewart, former publican and owner of the North Brisbane Hotel, still owned the neat two-roomed cottage in Adelaide Street behind the hotel which he decided to use as a school. Mary and Margaret, now 18 and 16 respectively, would be kept occupied and away from the negative influences of the hotel. The school had 22 students, including the Sneyd children with Mary and Margaret as teachers. Daily lessons took place in the largest of the two rooms, the other being set aside as a private sitting room. Once a month afternoon teas were held in this room for the students and their families. On Saturdays, Mary would take some of the students for walks over the Green Hills (today the ridge of Petrie Terrace). Stables and a grazing paddock completed the hotel grounds, and Walker kept a fine horse that complimented his military bearing.

At the back gate of the cottage garden was a creek with a bridge wide enough for a dray. Mr. Brennan, who worked at the hotel, used the bridge to cross into the back of the hotel carrying the daily load of water casks filled at the reservoir (today the Roma Street rail yards) at a cost of two shillings per cask. The water was very yellow and alum was added to clear it, although it probably still smelled unpleasant. Firewood was collected from the bush which in those days was no further away than Ann Street (about two blocks). Bread was delivered daily from across the river at Kangaroo Point and milk from Tom Haye's dairy just around the corner in Albert Street, where the cows grazed contentedly alongside the Australian Hotel.

Gas lights were years away and linseed oil fuelled the lamps. Pauline Seal recalled her mother describing Brisbane as a place where the nearby hills were still covered in forest, aborigines camped where city streets now run, and bananas grew in Queen Street. Other identities of that time recall the sounds of aboriginal corroborees drifting down from the hills surrounding the town and the blaze of numerous camp fires belonging to the local tribes.

The Walker years at the North Brisbane Hotel would be marked by adventure, joy and tragedy. Second daughter Margaret Victoria, an enthusiastic rider, frequently travelled from Sandgate where she held the position as governess with the Slaughter family, to her father's hotel. At times, she and Miss Slaughter became lost and feared encountering natives on their way into town. Albert Ernest Walker, the last child and only son, was born at the hotel in 1857 but he was to tragically lose his mother just a year later when Jane Walker died of a gastric complaint on 17 July 1858 aged 39. Jane Walker had spent 21 years supporting her husband Matthew through some of the toughest times in Norfolk Island's history. Even the balmy climate, abundant sub-tropical forests and rich agriculture of Norfolk Island could not have made up for the human toll.

Before she died, Jane was able to see one of her daughters settled. Rather than keep the girls from the hotel life, their school and home still brought them in touch with the visitors and lodgers.

One young man, James Bartley, a customs officer and resident at the North Brisbane Hotel, caught the eye of the eldest girl, Mary Anne Walker, and they were married in 1859. Late one night shortly after the Walkers had settled at the hotel, four young musicians, including an exotic foreigner, Andreas Siegel, called at the door looking for a practice room. Dour disciplinarian and conservative Scotsman, Matthew Walker, replied with the words:

> Tut, mon, I would noo allow my hotel to be made a public show of by musicians drawing crowds to my door.[2]

Little did he know he was sending his future son-in-law off into the night. Andreas Siegel, or Alexander Seal, as he preferred to be known in the new colony, became a respected musician around Brisbane. He opened a music shop and eventually was known as 'Professor Seal'. In 1862 he married Margaret Victoria, Walker's second daughter, and they had eight children, one of whom was Pauline whose reminiscences of the 1920s provided a unique insight into their lives.

Matthew left the hotel just months after Jane's death, his two eldest daughters remaining in Brisbane. He returned to the prison service in New South Wales and married 29-year-old Ann Fackney just over a year later in 1859. He and Ann served as jailer and matron respectively at Braidwood Gaol and then at Goulburn Gaol, where he held that position for 18 years. In his obituary in the Goulburn Evening Penny Post on 15 August 1882, Matthew Walker was fondly remembered as 'highly respected … and held in kind regard by everyone who came in contact with him'. Teaching prisoners practical skills and en-

Chapter 6 — North Brisbane Hotel

couraging them to compete in the Sydney International Exhibition in 1879 (held over seven months in specially constructed buildings in the Sydney Domain) meant that 'many a reclaimed prisoner must be deeply indebted to him.' Anne Walker died on 15 March 1891 at East Maitland aged 61.

George Dickins, formerly a butcher from Fortitude Valley, brought his wife Jane and sons Thomas aged 15, John 11 and George 5 to the North Brisbane Hotel in about September 1858, taking over the licence from Matthew Walker. The Dickins family, who had arrived aboard the *Chasely* in 1849 as immigrants, had been forced to find work and new businesses after discovering that the land orders (legal tender for the purchase of land at auctions) promised by Dr. John Dunmore Lang were worthless. Lang had enticed immigrants to Australia on the ships *Fortitude, Chasely* and *Lima*, by selling land orders not ratified by the New South Wales government.

In later years as Dr. Lang sought recompense from the government for his failed scheme, George Dickins wrote a letter to The Brisbane Courier outlining the grudge the immigrants had against Dr. Lang. The scheme created by Dr. Lang was designed to encourage non-Catholic settlers to Brisbane and also to promote the possibilities of growing sugar and cotton. The Cooksland Colonization Company, of which Dr. Lang was the instigator, sold land orders which guaranteed free passage to Brisbane. George Dickins paid £100 for the purchase of 80 acres and secured passage for himself and his family. Dr. Lang never completed negotiations with the government in Sydney or notified the authorities in Brisbane of the impending arrival of the first ship, the *Fortitude*. Its arrival came as a surprise to the new Brisbane colony. Police Magistrate Captain John Wickham took pity on the new arrivals and, realising the benefit of so many able-bodied skilled people, hastily arranged accommodation for the immigrants even though he had been expressly ordered not to do so.

It quickly became obvious that the land was not available and never would be. In his letter, George Dickins outlined what would have been a better plan – to purchase a passage for each person for £20 which would have secured a government guaranteed 20 acres (8.09 ha).

However, the industrious immigrants all immediately found work or started a business, succeeding despite Lang and his schemes.

In 1861 George Dickens left the North Brisbane Hotel. It couldn't have been easy for the family, exposing children to the constant drunkenness and unruly behaviour of patrons. Early Queen Street buildings were quickly and sometimes shoddily built, but inside it was a different story. When he left, George Dickins auctioned off the contents of the North Brisbane Hotel. There were dining and dressing tables, beds, washstands, cedar chairs, marble statues, engravings and pictures and a quantity of books among which were 20 volumes of Encyclopaedia Britannica, three volumes of Gallery of Nature and Art and 26 volumes of Medico Chirurgical Review (a British medical journal)[3].

Lacking public spaces, the colony relied on hotels to provide many other services aside from alcoholic drinks, food and accommodation. They were used for planning sporting events, displaying the wares of commercial travellers, holding public meetings and fundraisers, counting electoral votes, auctioning goods and livestock, selling land and holding inquests. Even visiting dentists were known to open for business, no doubt hoping their clients had semi-anesthetised themselves in the bar before arriving for treatment.

The Dickins family returned to the butchering business and their former immigrant friends in Fortitude Valley. Not completely over the hotel business, by 1863 George Dickins was at the Royal George Hotel which still stands today on the corner of Ann and Brunswick Streets in Fortitude Valley. Two years later George stood for election as Alderman for the Valley Ward in the Local Council elections but was beaten by John Petrie (son of Andrew Petrie the first Superintendent of Works in Brisbane).

In 1870 George and his family sold all their possessions by auction including bedsteads, tables, chairs, crockery, kitchen utensils, garden tools, their poultry and even the saddle horse. George found employment with the Railway Carriage Department of the Queensland Government in Rockhampton. His wife Jane died in July 1878 in Brisbane. It appears that at the ripe old age of 65 George married again to another Jane, Jane Worton. Their time together was short and George died in the Benevolent Asylum on North Stradbroke Island of cancer in 1886, aged about 66, and is buried in Dunwich Cemetery.

Following George Dickins at the North Brisbane Hotel was another veteran of St. Patrick's Tavern, John Jones of Wales who, by 1860, was acquiring hotel properties. He built the North Australian Hotel which was in Adelaide Street a short distance from Albert Street, while he was still running St. Patrick's and, in 1862, purchased the North Brisbane Hotel.

When John Jones left Brisbane two years later, John and Honora Thomas acquired the license to the North Brisbane Hotel. At the time of the fire in April 1864 John Jones was the owner of the property and Honora Thomas, the licensee.

Jones returned to Brisbane and married Sarah Hitchings in May 1867, but five months later she died aged 49 at the North Australian Hotel. It was common then for there to be little time between one marriage and the next. The bereaved widower was quick to find a new mate who would act as housekeeper and often mother to children left behind. John Jones married Harriet Grant in 1868, but died in the first week of December the same year. His grieving widow, already a heavy drinker, died just over a week after her husband as 'the result of natural causes, but accelerated by her own conduct.'[4]

On Sunday 3 April 1864, John Thomas, new licensee of the North Brisbane Hotel, and ex-11th Regiment soldier, was enjoying the fine surroundings and convivial cheer of his patrons. He retired late to bed, feeling a little unwell. Shortly after midnight he was discovered dead, probably by poor Honora. He was only 38. His funeral took place the next day, Monday 4 April in the presence of Sergeant Hawkes and several members of the 12th Regiment mustered in uniform at his graveside who paid respect to their companion in arms who had served in the 11th Regiment They would gather again in just a week's time to tear down the North Brisbane Hotel to help prevent the spread of Brisbane's first great fire.

Honora, who was only 30, moved on, relocating to the Forresters Arms Hotel in Fortitude Valley where she transferred her North Brisbane license on 20 May 1864. Not requiring many of the contents that were saved from the Hotel and having nowhere to house them, they were auctioned off just two weeks after the fire. They included mahogany sideboards, iron bedsteads, leather chairs, dressing tables, washstands, cedar tables, oil paintings, engravings, kitchen utensils and equipment, a beer-making machine, casks of wine, brandy, ale, rum and gin. Considering all these items were removed from the hotel on the day of the fire, it is astonishing how much was saved in such a short time.

Within the year, finding the hotel trade difficult on her own, Honora Thomas had remarried, choosing Matthew Murray, a cab driver six years her junior. Murray was a violent young man who, with his accomplice William Hayes, proceeded to move from one arrest to the next. The hansom cab Murray drove was a surprisingly manoeuvrable carriage capable of carrying two people with two large wheels pulled by one horse with the driver sitting at the rear. The cab business in Brisbane was highly competitive and frequent fights broke out between drivers, and police were often assaulted when intervening. By March 1866 Murray had been convicted five times in six months resulting in the cancellation of his licence. These charges included disorderly conduct, assaulting a constable and furious driving (being in charge of a carriage where wilful neglect or conduct caused bodily harm to another person) resulting in 14 days in jail.

Removing his licence had no effect and in July 1866 an aggravated assault charge saw him spend two months in prison. Matthew and Honora drifted north after his disastrous start in Brisbane and ran the Criterion Hotel in Rockhampton before taking on the Picnic Hotel in Charters Towers. During their time in Brisbane they had a daughter, Mary Ann, who went on to marry and have a large family with

Charters Towers publican Richard Randall. Matthew seems to have eventually mended his violent ways, perhaps under the steady influence of Honora who died in1889. However, like many publicans before him, drink was his eventual undoing. On April 2 1890, after heavy and persistent rain, Murray, a little under the weather himself by the accounts of witnesses, tried to cross the swollen Millchester Creek (just outside Charters Towers) against advice from onlookers.

On horseback, he waded into the creek until it reached his knees. Almost immediately the horse rolled and he was thrown into the swirling creek. A couple of bystanders raced to his aid at a bend in the creek and grabbed hold of him. They were forced to let go as the current threatened to drag them in. His body was found the next day.

Back in Brisbane The North Brisbane Hotel was never rebuilt. John Jones, the owner at the time of the fire already ran the successful North Australian Hotel. After the second fire in December the same year, Alexander Stewart and William Hemmant (see Chapters 17 & 18) purchased the property and built a shop and warehouse.

In its short 13-year history, the North Brisbane Hotel had played host to many varied characters and events from Brisbane's past and provided a home and refuge to families, travellers and immigrants. One accidental spark wiped it from history, but the stories that remained ensure it will not be forgotten.

Brisbane Burns

Chapter 7

'Useless', said the Press

The Brisbane Volunteer Fire Brigade

Brisbane's volunteer fire brigade had only acquired a fire bell in July 1863, mounted on a tower in the yard on Gaol Hill next to a shed housing a single fire engine and a generous assortment of ropes, grappling hooks, ladders and hefty tools, reflecting the mid-19th century fire fighting approach of demolishing structures to starve a fire. It was this bell that pealed the warnings when the fire first took hold in Fegan's store.

By the time the engine made it down to Queen Street four buildings had already been consumed by the fire. The presence of the brigade in an already crowded street would hardly make much difference. The only water available, from a tank behind *Perry Brothers* across the street, was pumped onto the flaming wall and by now blanket-covered shingle roof of Kingsford's store. But the reserves were soon spent and the heat and breeze combined to quickly overcome all attempts to dowse the flames and protect the roof. The fire fighters were left to join the soldiers of the 12th Regiment in tearing down the shops still in the path of the fire.

> The engine was next to useless, sending only a "feeble squirt" into the fire..[1]

In 1860, soon after separation from New South Wales, Brisbane had seen free settlement for the last 20 years. Buildings and business had sprung up and recent immigration had swelled the population, but there was no fire brigade. A small population, limited financial resources, apathy on the part of the residents and the failure of the NSW government to show any interest, accounted for some of the problem. The Moreton Bay settlement had always been starved of money and the new Queensland government and the fledgling Brisbane Municipal Corporation had few funds and a long list of projects.

In 1860 fire destroyed a cabinet making workshop on the corner of George and Elizabeth Streets despite the heroic efforts of a volunteer brigade. Reflecting on the possible serious outcome of such a fire in the future, newspapers criticised the poor leadership and haphazard efforts of volunteers. They highlighted the inadequate water supply, lack of organisation and the urgent need for a fire appliance.

At a public meeting in October 1860, the Brisbane Volunteer Fire Company was formed and 36 men enrolled. They hoped for funding from the Corporation, the insurance companies and from public subscriptions. The Corporation was not forthcoming, the insurance companies seemed to be waiting for the Corporation to take up the matter, and the public subscription failed as many people rightly thought it was the responsibility of the Corporation or the insurance companies.

A paltry £32 was subscribed to the fund, much of it from the weekly subscriptions of actual members of the brigade. It was no surprise that the brigade was disbanded in July 1861 and the money returned. Brisbane was to be without a fire brigade for another year.

The next attempt at a brigade was prompted by the establishment of the Queensland Insurance Company in 1862. Investors in the new company agreed to import an engine which duly arrived in July 1862 costing £200. (The 'fire engine' was a steam driven pump with a hose on wheels drawn by men or horses that could draw water from creeks or tanks.) The fire engine was offered for the use of any volunteer brigade and the Corporation was coaxed into repairing a shed on Gaol Hill (later the site of the General Post Office) to house the vehicle. Another group of concerned citizens stepped up and the Second Volunteer Brigade was born.

Despite the fact that this group fought serious fires within the North Brisbane district, it attracted much more criticism than its predecessors. The newspapers, citizens, and even the Corporation seemed to forget that these men were volunteers who were once again having to beg for funds. Even though the recently acquired fire engine enhanced their fire-fighting capabilities, its every movement and action was condemned in the press.

In February 1863 a huge fire broke out in Ipswich's business district. Although not the responsibility of the Brisbane Municipal Corporation, it was an ominous event. With wooden buildings packed close together and no fire engine or fire brigade, a whole block (the western side of the Ipswich Mall) burnt to the ground. (Mr. Robert Bulcock, who was to lose his store in the April 1864 fire, owned a seed store in this block which was destroyed.)

The remnants of the Volunteer Brigade were called out again in March, 1863, fighting yet another fire for which they would be roundly castigated.

> It is a painful reflection that in a city like Brisbane there is not an organised body of men whose services could be availed of in such an emergency to render anything like efficient assistance. If any of the Volunteer Fire Brigade were there, individual effort may have distinguished them, but certainly united effort did not.[2]

Apparently the fire engine was useless as well. Even the tardiness of the church bells rung as an alarm attracted the attention of the press. Not surprisingly, the next day, two angry letters appeared in response – one from a volunteer and one from the secretary of the Brigade, Mr Howard Smith.

Few men, declared the volunteer, were willing to offer up their time and efforts to a brigade that was so criticised by the public.

> They have been called lazy scoundrels, idle rascals, and many similar or worse names, by those who, from their position in the city one might have expected more courtesy, if not more sense.[3]

He further offered that no body of men, no matter how well trained, scattered throughout the city would know that a fire had broken out unless some general alarm was raised and without the alarm 'fire engines could be but of little use.'[4]

Howard Smith waded into the argument, defending the Brigade. He pointed out that there wasn't enough water in the creek for the fire engine, and all efforts to use it resulted in it being clogged with mud. Also, as the Volunteer Fire Brigade had no uniform, its members were indistinguishable from other citizens, impeding their ability to command and organise.

There were two more fires, both at the Victoria Hotel in Queen Street. In May 1863, the billiard room was threatened by a fire which broke out in the bedroom above. Water was quickly obtained and smart work by some volunteers (not the brigade) extinguished the blaze. By the time three members of the Fire Brigade arrived, one of whom had hurried from church, it was all over. Once again the necessity of a bell to raise the alarm and summon the brigade was debated in the press.

In June, the Victoria was again the victim, but this time the billiard room and the stables were lost. The Volunteer Brigade was finally able to put the engine to good use with water from tanks at the Sovereign Hotel. Buckets of water were also thrown across the roofs of adjoining buildings, but to no avail. There was indiscriminate removal of belongings and furniture, some disappearing in the confusion, and many buckets of water dumped 'on places they were not wanted.' The case was made again for some improvements:

> It must have been apparent to every person who was present at the fire last evening, that there is a necessity for having a well organised brigade.[5]

> It is true that there is a Volunteer Fire Brigade, but it cannot be expected that young men, however zealous they may be, can neglect their business and rush to the engine at a moments notice. Whilst giving the brigade every credit for the zeal they have shown on occasions on which their services have been required we feel compelled to say that all their efforts will be fruitless until they adopt a better system of organisation.[6]

Finally a fire bell was acquired in July 1863 and mounted on a tower in the yard on Gaol Hill next to the shed housing the fire engine. It was this bell that pealed the warnings for the first big Queen Street fire nine months later on 11 April 1864. No further mention of the brigade is made in the following day's newspaper article.

A public meeting the next day (12 April, 1864) decided on a more effective fire service with the formation of the Citizens' Fire Committee. There was an aura of déjà vu, as the committee met to discuss a new agenda – water supply, building regulations and the lack of authority to raise funds. The State Government now had control of the water supply and the committee had to negotiate with two warring authorities. At the inquest into the April fire, the coroner finished with the fateful words:

> I also strongly recommend to the Corporation of this city that measures should be immediately taken for the formation of an efficient brigade, and adequate supply of water, to prevent the recurrence of a similar catastrophe.[7]

Still the Citizen's Fire Committee battled on. With the arrival of George Cutbush, a man with professional fire-fighting experience, and the calm resolve of Edmund MacDonnell, manager of Flavelle's Jewellery, the Third Volunteer Fire Brigade was formed. The Brigade, however, was still without support until a deputation of volunteers approached the Corporation and again pressed their case. Perhaps with the advice of the coroner still ringing in their ears, the Corporation agreed to fund a brigade. With a collective sigh of relief, the volunteers decided to disband.

But sadly, apathy, disorganisation and ignorance continued to haunt the Corporation and ultimately no further action was taken. In desperation the volunteer fire brigade reformed without funding and continued to operate as best they could. Its paltry fire-fighting equipment had been purchased by subscriptions obtained from members of the brigade and other concerned citizens. So small was the budget of the brigade that the equipment amounted to some pole hooks and axes, a length or two of rope and chain, some buckets and ladders. By November there were only 23 members left, and it was this group of men who raced to aid of the city on the night of 1 December 1864.

Following the December fire the Corporation, and its attitude to fire prevention and fire brigades, was vigorously discussed in the public domain. By the end of 1864 the volunteers at least had a uniform — supplied at their own expense — of white flannel with red facings, a black belt and a white glazed hat, but no helmet.

The Third Volunteer Brigade again disbanded when no Corporation support seemed imminent. By January 1865 however in response to criticism, the Corporation passed a number of by-laws relating to extinguishing and preventing fires which included a properly formed and paid brigade. With William Watts at its head, the brigade still included Edmund McDonnell and George Cutbush.

Finally, the fire brigade achieved a level of recognition and support that had long been their due. On 3 April 1865, led by a noisy band, the snappily attired firemen in bright red uniforms marched through the streets with a brand new fire engine as part of a torchlight parade to honour a visiting theatrical celebrity. They were presented with a magnificent banner inscribed with the words 'City Volunteer Fire Brigade' and the motto 'Ready, aye, Ready'.

Chapter 8

Unruly Redcoats

The 12th Regiment

Under the leadership of Sergeant Hawkes, the entire 12th Regiment, garrisoned nearby to the city centre, begun their own fighting response to the fire as the flames beat against the brick wall of the North Brisbane Hotel. First they worked to remove as much furniture and belongings as they could from the Hotel, then as fire took hold of the interior they shifted their attention to demolishing two small timber shops next door.

Resplendent in their high-collared, single breasted, scarlet tunics, white sash, dark blue trousers, and smart single peaked shako of blue ribbed cloth (a tall cylindrical cap with a visor and the ornamental regiment badge on the front), the men of the 12th Regiment of Foot East Suffolk arrived in Brisbane with their chief officer Lieutenant David Thompson Seymour on 13 January 1861. There were 27 'Redcoats' including a drummer and a sergeant, accompanied by three women and nine children.

It had been 17 years since the colony had seen a full company of regular soldiers. After separation in 1859, Governor George Bowen had been quick to recognise that the new colony needed some form of defence. Letters to the Editor of the day reported fears of 'gunboats running up the Brisbane and Mary Rivers', and the dangers of the 'hybrid population of "Nouvelle Caledonia".[1] No doubt the long-seated English fear of the French prompted such dire warnings.

Previous detachments of 'Redcoats' in Moreton Bay had been charged with prisoner supervision and punishment, but with the cessation of transportation to east-coast Australia, the new incarnation of soldiers were now honoured representatives of the British Empire fulfilling the roles of protectors and ambassadors. Although the soldiers were not officially supposed to take on the role of policemen, the reality of colonial economics meant that the cost of the detachment of the 12th Regiment was less than the annual wages of four police constables. Police were paid by the fledgling Queensland colonial government; soldiers by the British Government. Initially the Regiment was stationed in the William Street Barracks, but in 1864, it moved the new Barracks at Petrie Terrace.

Police whose work had included guarding prisoners and providing security at Government House were relieved to be able to return to normal duties. The citizens of Brisbane were looking forward to increased police vigilance and a reduction in unruly behaviour, while local socialites relished the glamour that the new commanders in uniform would bring to their soirees. While the arrival of the 'Redcoats' had been anticipated with some excitement, their first few months in Brisbane proved anything but uneventful. Within days, the *Moreton Bay Courier* was reporting on their drunken behaviour, 'they are likely to become a public nuisance instead of a benefit.'[2]

Many of these soldiers, including their commanders, were either newly arrived to Australia, had seen service at Ballarat during the Eureka uprising in 1854 , or had been present at the Lambing Flat riots (violent protests on the New South Wales goldfields) in 1861. Their resentment at being sent to such a backwater was fuelled by the knowledge that the regiment was to remain in Brisbane for five years without rotation. Drunkenness and unruly behaviour was already a major problem in the fledgling town with two or three hotels per city block. There was little real soldiering for the regiment to carry out. They resented being mere orderlies for the Governor and continually picked fights with the regular police.

Arriving in Brisbane in hot, humid January was a shock for the soldiers and their families and the requirement to wear the regulation uniform of woollen tunic over serge (woven wool twill) trousers caused extreme discomfort. Lieutenant Seymour wrote to Sydney requesting a change to 'a white loose uniform'.[3] Dr. William Hobbs, a leading medical officer at the time, added his weight to the argument claiming that the uniforms would seriously affect the health of the troops. No action was taken (definitely a too-hard basket item). This probably led eventually to Lieutenant Seymour looking askance at the men's habit of wearing 'mufti' (civilian clothes) during the day.

By June 1862, soldiers were often found working as labourers and mechanics dressed in plain clothes and returning to the Barracks at night where they would parade and drill in regulation uniform. Desertions were common, with almost a third leaving during the first two years requiring the posting of new recruits from Sydney to fill the depleted ranks. More often the men were guilty of the lesser charge of being absent without leave, many attempting to supplement their meagre wage with a day's work. Those that were determined to flee went west, often being recaptured in Ipswich or on the Darling Downs.

Despite the behaviour of the rank and file, Lieutenant Seymour, Ensign William Crosbie Siddons Mair and Sergeant Thomas Devonshire Penrose Hawkes maintained enough order, and the officers began to contribute as the colonial society had hoped. Both Seymour and Mair became prominent members of the North Australia Club and the Queensland Club.

Until Governor Bowen's request for a full company of regular soldiers could be granted, a temporary arrangement for the drilling and instruction of a volunteer force was made with the presence of Colour-Sergeant William Green of the 12th Regiment, a respected man with a pleasing manner. He was replaced in 1863 by Sergeant Hawkes who continued to work enthusiastically with the volunteer force.

Complimenting the volunteer movement was the Queensland Rifle Association which began in 1861 and eventually became synonymous with the Volunteer Corp. Rifle shooting contests between the Volunteers and the Regiment were common, hotly contested and often reported in the press, with the Regiment displaying considerable marksmanship. A wandering cow was the only reported casualty.

> It was, however, purely accidental, the animal happening at the time to be too near the target, and indistinguishable amongst the trees.[4]

The 12th's marksmanship reputation was also missing the day one of their number decide to take a pot shot at a pelican minding its own business near the South Brisbane ferry despite the rules about discharging firearms within the town. The pelican gently lifted into the air, the bullet missed its mark, continued across the river, straight up Russell Street and lodged in a post. Happily for the clumsy marksman, nobody happened to be in the road.

The 'Redcoats' had many talents. Sergeant Carroll of the 12th demonstrated his skill with a broadsword and bayonet in Professor Parker's Grand Assaut de 'Armes in May 1862. Sergeant Hawkes put his organisational skills to work in planning celebration balls and was the Master of Ceremonies for the Inauguration Ball of the Brisbane Recreation Society, and managed the ball for Queen Victoria's Birthday in May 1863.

No half decent Corps of soldiers is complete without a brass band. And so, in March 1861, calls went out for more volunteers, this time of the musical variety. Eventually six members were secured on the understanding that they would provide their own instruments except for drums, which would be provided by the Corps. The Brisbane Volunteer Band was born.

The first soldier to die in the Colony of Queensland was the 12th regiment's Frederick Dutton who passed away on 4 March 1862 from a lung complaint. He and his wife Emma Bailey had 10 children of which only four survived past the age of four. Dutton had been posted to Ballarat during the Eureka uprising in 1854. Lieutenant Seymour complimented the Volunteer Band at its first public appearance at the solemn funeral as 'well-performed and effective.'[5]

Further cementing the 12th Regiment's relationship with Queensland, Lieutenant David Seymour married Matilda Caroline Brown, daughter of W. A. Brown, Sherriff of Queensland, in St. John's

Chapter 8 — The 12th Regiment

Church on 28 January, 1864. Lieutenant David Seymour had so impressed the Government of Queensland that when they looked around for a new Police Commissioner, someone to take charge and reorganise the infant force, they went no further than the Officer in Charge of the 12th Regiment detachment.

> The selection of a gentleman so well qualified by his antecedents to fill such a post, must, we feel assured, be received with unmixed satisfaction by the colonists at large, and may be taken not only as a proof of their patriotism, but as a complete refutation of the charge of favoritism so frequently brought against the government when filling up vacancies in the public service.[6]

His appointment as acting Police Commissioner of Queensland was gazetted 1 January 1864. He finally resigned from his commission in the army in July 1864 and was appointed Police Commissioner from 1 July 1864.

Born in 1831 at Ballymore Castle County Galway, Ireland, son of a gentleman, David Seymour entered the army in 1856. He rose quickly through the ranks before arriving in Sydney July 1859 as a Lieutenant and Officer in Charge of a company of the 12th Regiment. He threw himself both into the colonial life of Sydney, gaining a reputation as a dancer and ladies' man, 'which led to his being favourably noticed in the photographic albums of the young ladies of the day'[7], and into the life of the Regiment, serving on countless committees.

Duly noting this advantageous mixture of skills, the commander-in-chief selected Seymour as the leader of the Brisbane detachment. While his men were supplementing their army pay by working day jobs, Seymour was also taking on extra shifts as Aide de Camp to the Governor, for which he was paid. Keeping up appearances even in the colonial society of Brisbane was a costly business. No doubt he jumped at the chance of

David Thompson Seymour.

Commissioner of Police and for a time he held both positions. Rumour was that he was reluctant to resign his commission while his Regiment was engaged in active service in New Zealand (a long running conflict between the colonial New Zealand government and the indigenous Maoris). Eventually he was persuaded by a mentor to overcome his scruples, resigning his commission on 12 April 1864. Recently married, there were many pressures on the young man – honour, duty, service, place in society, and devotion to family.

David Seymour went on to serve as Commissioner for Police for 31 years, retiring in 1895. When he took over the job in 1864, the Police service consisted of numerous Police Magistrates operating as Inspectors in control of a small number of constables. There was no overseeing officer and David Seymour initially had the task of bringing all the disparate parts of the force together including the Native Police totalling 287 men in all. When he retired, the force had trebled to 921 serving in 222 stations.

Seymour was a forthright and determined man, with a reputation for harshness and little tolerance of interference in his force. A fan of horse racing, he was a foundation member of the Queensland Turf Club. He and his wife Matilda had six girls. Taking the Commissioner's job had indeed improved David Seymour's position, not just in monetary terms but in the social whirl of Brisbane. With six daughters, he had many opportunities to extend his influence through strategic marriages. His eldest daughter Margaret Matilda married Duncan Alexander McNeil, Sub-Inspector of Police. Starting as a share and stock broker and branching out as a mining and financial agent, McNeil was also a Lieutenant in the Moreton Mounted Infantry.

Eleanor May married Major Charles Hamilton Des Voeux, who later became Lt. General. She accompanied her husband to India where he served with the 37th Regiment of Foot for almost 17 years. Her youngest son Harold died tragically at the Dardanelles in 1915. Seymour's third daughter Ethel was the second wife of Boyd Dunlop Morehead, 10th Premier of Queensland. Morehead's niece was P.L. Travers who wrote Mary Poppins.

Not content with his success in marrying off his daughters, David Seymour remarried after the death of Matilda in 1884. He was 57, and his new bride, Sarah Stevenson, just 23. They were a striking couple at the many society events demanding attendance of the Police Commissioner. A young wife means a young family, and David Seymour started all over again with at least four more children, two of whom died in infancy. He retired in 1895 and died in London aged 85 in 1916.

On October 15 1866, with its posting completed, the 12th regiment was sent to New Zealand, and replaced in Brisbane by the 50th Regiment which had been fighting in the Maori wars. Prior to their departure, members of the 12th were presented with a testimonial and a small monetary gift from the employees of Government House in appreciation of the conduct of the soldiers who had provided guard duty. Captain Mair, on behalf of the soldiers, said that he wished at some time in the future he would again see many of these people 'among whom we have spent so many of our balmy days of soldiering.'[8]

While it would be the last Brisbane saw of Mair and Hawkes, many of the soldiers of the 12th had such fond memories of their balmy days that they returned to Brisbane. Some brought back their families and others started new ones in Queensland, reaping the rewards of the opportunities available in the expanding colony. Patrick Clancy was one of those who came back from New Zealand to Brisbane where, in 1867 he joined the Police Force serving for 21 years. Daniel Cahill was another who returned from New Zealand. He also joined the Police Force but only for two years, becoming a Letter Carrier for the General Post Office where he served for many years. Clancy and Cahill would have been in Queen Street fighting both the April and December fires in 1864.

Fellow ex-soldier William Craft also joined the General Post office and served as a Letter Carrier in Brisbane, Mackay and Rockhampton for over 30 years. Upon discharge, Privates Joseph Tristram, William Kilner (who married the widow of Frederick Dutton, the first soldier to die in Queensland) and Thomas Walker settled in Brisbane. Patrick Kearns, who is buried at Toowong Cemetery, was for many years a respected porter at Parliament House where he proudly wore his regimental medals on special occasions.

Brisbane Burns

Chapter 9

A pesky pork sausage maker

John Phillip Jost 1835–1921

A now considerable combined force of soldiers, firefighters and volunteers was attacking the fire as it continued burning away from its ignition point in opposing directions up and down the street. The 12th Regiment, working at the southern end seemed the most organised and soon had passed ropes over the low timber dwelling housing the adjoining shops of Mr. Berkley, the chemist, and Mr. Jost, the pork butcher. At imminent risk of bursting into flames from the inferno next door at the North Brisbane Hotel the building's destruction would starve the fire of fuel. Fortunately most of the stock was by now out on the street or piled up in a nearby yard. With the assistance of 'a hundred stout and willing hands clapping on'[1] the building gave way, crashing to the ground in a jumble of splintered timber and loose shingles.

As the remnants of John Phillip Jost's pork butchery succumbed to the now reducing flames there would have some onlookers not sorry to see its demise. Since opening his shop in 1860, Mr Jost had been a source of irritation to his neighbours, city authorities and the police.

Born in Darmstadt in the Grand Duchy of Hessen, Germany on 7 November, 1835, John Phillip Jost learnt the butchery trade from his father. He arrived in Moreton Bay in 1856 aged 21 and, unable to find suitable work, spent a year in a sheep processing factory on the Clarence River in northern New South Wales. Jost then walked more than 200 kms overland to Ipswich where he found a job as a butcher.

On 1 February 1859 in Brisbane he married Catherine Leahy, an Irish immigrant, and the following year opened his butcher shop in Queen Street on the western side between Albert and Edward Streets. There was no refrigeration available and so butchers had to slaughter regularly to maintain fresh supplies. Keeping animals close by was convenient and economic.

In January 1860 Mr Jost first came to the attention of the authorities when he was charged with letting four pigs run wild into Adelaide Street. Far from being contrite he claimed that the animals were 'docile as lambs, and that 'he had never known them to stray further than Dr. Ball's residence.'[2] Dr. Ball's house was a block away on the corner of Queen and George Streets.

A charge of 'Furious riding' (the equivalent of speeding today) followed some time later, along with leaving a horse and cart unattended in the street and erecting a signboard across the footpath. Each time Jost was found guilty and fined.

Once again in October 1862 the pigs were a problem when he was fined for keeping them within 40 yards of the street. Five months later, failure to empty his water closets (toilets) was the issue. Just five months before the first big Brisbane fire in April 1863 he used threatening language towards his neighbour, wife of the publican of the North Brisbane Hotel Honora Thomas, and was fined £20 and bound to keep the peace for six months.

The ongoing disputes with his neighbours were the result of noxious smells emanating from Mr Jost's shop and yard. Inspector of Nuisances, Sergeant Coffey, visited the property numerous times and issued an order that the 'quantity of offal' in Mr Jost's yard be removed. Sergeant Coffey described the smell as 'a frightful stink; that arose from decomposed meat.'[3]

Another neighbour, John Buxton, stated that it consisted of the smell arising from bones and offal; cleansing meat, and making and curing sausages.

At the last minute, the prosecution withdrew their charge because of insufficient paperwork but declared their intention to continue with the prosecution at a later date. Much to the relief of Jost's neighbours, the threat must have worked as no further complaints arose before the fire carried out the ultimate cleansing act.

Two days after the inferno, Jost was back in business and once again annoying Mr Buxton. Jost had erected a flimsy wood and calico structure in which he intended lighting large fires for sausage making, boiling and curing meats. In a letter to the Mayor and Aldermen listing his complaints John Buxton added:

> I have offered to pay Jost a large sum of money to remove the shop from the ground he now occupies, rather than be in continual dread of another fire.[4]

Jost remained Buxton's neighbour when a new butcher shop was built. The North Brisbane Hotel was not replaced.

Police were called to Jost's new premises the following year when he reported the discovery of the body of a new-born baby in his outdoor toilet. Investigations revealed that the mother was Jost's servant, Eliza McComb, who had managed to conceal her pregnancy and confinement from the household. The only other servant was a German woman who spoke no English and denied knowledge of, or even suspecting, Eliza's pregnancy. Jost's wife Catherine also stated she had noticed nothing unusual in Eliza's appearance or behaviour – a curious scenario in a small house with four adults and three small children. Eliza was charged with concealing the birth of a child but not convicted.

The new building and increased vigilance of the authorities prevented further complaints against the Jost family. In 1869 their fifth child, Francis John was born. He joined his siblings Catherine ten, George eight, William four and Mary two. Further servant trouble was still to follow however. Mary Booth was employed as a nursemaid to care for the children and shared a room at the top of the house with another servant, Bridget Duggan. Mary awoke one evening to find Jost's servant, William Stevens, clad only a shirt, attempting to get into bed with her. The two girls screamed, Stevens assaulted them and fled back to his bed where Jost, awakened by the noise, found him pretending to be asleep. William Stevens was charged with indecent assault. At the trial, evidence was given that Mary Booth was 'intimate with the prisoner, and went to dances with him sometimes.'[5] Stevens was found not guilty.

In 1876, after 18 years as a butcher, John Phillip Jost sold his shop. A celebration was attended by 40 former employees and Mr & Mrs Jost were presented with a silver cup and salt cellars. The couple retired to a 10,000 acre (over 4000 ha) property near Grandchester west of Ipswich called *Jostvale*.

Here, through the 1880s, J P Jost was able to indulge his passion for horse racing – buying, breeding and racing some of the most successful horses. Parliamentarian Sir Joshua Peter Bell was credited with revitalising the racing industry in Queensland, breeding many champions on his estate near Ipswich. On his death, some of his best horses and their progeny were sold to J P Jost.

Jost was instrumental in the revival of Tattersall's Club in Brisbane and served on the first committee. He supplied the initial Tattersall's Club Cup, a gold and silver trophy worth £50, along with many of the other prizes for the first meeting, held on 10 December 1884, including three Ladies Bracelets, much admired and envied amongst the female racing fans. Such were the quality of J P Jost's own horses there was speculation that the Cup and many of the lesser prizes would return to him. On a scorching, dusty afternoon at Eagle Farm, at Tattersall's first meeting, Jost's favourite, Elsinore, was beaten by his rival John Finnie's Medusa. As expected, Mrs Jost carried off two of the three bracelet prizes much to the envy of the few other women who turned out that day, and Mr Jost won £119 in prize money.[6]

In an 1884 article, the sporting columnist of the *Queensland Figaro* called Jost a 'pork-sausage maker'. Keen to report on Jost's response, the racing columnist from the opposition paper, the *Queenslander* suggested Jost investigate the potentially libellous piece.

Jost visited the *Queensland Figaro* and after sharing a drink with the columnist and reading the article, the *Queensland Figaro* reported that 'after laughing until his eyes bulged out like those of an apoplectic fish', Jost replied

> I wish I had stuck to de making of pork sausages. It would haf been better for me and de people of Brisbane, too. I should haf made more money dan ever I did by following up sport and

>   running racehorses; and de people of Brisbane would haf been able to buy a descent sausage, which dey cannot do now![7]

John Phillip Jost's horses competed all over Queensland. He had stables at Hendra and a residence nearby. His wife Catherine died aged 58 after a long illness on 28 January 1895. The huge *Jostvale* estate was sold in March 1901 for £21 000 (a multi-million dollar return in today's values). Jost moved to Toowoomba investing in local property and hotels. He travelled to Europe for an 18-months tour returning to Brisbane in June 1902. In his early 70s, but not yet ready to retire, he purchased another property, which he also called *Jostvale*, about 3km from Oakey.

He died on 4 July 1921 aged 86 and was buried at Oakey. His property was sold and the money invested for his grandchildren. Small annuities were left to Alice Jost (daughter-in-law and wife of William) son George and daughter Catherine. Mary Jost had died aged 42 in 1909 and Frank Jost (Francis John) was never mentioned in the will. In 1923 Jost's beneficiaries sought the help of the courts in interpreting the complicated will. An illegitimate granddaughter, Myra Woods, was deemed to have equal shares to that of the other six grandchildren of Alice and William Jost. Whose child she was remains unclear, and the reason for Frank Jost's exclusion from the will was never explained.

Brisbane Burns

Chapter 10

A shrewd politician

Robert Bulcock 1832–1900

While the battle against the fire raged at the southern end of Queen Street, the intense flames that had erupted from the roof and verandah of Kingsford's two storey brick haberdashery toward the northern end were also requiring significant resources. Next door to Kingsford's was a two storey timber structure. Lacking an attic it stood not quite as tall but just as flammable with light woods, including Baltic pine, which 'blazed up like greased cardboard'.[1] It contained three shopfronts, Mr. Bulcock's Fruit and Vegetables, Mr Mandel's jewellery business, and Mr Keith's ironmongery and tinsmith factory as well as number of small upstairs offices. Prompt attention was paid to the 'adoption of measures for the preservation of contents', some of which could not eventually be saved and some of which, in the case of Mr Mandel's jewellery 'were scattered beyond his ken'. The extensive seed, grain and fruit stock of Bulcock's were destroyed with losses estimated at £1000 over and above the total amount of insurances.

Robert Bulcock was a stern, conservative immigrant from Clitheroe, Lancashire, England who, at the tender age of eight, swore a vow of temperance. On 11 April 1864 he faced financial ruin for the third time in two years, but like many of his fellow Queen Street traders he rebuilt the business which flourished on the same site for many decades. Bulcock was also an enthusiastic politician serving in both houses of Parliament in Queensland and was the foremost election organiser of his time.

He arrived in Brisbane with his wife Elizabeth Grandige and first son William aboard *The Light of the Age* in late 1854. His cousin Benjamin Bulcock, brother William and wife Margaret, and sister Jane had all arrived on the *Fortitude* in 1849 as part of Dr John Dunmore Lang's immigration program. Accompanying Robert Bulcock and his family were his brother Richard and sister Alice.

Dr Lang's promise of land and a prosperous future in the clean air of Moreton Bay had beckoned the Bulcocks who had been working in the cotton mills of industrial Lancashire for almost ten years. Robert Bulcock senior was a power loom overlooker (maintainer of the looms and staff overseer) as was Robert junior before his departure to Australia. Dangerous working conditions in the noisy, humid, cotton dust-filled mills caused deafness, lung disease, and tuberculosis. Injury and death from accidents with the swiftly moving machinery also haunted the workers. The cramped, unsanitary living conditions in the crowded cities and towns further contributed to the spread of disease.

Life in the new settlement of Brisbane also had its difficulties. The *Fortitude* immigrants never saw the land Dr Lang had promised them and began life living in tents, forced to find their own employment. When Robert and his family arrived, brother William was living at Eagle Farm (about five km north east of central Brisbane) eking out a living from agriculture where he drowned in 1855 after a suffering a seizure, leaving behind a young family. Eliza Bulcock (Robert's wife) recalled 'protecting herself and young family from an attack from the blacks on her home at Eagle Farm.'[2]

The family moved to Ipswich where Robert began his business career 'as a carter of wood and water'. The water was carried from the Bremer River to households in horse-drawn water trucks for 1 shilling per cask. He later started a very modest fruit and greengrocery business, his shop sign being a bunch of bananas, hung out on a gum sapling. It proved to be a success however and he eventually relocated to a small rented shop in Brisbane Street, Ipswich continuing to sell fruit and vegetables. In partnership with his brother Richard, Robert ran both the store in Ipswich and a Queen Street store in Brisbane. In February 1863 a large fire on Nicholas Street Ipswich burnt Bulcock's Fruit and Produce Shop. Just weeks later, Wheat Creek (by then a major drain) behind Bulcock's Brisbane store, overflowed during a storm and the water was so deep behind the shops that Robert Bulcock had to swim to the stables to save the horses. Four tons of bran, hay and corn were ruined. This was followed by the devastation of the 1864 fire.

Richard and Robert Bulcock eventually sold the produce section of the business in 1871 and expanded into other ventures, including a tannery. The partnership was finally dissolved in 1876. Robert Bulcock owned houses and retail premises throughout Brisbane and most famously purchased 277 acres (112 ha) at Caloundra in 1875 which was later developed by his son and named Bulcock's Beach.

In 1888 Bulcock fought a libel action against the *Boomerang* (a weekly Brisbane-based rascist pro-worker newspaper) for an article, which among other things, said he was 'always at hand when money is to be made without hard work or too much risk' and

> whose contribution to the wealth of the community consists of grabbing every likely bit of land he sees and holding on to it until some industrious man pays toll for its use.[3]

Such astute investments allowed his retirement from active business life in his late 40s and he was elected to the Queensland Parliament in the seat of Enoggera in 1885.

Politics became his passion. Although conservative in his views, Robert Bulcock never attached himself to a particular party and *The Worker* noted:

> Always a keen politician, but without fixed political principles, the hon. Bob has weathercocked all round the compass. …Bobby has a vivid imagination, and sees blood and revolution in all opposition to the dominant party.[4]

Whichever party had his current allegiance didn't question his principles but was glad to have him of their side as he was known as having 'an absolute genius for conceiving and compassing electioneering tactics.'[5] He strictly controlled the electoral rolls, one side applauding his determination and the other accusing him of stuffing or 'Bulcocking' the rolls. Judging which candidate suited the seat was another skill valued by his allies and he was credited as possessing

> a power of being able to forecast the result of a contested event with almost mathematical exactitude.[6]

> From the day of dissolution of Parliament until the assembling of the new House his finger is on every pulse of public action and reaction.[7]

From his campaign for a strict party organisation through the Queensland Evangelical Standard in the early 1880s, his involvement with the temperance journal *Joy Bells* through 1887–1888, and the establishment of the Patriotic League in 1891, he exerted serious influence over the Queensland government. Despite having many critics, a high political profile and being the butt for many years of newspaper and journal cartoonists he was asked to join the Queensland Legislative Council in 1894.

On 10 May 1900 he died suddenly of peritonitis aged 68. He was survived by his wife and six of his 11 children – William, Robert, Edwin, Arthur, Ernest and Sarah Isabelle. Emily Hemens Bulcock OBE, a poet and journalist, whose works were published throughout Australia over 70 years, was the wife of Robert Bulcock junior, developer of Caloundra and Bulcock's Beach. Elizabeth Bulcock, widow of Robert senior, died in Brisbane in 1908.

Chapter 11

Dented but not defeated

William Keith 1825–1885

The fuel supplied by the three timber shopfronts and first floor offices, known locally as Bulcock's Buildings was indeed efficient. Hardly more substantial was the block of shops and offices next in line of the fire – three rickety timber stories housing a bookseller, crockery dealer and various professional services. As the blaze from the buildings combined and intensified the heat generated began to blister the shutters of shops on the opposite side of the street and damaged some of the copious amounts of varied stock now piled up in the middle of the street. For tinsmith William Keith the inferno claimed most of his stock. He was only insured for £500.

Today we use plastic. In the mid 19th century many household utensils, pans, canisters, pails and even baths were made of tin. Composed of iron dipped in melted tin and then milled thin and flat, tin-plate was the raw material of the tinsmith. Using shears, anvils and hammers the tinsmith could manufacture numerous household items, farming implements and containers. While glass and earthenware was also popular, tin was cheap, light, durable and easily carried by people and horses.

William Keith, his wife Mary and children Isabella, William, James, Mary and John arrived on the *Glentanner* in 1859 from Aberdeen

Scotland. Within two months he had begun his tinsmith business in Edward Street.

> William Keith has opened the third shop in Edward Street, off Queen Street, as a Tin-plate, galvanised iron, and zinc worker and hopes by keeping nothing but first-class goods, and by strict attention to business, to merit a share of public patronage.[1]

He moved the business to Queen Street in 1862 and described it as:

> a large and extensive workshop, the best and most experienced workmen, and a plant of the most modern improved machinery, unequalled in the colonies.[2]

Traditional hand-tools of the tinsmiths' trade were not up the task of providing the quantity of tin goods required by the growing settlements and from the 1860s many tinsmiths such as Keith had introduced newly invented American equipment to mechanise the process. Keith had also expanded into galvanised products and imported general ironmongery to stay ahead of the other tradesmen.

A year before the April 1864 fire William Keith had insured his stock and property for £500. His business premises were rented from Robert Cribb. After the fire, Keith claimed that he had £2100 worth of stock, part of which he had received only days before the fire. Some of items stored in the cellar were saved and the insurance company took possession of these and auctioned them off at a greatly reduced value. William Keith took the insurance company to court to recover the proceeds of the sale. The court ruled in his favour to the extent of just £76, far less than the true value. Together with the £500 payout, this was not enough to cover the destroyed property. Two months earlier the family had lost their infant son Joseph Charles and they were left struggling to come to terms with the double disasters.

Like many other of his fellow businessmen, he took advantage of the temporary buildings hastily erected after the fire further down Queen Street known as Refuge Row and recommenced trading. Although he had suffered an economic blow, he had saved many of his tools and machinery and quickly imported new stock from Sydney – a variable assortment of wire, barrow wheels, zinc, frying pans, shovels, fencing wire, buckets, axes nails and camp ovens.[3]

Four months after the fire William Keith had returned his business to its original site in Queen Street. In an effort to remain competitive, he expanded the business to included general ironmongery including furniture such as lamps and bedsteads. Cheap imported goods reduced the requirement for locally manufactured items. Three years after the fire, in October 1867, William Keith narrowly avoided bankruptcy by selling the stock and business to F Lassetter & Co in repayment of a debt. Undeterred he moved across the road and set up shop again. Within a year he had returned to his old premises on the western side of Queen Street. In 1869, Keith's were promoting newly invented and locally produced articles including an atmospheric churn for the dairy industry and sulphurising bellows for vine-growing. By 1873 he had secured contracts to supply tools and materials to the Brisbane Council and the Lady Bowen Hospital. In the following years be became an agent for the 'Home' brand of sewing machines and continued selling general ironmongery and furnishing while still maintaining a tin-plate workshop.

> **WILLIAM KEITH,**
> **PLUMBER,**
> Tin Plate and Galvanized Iron Worker,
> QUEEN STREET,
> **BRISBANE,**
>
> ANNOUNCES to the Public of Queensland that his Establishment is furnished with all the newest and most improved MACHINERY, and that he is now in a position to make and supply, on the most reasonable terms, and on the shortest notice, GALVANIZED IRON GUTTERING, half-round and O.G. TANKS, from 100 to 1000 gallons.
>
> Storekeepers and Squatters supplied, at the cheapest rate, with Tinware of every description.
>
> *All Orders promptly and punctually attended to.*

Despite William Keith's determination and application to his business and his willingness to change with the times, by 1878 disaster was not far away. Fighting local competition – Perry Brothers Ironmongers across the road, another ironmonger two doors down and a tinsmith in the next block – Keith imported 65 packages of hardware including bedsteads, cutlery, tools, lamps, stoves, grates and fenders. He managed to pay for these goods, but by March the following year his debts were over £1500 and, claiming 'losses in trade and falling off of business and pressure from creditors'[4], he filed for insolvency.

An itemised stock inventory filled 57 foolscap pages with a total value of £1374. His horse, cart, buggy and harness were valued at £90 and his workshop tools at £70. Cleverly, and like many other businessmen in town, his home in Brunswick Street and land in Sandgate Road were in his wife's name.

The business resurfaced about a year later in Elizabeth Street as W Keith & Co and continued under the stewardship of sons James and John and was still advertising in 1905 after moving to Charlotte Street.

William Keith died on 25 April 1885 aged 59 and his wife Mary died in 1902 aged 80. By the end of the 19th century galvanised iron had replaced tin, and the 20th century saw the invention of plastic. Mechanisation made the tinsmiths' skills redundant and their trade disappeared only remaining today as a hobby or curiosity in a heritage display.

Chapter 12

The ironmongering tailor

John Markwell 1823–1881

> *The fire, as if impatient of delay, communicated, almost simultaneously, to the store of Mr. Markwell, the ironmonger.*[1]

Raging unchecked through the row of flimsy timber buildings as it spread toward the Edward street corner the fire now confronted the solid, low slung brick construction of the premises of John Markwell & Co, built only three short years before. Here was finally a chance for the tired fire fighters to gain the upper hand. The next building on from Markwell's was also constructed from brick and reared three stories above the ironmongery. With flames now leaping up from the roof of Markwell's there was no time to be lost in setting a proper line of containment.

The decision was to cost the ironmongery's proprietor his fine young building and the greater portion of his stock as attention was placed on its larger neighbour.

Markwell's was the last building entirely destroyed by the fire.

William Morley (John) Markwell didn't start out his retail life as an ironmonger. Born in Wainfleet, Lincolnshire in 1823, he was apprenticed as a tailor in London where he married his master's daughter, Mary Ann Izard, in 1841. Together with his brothers, Isaac and Samuel and their families, John (the name he quickly adopted in the new colony) Mary Ann and their children Ellen and Henry (infant daughter Emily died at sea) arrived in Brisbane

John Markwell.

aboard the sailing ship *Chasely*, in May 1849.

Within weeks Markwell began a tailoring business in Queen Street. By March 1851 he had moved to a larger shop, expanded into general drapery and taken on a partner, William Smith. He promised his customers to:

> carry on the tailoring business in all its branches, and on such a system of extent and economy as will defy competition.[2]

John Markwell and Co sold a wide variety of items such as trousers for men and boys, hats, dresses, diapers, stays, bonnets, ribbons, blankets, gloves and hosiery. In addition they carried lengths of cloth which varied from twill, tweed and drill to doeskin, cashmeres and moleskin. Tailoring and drapery at that time had become a competitive business. Aggressive and novel advertising appeared in every newspaper issue. John Markwell relentlessly continued this practice, eventually placing some of the earliest display advertisements in a time when most advertising consisted of rousing sentences about the utility and benefits of a product. The business expanded into a neighbouring shop and by June 1851 the partnership with William Smith was dissolved.

In April 1853 Mary Ann died aged 30 after a long illness leaving John to look after their two children, Ellen 11, and Henry 9. This was not a situation Markwell could afford to encounter for too long. His eye soon fell to sixteen-year-old Georgina Edmondstone, who, with her younger sister Elizabeth were frequent visitors to their father's butchery opposite Markwell's shop. Thirty-year-old John saw an opportunity in Georgina for a new wife, a handsome marriage settlement and, through her father George Edmondstone (see Chapter

24 of this book), a highly respected early settler to Brisbane, an introduction to the elite of Brisbane's society.

Not only did George quickly grant his permission but he also gave the couple 18 acres on the river at Toowong and an inner city block in Edward Street. They were married in December 1853, a scant eight months after Mary Ann's death. They would go on to have ten children.

Extending across two columns and down two-thirds of a page of the *Moreton Bay Courier*, John Markwell's splashy display advertisement in January 1855 announced yet another new premises, that of *Victoria House* on the corner of Queen and George Streets opposite the Bank of New South Wales. He thanked his customers for:

> the more than liberal support he has received since commencing business; and whilst soliciting a continence of their favours, would observe that the business at the New Premises will be conducted under the same principles which have already gained for him one of the largest trades in these Northern Districts.[3]

With William Grimes, a fellow *Chasely* immigrant, he opened another tailoring department upstairs in *Victoria House* in 1856. Business was booming. In October 1857 advertisements appeared for the sale of the Markwell's household furniture from their home in Edward Street stating that John Markwell was "leaving the colony for England"[4]. Markwell took the eldest two children to Sydney in November 1857 and Georgina and the youngest two followed in January 1858. Yet for some reason there was a change of heart about returning to England and two months later the family was back in Brisbane. Georgina's third child was born in September 1858 at their new house, *Moorlands Cottage*, on the property at Toowong.

Georgina Markwell.

Tailoring was taking a backward step in Markwell's expanding businesses which now included retail and wholesale groceries. In 1861 with his eldest son Henry aged 17 as a partner Markwell opened the ironmongery shop in Queen Street that would eventually succumb to the April 1864 fire. Although losing considerable stock from the fire John Markwell & Co were able to return to new premises on the original site after a 10-month stint in Refuge Row and recommenced trading.

Markwell was elated, as most Brisbane businesses were, at the opening of a temporary bridge across the river in June 1865. The ease of access for businesses trading on both sides of the river was an exciting prospect, but the bridge had come at a price. The new government had over-extended itself with numerous capital expenditure projects including the construction of the first railway line to Ipswich. In June 1866, the government's bankers in London closed their line of credit, and banks and building societies in Brisbane closed their doors. Local businesses encountered a severe slump and many of those that had been teetering on the edge after the fires of 1864, collapsed.

In February 1867 John Markwell & Co, the business John shared with son Henry, was put into receivership, but the grocery and drapery concerns continued. Stock was sold and Markwell auctioned several properties in Spring Hill, but it was to no avail and the ironmongery business became insolvent in September 1867. Henry, with help from his father, purchased the remaining stock from the receivers at a bargain price and reopened the store in Queen Street as H J Markwell & Co, general and furnishing ironmongers.

With the ironmongery enterprise resurrected, life seemed to return to normal, but 1868 was to be a year of tragedies for the Markwell family. On 21 February seven-year-old Frederick Markwell and his younger brother Edmondstone were playing in a creek near their home. Crossing a bridge without railings, Frederick tried to touch the water with his toe, slipped and fell. Unable to swim, he struggled and momentarily caught hold of a branch which broke. He was dragged from the water but desperate attempts to revive him failed. Disaster again befell the family in October when eldest son Henry was killed in an accident.

Henry had enjoyed a few drinks with friends after closing time and at about 10 o'clock was seen riding up Queen Street. A short while later a horse and rider galloped along the road to Milton past George Edmonds, who worked for Henry's grandfather George Edmondstone. Within minutes, George Edmonds found the rider unconscious on the footpath with head injuries. The victim's face was unrecognisable, but on searching his pockets George found letters addressed to Henry Markwell.

Henry was carried a short distance to his father's house but died a few hours later despite medical attention. He was 24 years old and left a wife, Annette and an infant daughter.

> His family here so generally liked by all the old residents of Brisbane, that this misfortune elicited unusual sympathy. A number of shopkeepers in Queen Street put up their shutters as a token of respect.
>
> He was a smart businessman, a genial companion, and had the esteem of a large circle of friends.[5]

Less than a year later, H J Markwell & Co was sold to Brookes and Foster who continued the ironmongery on the same site. Looking for a fresh start, John Markwell set up as a house, land and stock agent in January 1870 and in July nominated for election to the city council which he failed to win. With their youngest child just 15 months old, Georgina died, aged 33, on 4 October 1870, leaving John once again with a motherless young family.

In December of the same year, Markwell's application for a land selection at Beaudesert, 90 kilometres south of Brisbane) was successful.[6] He stocked the land with cattle, hired labourers and cattlemen and, on 13 June 1872, married 20-year-old Harriet Hunt Beal. John, now 48, young Harriett, and eight of Georgina's children aged from four to 18 leased *Moorlands* and moved to Beaudesert. By late 1873 Markwell's property was described as 'a fine estate of some three thousand acres' being mainly rich river flats where he ran about 400 head of cattle for breeding and fattening – a dramatic change from sewing suits and selling gardening tools, buckets and bedsteads.

> His house makes no great pretensions to outside appearance, but is snug and pleasant within.[7]

John and Harriet Markwell would have six children together. None of them were born at Beaudesert, Harriett choosing to travel to Brisbane for the birth of the first two to secure their safe arrival. Ten-month-old Arthur, John and Harriet's first child, died at Beaudesert in 1874, souring their idyllic country lifestyle. Although the cattle business was a success, the ever-expanding family returned to Brisbane in 1875 selling the Beaudesert property.

> He will be much missed by the inhabitants, as they have all found in him a good friend and neighbour.[8]

Too many bad memories existed at *Moorlands* in Toowong, and the Markwell family settled back into another property close by, calling the new house *Morley*. The land surrounding *Morley* was subdivided into the *Morley Estate* in 1875. Moorlands itself was sold to the Mayne family in 1876. In 1892 the Maynes built a new house on the same site. The new *Moorlands* remained in the Mayne family until 1940 when it was bequeathed to the University of Queensland. From 1947 to 1971 it was owned by the Brisbane Legacy War Widows and Orphans Fund. In 1971 it was purchased by the Uniting Church and is now the site of the Wesley Hospital. No longer pressed by day to day business, Markwell and his large family lived quietly at Toowong. As was the case for many families of the time though tragedy was never far away. Three-month-old Gwendoline died in March 1877.

Shortly before his death at *Morley* on 26 October 1881 aged 57, John Markwell finally achieved a civic post, being elected to the new Toowong council. His last, and 18th child, John Benjamin was born three months after his death.

John Markwell, his brothers and extended family were some of the original pioneers of Brisbane and its hinterland, demonstrating entrepreneurial spirit, resilience and endurance. Their immeasurable contributions are remembered in street and place names throughout the area.

Chapter 13

An indefatigable quiet achiever

John Alexander MacDonald 1823–1895

As Markwell's floor stock caught alight from the collapsing roof, the fire's progress toward Edward street finally slowed as it was denied the easy fuel provided by timber framed walls. The fire fighters now had time to scramble into the attic of the next building facing ruin, Flavelle Bros jewellers, a three-story brick construction also housing the home of one of its proprietors. Leading the charge was Inspector John MacDonald, of the Water Police.

> *It was here that the most gallant and successful effort was made to arrest the fire. Inspector MacDonald mounted to the upper part of the house, three stories high at the street front, and got into the attic, whence he cut his way with an axe through the roof.*[1]

Removing the combustible shingle roofing would prevent the flames from Markwell's establishment spreading to the jeweller. But there was a complication.

MacDonald had been made aware that included in the stock now engulfed in flames within John Markwell & Co. was fifty pounds (22Kg) of dynamite. This was something he did not initially mention to his men as he called them up to the roof, fearing they might not follow. The deception succeeded however, as the group worked quickly to cut away the shingling and woodwork of the south gable of the building just as the flames began to take hold. A fire hose was then brought up to the men allowing them to concentrate what little water they had access to down upon the burning roof of the ironmongery, extinguishing the fire before it could reach the stored dynamite. Reports at the time do not say exactly when MacDonald told his men about the dynamite or their reaction but note that it was eventually removed from the smouldering ruins and placed underwater in a nearby drain.

John Alexander MacDonald is best remembered in Brisbane history as first Superintendant of the St. Helena, Moreton Bay penal settlement, a position he held from 1867 to 1882. Long before this appointment John MacDonald had been prominent in Brisbane affairs often displaying courage, bravery, careful consideration and excellent leadership. Like many ex-military men of the time he was well suited to the Civil Service and eagerly sought after by such employers.

Born in Scotland, John MacDonald had served with the 93rd Sutherland Highlanders Regiment of Foot and saw active service in the Crimean War as a private, non-commissioned officer and subsequently a Commissioned Officer on the staff of Lord Raglan. During the Crimean War (1853–1856) General Raglan had overall command of the British Forces during the ill-fated Charge of the Light Brigade in October 1854 which resulted in large British casualties. The Regiment distinguished itself at the Battle of Balaklava in 1855. As the formidable Russian cavalry advanced towards the 93rd Highlanders, the regiment drew themselves up in a long line, two deep. They fired two volleys at the approaching Russian charge and held their line, immortalized in history as 'The Thin Red Line'. The Russian cavalry charge split left and right and finally retreated.

In 1856 the 93rd Highlanders returned to Britain. John MacDonald, still a young man, decided he'd had enough excitement and left the army arriving in Victoria and, like thousands of others, made his way to the gold fields. He married Alice Malcolm in 1860 and moved to Queensland. Almost immediately he was snapped up by the Civil Service and promoted to Sergeant in charge of the Brisbane Police Station. At that time in Brisbane, apart from the Police Magistrate, there was one chief constable, three sergeants, one acting sergeant and 18 constables.

Chapter 13 — John Alexander MacDonald

On 31st May 1859 the first Water Police Magistrate for Moreton Bay was appointed. The Water Police had always been a separate entity to the ordinary police and were controlled from NSW until 1863. John MacDonald was made an Inspector to the Water Police in October 1862 under its new head, William Thornton. Thornton outlined the structure and duties of the Water Police to a Select Committee inquiry, saying:

> The Water Police consists of an Inspector, a coxswain, a carpenter, and five constables one of whom acts as cook. There are no other water police in any part of the colony. The water police are stationed on board the hulk at the mouth of the river.

The hulk referred to was the *Proserpine*, a decommissioned brig also used to house prisoners. Other duties of the Water Police included maintenance of the dredges at the mouth of the river, generally keeping order of shipping in the bay and on the river, acting as Customs and Health Officers, and assisting the Tide Surveyor.

On the morning of 9 April 1863 as John MacDonald pulled his small boat alongside the newly arrived *Queen of the Colonies*, he was informed of a disaster that had occurred just three days earlier. The clipper ship under the command of Captain Cairncross, had just completed a voyage of 110 days from London, via Ireland. Having left with 460 passengers and 1200 tons of cargo, the voyage had already been eventful. Measles broke out, six children died, two women died from the complications of childbirth, one infant from convulsions and one adult from falling into the ship's hold. If that wasn't enough, 26 stowaways were discovered, there were seven births and one marriage. Captain Cairncross must have been very relieved to spy the headland of Cape Moreton, but sadly his greatest challenge of the voyage began here.

Mrs Barnsfield, one of the passengers, had died in childbirth and the Captain anchored off the lighthouse at Cape Moreton with the intention of sending the lifeboat ashore with Mrs. Barnsfield's body for burial. It was against the law to bury a body at sea within the confines of the harbour of Moreton Bay and the process of arrival, quarantine and health checks meant that it might be a week before anyone could leave the vessel, and without refrigeration the

Captain had no alternative but to send the corpse ashore despite worsening weather.

On board the lifeboat with the body were Captain Hill, five passengers including Mrs. Barnsfield's husband, and six crew. There was a strong south-easterly wind blowing. The boat was seen to make the shore and the lighthouse keeper was able to report that he had seen Mrs Barnsfield's grave. The lifeboat returned to the *Queen of the Colonies* and passed under the stern ready to be retrieved by the davits. In the darkness and increasing squall, it missed the davits and drifted astern out of sight.

When apprised of the calamity John MacDonald immediately notified his superior who passed the information onto the Acting Colonial Secretary to await further instructions. It was the opinion of experienced Moreton Bay hands that the lifeboat had by now either sunk or been swept away to the northern end of the bay. A rescue mission would be mounted.

The following day, The *Brisbane*, a government steamer, was dispatched to Cape Moreton to search for the lifeboat, but the strong winds and rough seas forced it to return to the river. For the next three days the weather remained too dangerous to venture back across the bay allowing the *Brisbane* only the task of ferrying passengers from the *Queen of the Colonies* up the river to the city.

Meanwhile, the men adrift in the missing lifeboat had indeed washed up ashore northwards of the bay past Bribie Island on the afternoon following the burial. Landing safely in an uninhabited area near where Caloundra is today, they had found bottles and containers on the beach to collect water and were living off shellfish. They sheltered in a tent constructed from the remains of a wreck, and built signal fires from driftwood.

A week after the lifeboat and its occupants had disappeared, the *Brisbane* was ordered to prepare for another search, by taking on enough coal for 30 hours steaming. Meanwhile, the castaways were beginning to fear they had been left to their fate. They decided to launch the boat through the surf and attempt to row to safety. Swamped by the large surf, the boat overturned and the men scrambled back to shore. A quick headcount revealed that Mr. Barnsfield, the husband of the woman buried on Moreton Island, was missing. His companions watched and waited. After seeing the huge fins of patrolling sharks beyond the surf, they assumed the worst.

With escape by sea now seemingly impossible, the castaways decided that three of them would attempt to walk to Brisbane, about 95 kilometres south, and left the main party the next day.

By Thursday April 16 the *Brisbane* had finally secured enough coal and a marine pilot who knew the Bribie Island area, to depart yet again on its search mission. In a cruel twist, just after the *Brisbane* departed, a group of aboriginal men native to the north coast area arrived in Brisbane with news of 14 'new chums' stranded up the coast. The news of the survival of the men from the lifeboat cheered the newly arrived immigrants and the crew of the *Queen of the Colonies* but it missed the *Brisbane*. John MacDonald and a crew from the Water Police were onboard the *Brisbane* as it sailed for the Bribie Island search area using information gathered from experienced Moreton Bay sailors. Thus began an ordeal for John MacDonald that was to last a week.

As shoals and sandbars prevented the *Brisbane* from going in close to Bribie Island, John MacDonald and a few men rowed ashore in a small boat. They crossed the island and searched the beaches fruitlessly. The next day they returned to the boat and rowed on to the mainland near Caloundra. From here, the search party walked five miles before stumbling upon the eight castaways, amazed to find them resting in the shade, after morning prayers. Of the survivors, one needed assistance to walk. MacDonald led the men to the rowing boat where they hungrily devoured a meal of bread and cheese. Relieved at being rescued, the moment was clouded by news of the apparent death of Mr Barnsfield four days earlier. At 3.30pm MacDonald and the castaways set out for what was to be yet another dramatic chapter in the saga – a perilous 24-hour haul through the heavy seas and a black night to the safety of the *Brisbane* anchored off Bribie.

Having finally returned the survivors, the *Brisbane*, along with John MacDonald and his coxswain Mr. Mason, who had left without even changing his clothes from the previous rescue, departed once again for Bribie Island to see if there was any trace of the three men who had tried to walk to Brisbane. Two days later MacDonald and a small party rowed ashore from the *Brisbane* ashore at the northern end of the Bribie Passage, intending to camp for the night. With one of his men, MacDonald, walked back to where they had found the eight other survivors four days earlier on the chance that the missing three had returned and found a note he had left for them. Amazingly there they were, asleep on the ground, exhausted, having failed to make it very far south and backtracking to the camp.

For nine consecutive days John MacDonald and his coxswain, Mr. Mason, had heroically kept up the search and rescue mission and brought back all but one of the burial party that had set out from the *Queen of the Colonies*.

The Brisbane Courier declared

> We cannot here refrain from expressing our appreciation of the energy and 'pluck' displayed by Inspector MacDonald throughout the whole of this arduous undertaking.[1]

Inspector MacDonald was rewarded with a presentation from the Government of £100, and the Black Ball Line, owners of the *Queen of the Colonies,* presented him with a tea and coffee service valued at 100 guineas.

During the following year, Inspector John MacDonald and the Water Police dealt with many incidents including stabbings on board visiting ships, crews refusing to obey orders, desertion, stowaways, breaches of harbour regulations, crews stealing from cargoes, an assault on the chief officer of the *Queen of the Colonies,* and a captain found drunk behind the wheel of a steamer weaving erratically across the bay. All the while he displayed the quiet determination and leadership that brought the Water Police into such high regard and led to his bravery during the fire of 11 April 1864.

The Brisbane Courier applauded the conduct of the water police during the fire though refrained from mentioning MacDonald's deception over the dynamite:

> Thoroughly disciplined, they obeyed every order of their superior officer, whose quick intelligence and cool intrepidity directed them not only where their services were most needful; but where danger was imminent

In early 1866, in his position as Keeper of the Hulk, John MacDonald was ordered to use prisoners to commence work on clearing scrub and erecting accommodation for a quarantine station on St. Helena Island in Moreton Bay. During one such expedition a prisoner absconded and was unable to be found. It was decided that the security risks were too great and a proper prison on the island would be more suitable. With the indefatigable John MacDonald as its Superintendent, St Helena was proclaimed a prison in May 1867

Thirty-year-old MacDonald moved himself, his wife, and 10-year old son into a neatly finished five-room house on the 500 acre (200 ha) densely-treed island and with the prisoners, continued to build the infrastructure of the gaol. Starting with 50 inmates, he overcame many delays, complaints and interruptions.

A well-organised, stubborn, stern leader, he struggled in the first few years with inclement weather, bad workmanship, isolation, absconding prisoners and thieving, drunken guards to build an efficient self-sufficient and even profitable penal establishment. Maize, sugar-cane and vegetables were planted and the government supported his experimental agricultural work. By 1868 there were 5 acres (2 ha) of cane and 10 more planned.

A sugar mill was purchased and installed and the crushing of the first harvest of four acres produced seven tons of sugar – quite a feat for a self-taught farmer. He acquired the setts (sections of mature cane plants) from Louis Hope farming in Cleveland and from George Raff's Caboolture property. Using up to the minute newspaper reports and books, he systematically built a thriving industry using prison labour. The total sugar production from 1869 to 1877 was 277 tons. This high-quality, high-yield cane was sent to Mackay and Maryborough forming the basis of their industries. A large sugar exhibit from St. Helena Island was the focal point of a display of Queensland sugar at the 1879 Sydney International Exhibition.

Not content with a creating a successful mini sugar empire, MacDonald also branched out into silk farming purchasing mulberry trees from Albert John Hockings, the seed and plant merchant. Once the trees were mature, he acquired silk worm eggs. His cocoons and wound silk won prizes at exhibitions in Paris, Vienna and Philadelphia.

At one point he sent a 2cwt (50 kilograms) bale to the Colonial Stores in Brisbane, but through ignorance or apathy it was left to rot and MacDonald was asked to remove the bale as rats discovered it was ideal for nesting. Realising that his efforts were not appreciated, he let the worms die out and gradually the trees disappeared, many blown over in the sandy soil by the constant gales. John MacDonald truly deserves to be among the pioneers of Queensland's sugar industry.

Towards the end of his 15 years on the island, his wife became ill and in September 1881, Alice MacDonald died in Brisbane. Shortly after, in April 1882, John MacDonald retired from his position. He was presented with a silver claret jug made by Flavelle Brothers & Co. Jewellers, the very shop he had so bravely saved from destruction, almost 18 years earlier. The jug now resides in the St. Helena Museum. In a presentation by his peers on his retirement they stated,

> During that time you have, by your kindly bearing towards all with whom you have come in contact, endeared yourself to use by the strongest ties of friendship and goodwill and in begging your acceptance of this souvenir we trust you will long live to enjoy your retirement.[2]

Shortly afterwards, John MacDonald returned to Scotland, where he married Louisa MacPherson. They settled back in Brisbane and John died at their home in Hamilton in June 1895. Sadly, his only son, John Malcolm, had predeceased him in 1888, dying of the complications of a cold caught in Scotland.

Chapter 14

Taken from the northern end of Queen Street past the Edward Street corner, this photograph of the morning after the April fire shows the piles of stock, shop fittings and debris that were hauled away from the fire. The ladder John MacDonald used to enter Flavelle's large three-story building and finally stop the path of the fire is visible standing against the damaged but still intact structure.

The smoke clears ... for now

The last building damaged by the fire on the northern side of Queen Street was Flavelle Brothers & Co, which housed the jeweller's shop managed by Edmund MacDonnell. Internal fittings, and the plate glass window were removed and the shingle roof awning dismantled. John Buxton's stationary business on the southern side near to the Albert Street corner was also saved.

All that remained of the main business street of the young city was now a heap of blackened ashes, with here and there a charred brick wall or chimney.

Fourteen shops and two houses had been lost. Queen Street was littered with a combination of shop fittings, stock, household treasures and tangles of wood, rope and tools.

In the following days there was both praise and criticism. John Buxton placed advertisements thanking his saviours. To Sergeant Major Hawkes and the 12th regiment he added:

> but for your courage, coolness, and steady working, my premises, stock and probably many other buildings on the west side of Queen Street, must have been destroyed.[1]

He included the hapless Volunteer Fire Brigade in his thoughts, offering them his 'heartfelt thanks.' His comments were supported by a member of the public who complimented the Water Police and the 12th regiment in the paper the next day:

> There is no mistake, they worked bravely, and fearlessly, in most dangerous positions, and to them, and them only, do I attribute the saving of considerable property in Queen Street.[2]

Sympathy for the victims flowed as well as criticism for the council and the government:

> There are those among us who denounce in unmeasured terms the civic and colonial authorities for their apathy and neglect in not having long ago provided the means of extinguishing fires in Brisbane.[3]

A public meeting was duly called to discuss the formation of yet another volunteer fire brigade. Advertisements filled the newspapers advising temporary trading arrangements, auctions of damaged stock and pleas for missing articles to be returned. In particular, Rowland Illidge was searching for a large cheval mirror, a clock, a rocking chair and a bag of silver coins. Businesses that had lost accounting books begged customers to honour their debts.

Eleven larceny charges were heard in court the day after the fire. Quick work by the police rounded up the culprits, five men and six women, some being caught running away from the fire. The stolen items were mostly clothing and drapery. The defendants were fined or sentenced to between one and three months jail.

For the merchants now without a premises to trade from, temporary shops and sheds – ramshackle structures of wood and tin – sprang up down the street on vacant land bounded by Edward, Queen, Creek and Elizabeth Streets. Quickly christened by the local populous as 'Refuge Row', the block did its job and a semblance of normal commercial activity returned to the city centre. Within weeks plans were drawn for new buildings. Stone, brick and iron structures conforming to the council's recently passed 'first class' construction code replaced the old burnt-out wooden shingled-roofed structures.

The formal inquest into the disaster looked carefully at the timeline of the fire and which premises were affected, resulting in a hand drawn street elevation – a rare visual representation of the Queen Street of 1864.

The inquest ruled that the fire was accidental and originated in Edward Fegans' shop probably from a shelf of kerosene lamps along the wall adjoining Rowland Illidge's hairdressing and perfumery shop. While no lamps had been left burning, rats could have knocked over the still hot lamps and ignited matches kept nearby. Several cats had indeed been left on the premises for the express purpose of chasing the plentiful rats. The inquest also concluded with dire warnings of further disaster if problems of available water and an effective fire fighting unit were not resolved.

An ominous prediction indeed.

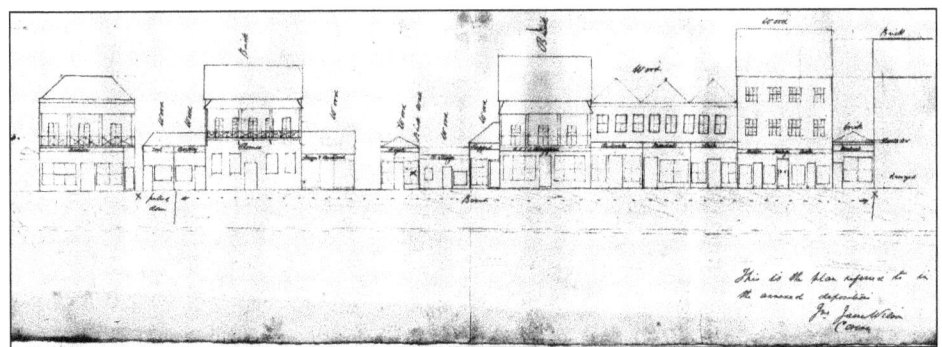

The fire inquest street elevation.

Brisbane Burns

Chapter 15

Refuge Row

In 1864 the block of land bounded by Edward, Queen, Creek and Elizabeth Streets was undeveloped except for the old convict women's prison which stood on a small rise, hence the local name for the area – Gaol Hill. The buildings were used for the Police Court and Land Office. On the levelled site today is the stately General Post Office. After the April Queen Street fire the council allowed the erection of temporary buildings on the Edward and Queen Streets corner – Refuge Row.

Ironically, as the city debated how to avoid another devastating fire, the refugee merchants were nearly burned again just five months later. On 4 September 1864, fire broke out in the Little Wonder bookstore in Edward Street run by Francis Marriott whose previous shop had been destroyed in April. By the time the fire brigade arrived, nothing could be saved of the bookstore and Robert Bulcock's neighbouring seed and produce shop was also ablaze. This was the third time in three years that Robert Bulcock had lost his stock and business premises. The rest of his store was demolished and the adjoining photographic store saved with water from a nearby tank. Fortunately this time the spread of the fire was prevented and disaster averted.

> There is little doubt that, (but) for the systematic course of action which was adopted, the whole of Refuge Row must have been rendered a heap of ruins.[1]

Yet the 'temporary' solution of Refuge Row would time and again prove more resilient to progress (or fire) than most had imagined.

By June 1865, the Government had recognised that the land now occupied by Refuge Row was being eyed off by hungry property investors. The whole block, officially Section 30, was subdivided into 17 small blocks. Eight went for auction, realising over £6000. Lot 33 was reserved for the new General Post Office. This was a significant return for an underfunded government desperate to finish infrastructure such as the railway to Ipswich, the Enoggera reservoir and the cross-river bridge.

Five years later, in 1870, five blocks on the corner were resold. The area now being considered prime city real estate, the press reflected the general view.

> It will no doubt be a cause of sincere pleasure to the citizens of the metropolis when the last of the tumble-down edifices in Refuge row, which are an eyesore in the principal business street of the city, is pulled down.

The Co-operative Butchering Company bought 47 feet (14 metres) of Queen Street frontage for £1630, the area being described as 'now one of the best positions in Queen Street.'[2]

Plans were made for a new General Post Office adjacent to Refuge Row in Queen Street. In 1871 the old women's prison was demolished and construction began on an Italian-style two storey building designed to suit the tropical climate with large windows, lofty ceilings and a second storey colonnade to protect the outer walls from heat and rain. Completed at the end of 1872, the building was the beginning of the gentrification of 'the meanest part of Queen Street'.[3]

By October 1875 some of 'the unsightly buildings which have for so long occupied Refuge Row Queen Street'[4] were due to be replaced by new buildings for the Mutual Provident Society designed by architect James Cowlishaw. Tragically, fire would visit Refuge Row once more before all the old buildings could be replaced.

On 23 March 1877 fire again erupted in Refuge Row. A leaking cask of rum was accidentally ignited in a grocery store. Alerted by the fire bell, the volunteer fire brigade arrived but no water was available. It was Friday, and the supply from Enoggera was turned off for the weekend. The brigade was reduced to using bags of salt to spread over the burning spirit. Volunteer fireman James Mooney was working close to the fire when another cask exploded spraying him with burning rum.

> His clothes becoming ignited he rushed out of the shop into Queen Street, where he was thrown down and enveloped in wet bags.[5]

James Mooney died two days later as a result of his injuries – the first fireman in Brisbane to die in the line of duty.

> The tolling of the death-knell on the fire-bell on Monday afternoon was the first intimation which many persons received of the melancholy event.[6]

His funeral took place the following day and the cortege, lead by members of the Volunteer Fire Brigade, stretched several city blocks. Immediately following the tragedy subscriptions were canvassed for the erection of a memorial stone over his gravesite in Toowong cemetery. Stewart and Hemmant, themselves victims of the December 1864 fire, were the first to offer a donation.

Simultaneously with the collection of donations for James Mooney, the council was planning a drinking fountain at the corner of Queen and Eagle Streets. With a grant of £300 the Council directed the Improvement Committee to deal with the fountain and a memorial to Mooney. It was nearly three years before the fountain was complete. In that time the Council lost sight of its intention to honour Mooney and the original plaque only dedicated the fountain to the 1879 Council members. Despite this oversight the fountain was always considered a memorial to James Mooney. It wasn't until 1988 when a new plaque was placed on the fountain that there was official acknowledgement of James Mooney and all fire fighters lost in the line of duty.

In July 1877 the last of the 'wretched shanties' that were known as Refuge Row were pulled down revealing 'a disgusting state of things.'

> That such a state of things could have existed in the main thoroughfare of the metropolis seems inconceivable.[7]

They were replaced by a magnificent three storey stone building for the Australian Mutual Provident Society (AMP) costing £8000. In the early 1930s this was replaced by the present nine storey building called Macarthur Chambers, named for its association with General Douglas Macarthur who used the building as the Allied forces South West Pacific Headquarters during World War 2.

Chapter 16

Set for Disaster

As dusk fell on the sweltering first day of December in 1864, the shopkeepers of Queen Street breathed a sigh of relief as they began to close up for the night. They pulled down the shutters, locked away the day's takings and, conscious of the ever-present danger of fire, carefully extinguished lamps, candles and lanterns. A few listless horses waiting to be unharnessed from their carriages and carts were led away to stables behind the shops. The last customers of the day gathered their parcels and headed home. For some, it was a long, tiring journey. The more fortunate, mainly business people, had only a short walk or ride up the hill to the splendid heights of Wickham Terrace and Spring Hill.

Elsewhere along Queen Street, hotels and cafes started lighting up. Over the bars and billiard tables, lamps and chandeliers were lit. Open fires and cooking ranges blazed, preparing evening meals. At the Sovereign Hotel at the top end of the street, publican, George McAdam was ready for yet another night's work. For nearly twenty years on and off George had been overseeing the Sovereign and its patrons. Beginning as a small single storey 'bush pub', it had retained its character over the years but had become a rambling complex stretching all the way through to Elizabeth Street.

Built mainly of timber, the long, low single storey building had a shingle roof and brick sides shaded by an overhanging roof. Entry to the property was through a gate covered by a tall iron arch, decorated with scrolls and topped with a hanging lantern. On each side of the entrance hallway were two parlours, both reached by a door from the verandah. In all, there were 15 guest bedrooms. The bar was in a separate building on the northern side. In the courtyard behind, there was a double-storey brick billiard hall with verandah. Completing the complex were the kitchen and stables.

Over the years the Sovereign's clientele had changed. It was still a place for squatters, graziers and stockman, but increasingly frequented by businessmen, merchants, traders and seamen. Gone were the rip-roaring days when drunken patrons dragged their horses inside the bar to bet on which ones could jump over the dining tables. Despite great hilarity, there were often serious consequences as 'jockeys', forgetting to duck, smashed their heads on the solid timber rafters above.

A few doors away at the Victoria Hotel the evening was in full swing. Publican George Mason ushered customers and patrons into the dining room. A passionate musician, Mason always provided entertainment, attracting out of town visitors and families. The Victoria, a low timber building which had stood in Queen Street for 20 years had grown steadily with each new publican. It boasted an excellent billiard table highly prized by its patrons.

In its early years the walls were thin and ceilings non-existent. A good night's rest depended on the level of revelry in the bar. One young sailor recalled leaving the raucous company of his mates to snatch some rest in his bedroom. His friends, miffed at his departure, banged on his door demanding that he return to the party. Ignoring them, he was stunned to find them later crawling along the open rafters above his bed yelling at him. Eventually they all went to bed except the ones that had fallen in a drunken stupor on to his bedroom floor. When the young sailor's ship next returned to Brisbane he chose to stay elsewhere.

Visiting doctors, dentists, salesmen and quacks often took rooms at the Victoria Hotel to conduct their business. This evening the hotel was host to a phrenologist, J. D. Kelley, who advertised advice "with respect to Choice of Occupation, Training of Children, Self-Culture, Marriage, etc."[1] as determined by examining the shape a person's cranium.

Chapter 16 — Set for Disaster

At Queen Street's stylish Café de Paris, preparations for the evening's meal were well underway. Proprietor Isaac Lenneberg checked that his kitchen and waiting staff were on duty. Upstairs in their residence, his wife attended to their toddler daughter and infant son. For the less affluent Brisbane residents, a few doors further towards Albert Street, the Oyster Saloon was open for business serving and selling the latest catch from Moreton Bay including fresh oysters from the islands and a wide variety of fish and crabs.

At Gaujard's Cigar Divan, the pipes were lit, the chess boards were out and those merchants not returning home for dinner were settling in for a quiet evening with a meal and spirited discussion. A few lucky last minute-customers scored a bargain from butchers George Edmondstone and James Collins as they cleared their leftover stock. Albert Hockings was packing away his stocks of young sugar cane, coffee, tea, banana plants, seed potatoes and pineapple suckers. Racks of garden and flower seeds were also on offer.

Augustus Kosvitz, a jeweller, had carefully secured his cases full of valuable stock, pulled down the shutters, locked the doors and retreated to his small residence in the back of the store for a well-earned drink. Donald Dallas, a saddler with a workshop close to Albert Street, had returned to his family in Boundary Street, Spring Hill. Further up Queen Street, another saddler, Nathaniel Lade, was putting away the tools and shuffling his apprentices out of the door. Harnesses and saddles, belts, bags, cases and boxes were all the work of the leather expert.

Dickson and Duncan, Auctioneers and Agents, were finishing the day's stock-take. In the last few days they had sold such varied items as a case of Enfield rifles with bayonets, eight casks of soda water, a quantity of sherry, sides of bacon and hundred pound bags of flour. Stock sold was expected to be removed immediately by the buyer, but some remained unsold or stored temporarily until transport could be found.

The new Masons Concert Hall behind the Victoria Hotel was nearly complete. A plain and fancy dress ball was planned for the opening night of 9 December to coincide with the Queensland Anniversary Regatta on the Brisbane River. All over Brisbane, costumes, dresses and suits were being sewed or spruced up for the night, making busy days for the drapers of Queen Street. One such draper, Stewart and Hemmant, on the corner of Albert and Queen Streets had just closed. Alexander Stewart had returned to his home in Wickham Terrace and William Hemmant was deep in discussion with Mr Hancock, the coroner, up in George Street.

Despite the competition between businesses, the owners and proprietors were friends and acquaintances. There were occasional spats over horses let run loose, signs blocking the footpath or noxious smells offending customers but overall, nods, friendly waves and an afternoon chat were expected courtesies in the tiny settlement.

This was Queen Street, Brisbane on the night of 1 December 1864 – the block bounded by Queen, George, Elizabeth and Albert Streets the beating heart of commerce. Behind the mostly wooden buildings, the shops and warehouses contained every imaginable item from the rarest cheeses, expensive wines to sheets of corrugated iron and buckets and shovels.

Anchored in Moreton Bay were the *Fiery Star* and the *Queen of the South*. Having disgorged their latest load of immigrants and cargo, the ships were being reloaded by steamers and lighters busily filling the holds with bales of wool for export to England. For £50 you could secure a berth in a saloon or £30 a cabin and £15 steerage for travel direct to England. A clipper ship could do the trip in an average of 82 days.

Further down Queen Street between Albert and Edward Streets, the finishing touches were being applied to new buildings constructed after the April fire. Some merchants and traders had already returned from their temporary premises in Refuge Row.

As night finally closed in and a whispery north easterly sea breeze brought the promise of respite from the heat of the day Edmund MacDonnell rested on the verandah of his Wickham Terrace residence overlooking over the jumble of buildings below that was Brisbane city. As newly-elected Superintendent of the Volunteer Fire Brigade his long-frustrated efforts to organise an effective fire fighting force had been rewarded at the previous evening's regular practice meeting with the police finally agreeing to allow police horses to be used to pull the fire engine. For three months he and George Cutbush, his second in command, and a zealous band of concerned citizens had agitated without success to improve the fire-fighting capabilities of the growing town. Water supply was still a difficult issue.

Many had declared the formation of an efficient fire service useless without an improved water supply. A temporary scheme was devised to pipe water from the nearby river so the more established part of town could be protected. As simple and logical as that sounds, in mid-19th century Brisbane it wasn't just a case of wandering down the road to the hardware store for supplies. A laborious system of ordering pipes through the post and waiting for ships and steamers to deliver the goods meant that by December 1864, there was still no easily available water. The first sod had been turned just three months earlier on the Council's project to pipe water from a dam at Enoggera but it would be another two years before a regular water supply arrived in the city.

Brisbane Burns

The Fire of December 1

Brisbane Burns

Chapter 17

The 'Royal' Scot

Alexander Stewart 1835–1918

As usual, Alexander Stewart was amongst the last to leave his drapers shop, Stewart & Hemmant. His partner William Hemmant was already at home. Stewart carried out his usual routine. As the last customer left the shop, one of two lamps left burning in the shop was extinguished and the other carried by the cashier, James Macintyre, to the cellar. Stewart remained in the darkened store waiting for O'Brien the porter to shut the door and draw the shutters. He and O'Brien went into the cellar, the porter fastening the window and locking the door while Stewart changed his boots. All lights were extinguished and the three men left the darkened building at just on 7pm.

It was a small timber shop, with the ground floor office and salesroom facing Queen Street. Where the land fell away in Albert Street, there was a cellar reached by internal stairs with an external door at the rear. The porter and Mr. Stewart later agreed that they had indeed extinguished all lamps; there were no matches in the cellar, no loose papers lying about and no-one smoking a pipe. All the proper precautions had been taken.

Yet something went wrong. As later reports confirmed, a group of young 'blackguards' as the press dubbed them – a dozen or so boys aged between 11 and 17 who regularly loitered at the shop corner – had been seen lighting pipes and cigars and throwing the 'lighted matches about in the most indiscriminate manner'[1] at the back of the store just outside the cellar.

By about 7.45 the city's fire bell was ringing and the cellar was ablaze.

Alexander Stewart had arrived in Brisbane from Perthshire, Scotland in 1858 aged 23. Having worked as a drapers' shopman since he was 15, it was a chance meeting with another draper, William Hemmant, which saw them hatch a plan to take on the competitive drapery market in Brisbane. Despite in later life adopting all the trappings of Scottish customs – full highland dress, playing bagpipes and displaying heraldic crests of the landed Stewart families of Perthshire – Stewart had come from humble beginnings. His father was a porter and shepherd. Alexander Stewart and his brother James, who also came to Queensland, were like other young Scottish men of the time, eager to seek a better fortune somewhere else.

Stewart and Hemmant compared experiences, exchanged ideas and scribbled away at business plans before taking on the well-established drapery stalwarts with an entrepreneurial flourish. Youthful self-belief and modern ideas paved the way for a successful business. Being the first to display prices in their advertisements, they also offered free ferry travel for customers from Kangaroo Point (across the river) and offered goods at Sydney's lower prices.

By June 1860, they had become so successful that anonymous rivals took out advertisements in the same newspapers as Stewart and Hemmant's lampooning a long list of bargains. Striking back at this jibe at their inexperience and youth, Stewart and Hemmant published another advertisement denying any connection with 'Skirt and Remnant' (as the jokers had nicknamed the store) and stating:

> To imagine for a moment, that these puerilities will deter them from advertising prices (which seems the great offence) argues but very limited common sense on the part of their anonymous assailants.[2]

Just a month later a mysterious advertisement appeared in the *Moreton Bay Courier*:

> Wanted. A FEROCIOUS DOG, accustomed to solitary confinement. Apply any morning before ten, with specimen at Stewart & Hemmant's[3]

Stewart and Hemmant were here to stay and prepared to fight off all opponents. (The dog never eventuated but, ironically, the presence of a one might have alerted others to the fire earlier.)

Their modern advertising strategy was however successful and by 1862 the business was sufficiently established for the opening of a branch store in Rockhampton managed by Alexander's brother James.

Financially secure, Alexander Stewart married Maria Vine Martin on 13 March 1862, the daughter of a Sydney builder. Their first child, Annie Elspeth,

Alexander Stewart.

was born in Brisbane on 14 January 1863. Around this time the young family moved to *Garth House* on Wickham Terrace, named by Stewart in honour of the home of his people in Perthshire, Garth Castle. Another Cowlishaw design, the house had been built in 1862 for William Munce. After the Stewarts, there were a variety of residents and in 1903 it was used as a boarding house for Somerville House School. Wickham Terrace, even by the early 1860s, was an exclusive neighbourhood. By now a man of means with a fine house and family, Stewart began adopting the many Scottish customs for which he became known.

> Here Scottish traditions were kept up, one being the blowing of bagpipes on special occasions by their coachman and gardener combined, one Mackenzie, in full Highland costume.[4]

Stewart and Hemmant moved into their new building in 1865 not long after the sudden death of Stewart's wife Maria aged 28.

With his daughter Annie only two years old at the time, Stewart was still a young man. Less than a year later he married 23-year-old Annie Killough of County Londonderry, Ireland. The new bride moved into the family home at *Garth House* in Brisbane's most fashionable street, Wickham Terrace. He and Annie raised six sons and a daughter. All, except the last, were born at *Garth House*.

With his partner William Hemmant involved in a political career, Alexander Stewart essentially ran Stewart and Hemmant on his own. The business survived the financial crisis of the banking collapse in 1866-67 and even opened a branch on the Gympie goldfields in 1868.

With its policy of value for money, the occasional 'Penny Table' sale and aggressive advertising, Stewart and Hemmant, now with the contacts cemented by Hemmant in London, were able to purchase directly from England, buying goods more suitable to Queensland's climate. By 1875, the firm was the largest of its kind in Australia with a turnover of £150,000. Forty people were employed on its expanded Queen Street site (later to be occupied by Woolworths followed by the Broadway Mall and now a global women's fashion chain). The following year Stewart and Hemmant sold the retail side of the business and continued as wholesalers and manufacturers on the same site.

With his large family – Annie 14, John 10, Mary 9, Charles 8, Alexander 5, James 3 and Alfred 1– Alexander Stewart needed more space. He had been buying up contiguous blocks of land along Enoggera Creek, west of Brisbane, eventually owning more than 280 acres in what became the suburb of Ashgrove. He called the estate *Glen Lyon*, supposedly in connection with the Stewarts of Garth in Glen Lyon Scotland. His connections to the aristocrats of the Stewart clan have always been hazy but he claimed connection, albeit through illicit liaisons, to the Royal Stewarts through both sides of his family.

Architect James Cowlishaw, who had designed the new Criterion Buildings in Queen Street and Rockhampton and Hemmant's *Eldernell*, also built Stewart' grand new home in 1876. The two storey building was constructed of bricks made on the site and then plastered to represent stone. There were verandahs on three sides with black and white marble floor tiles on the ground floor verandah polished with milk. Corinthian columns imported from England, a slate roof and bow windows (curved bay windows) completed the mansion. Inside, the oak woodwork complemented hand-painted Italian design ceilings and the magnificent staircase was lit by a stained glass window depicting a modified Stewart crest with a Scottish lion and thistle.

The approach to the house was through a grove of Bunya pines. The estate was designed to be self-sufficient with a dairy herd, a large lake supporting ducks and fowls, an enormous vegetable garden and an extensive orchard. The creek flats provided the fodder for the horses and a well and tanks stored the water. Stewart also had a stable of fine horses and an elegant carriage which he used every Sunday to travel to church (St. Andrew's) in the city.

With a large family to educate, Stewart was involved in a local campaign to secure a state school (Ashgrove State School) for the district's children. Stewart's three school-age children were among the first enrolments. Later additions to the property were *The Lodge*, built for the senior coachman, and a separate building housing a billiard room, gun room and cellar for his six sons. Slowly, the bush around the house was cleared creating a park-like garden with gravelled walks, extensive gardens and terraces. At one time the head gardener was Alfred Jolly, father of William Alfred Jolly, first mayor of Greater Brisbane in 1925.

Stewart continued his role as a respected member of Brisbane society as a freemason, and, for many years, a Trustee of St. Andrew's Presbyterian Church, being present at the laying of the foundation stone in April 1864.

The continued success of Stewart and Hemmant through the late 1880s to the early 1890s provided the finances for the expansion of *Glen Lyon* as well as the city store. In 1886 a five-storey bulk warehouse was built behind the Queen Street store fronting Adelaide Street. The economic depression of the early 1890s had little impact with the business expanding into clothing manufacture, taking advantage of increasing import duties. Hemmant sold his share to Stewart in 1893 but continued as the company's commission agent in London. The manufacturing side was set up in Fortitude Valley and in 1903 shifted to large premises in Ann Street. Shortly afterwards, the firm Alexander Stewart & Sons was formed as Alexander Stewart began to leave most of the running of the business to his sons.

On 13 January 1905 his second wife Annie died aged 62. Stewart was not done yet, and two years later, aged 72, he married for the third time to Edith Annie Best who had been the matron at the Hospital for Sick Children in Brisbane. They went to live at *Glen Lyon* where they enjoyed 11 years together before Alexander Stewart's death on 12 August 1918. He was buried at Toowong cemetery.

> It (the business) was materially helped forward by Mr Stewart's innate courtesy and by his ability to meet public requirements in his business sphere. Known throughout the country as a thoroughly capable and conscientious man, he carried the sincere goodwill of his fellow citizens. Imbued with a strong and unquenchable love for his native land, he rejoiced in the practice of Scottish customs.[5]

Alexander Stewart had spent nearly 60 years in Queensland leaving behind eight children and his third wife. The estate of *Glen Lyon* and the business, Alexander Stewart & Sons, had been signed over to his children as trustees in 1915. Stewart and his wife had remained at *Glen Lyon* as tenants. Shortly after his death, Mrs Edith Stewart left the estate and the entire contents were auctioned off in September 1918. The estate was eventually subdivided when trams began operating to Ashgrove in 1924. The house and a few acres of remaining land became the property of the Catholic Church, in particular the Marist Fathers, as a rest home.

Alexander Stewart & Sons did not survive the 1920s and was wound up in 1925, the valuable properties in Queen and Adelaide Streets being sold to Woolworths and the Queensland Property Development Co Ltd. respectively.

No blame for the 1864 great fire was ever laid at the door of Stewart and Hemmant. The inquest determined it was an accident of which the cause could not be determined. The boys who had been seen at the cellar door indiscriminately throwing matches were never identified. Even though confident that they had closed up correctly, niggling doubts nagged the two men, not just about the final few minutes at the shop but about each other. There is little doubt that suspicions created a lasting tension in their successful partnership.

Chapter 18

A purveyor of ladies and gentlemen's apparel

William Hemmant 1837–1916

Just on dusk, the light north-easterly sea breeze was beginning to cool the centre of Brisbane. As was usual, William Hemmant had left his business partner, Alexander Stewart, to close up their drapery shop, Stewart and Hemmant, 'purveyors of ladies and gentlemen's wearing apparel' at the corner of Queen and Albert Streets. After finishing supper at his home in Spring Hill Hemmant rode back into town to enjoy an evening chatting with friends and business acquaintances.

About 40 minutes later, William McFadyean, a near neighbour to the drapery shop, was enjoying the cool of the evening air when he noticed a light coming from Stewart and Hemmant's cellar. Ever wary of the danger of unsupervised fires, candles and lamps, his wife rushed to investigate and discovered the cellar was ablaze. McFadyean tried to break down the door alerting a passing police constable who immediately sent the news to the fire station. The station's fire bell rung out across the city.

Upon first hearing the bell, William Hemmant, ironically deep in discussion with Mr. Hancock who would be the coroner in charge of the inquest into the fire, dismissed it assuming it was only a drill. As the clanging became more frenzied and smoke began swirling into the night sky, panic swept across the city.

Fire chief Edmund MacDonnell raced to the Fire Brigade Station, joining other volunteer citizens where they donned the now familiar white and red uniforms and gathered their equipment.

Meanwhile, realising the fire was at the corner of Albert Street, Hemmant grabbed his horse and galloped to his shop as a group of men broke down the cellar door. Hemmant ran straight in, braving the fire to try and save his company's precious books.

> The office was so full of smoke that it was impossible to remain there more than a few seconds at a time; and, not having the key of the safe, I was obliged to give up hopes of saving the books.[1]

By the time Alexander Stewart arrived, also alerted by the fire bell, the shop was a mass of flames and the roof was falling in.

William Hemmant left his drapery in Cambridgeshire, England and arrived in Victoria in 1859, aged 21. For a short time he fossicked unsuccessfully on the Ballarat goldfields eventually moving to Brisbane where he met business partner Alexander Stewart. Together they leased premises on the south-east corner of Queen and Albert Street (Hungry Jacks today) from William Cairncross, imported the latest fashions from Sydney, and ventured into the fiercely competitive Brisbane drapery business.

Within a block or two of Stewart and Hemmant's there were nearly a dozen draperies. The arrival of the latest fashion magazines from England, which took three months by ship, meant that Brisbane men and women were as up-to-date and discerning as their relatives at home. Drapers who were originally just sellers of dressmaking, household and suiting fabrics and trimmings, had begun to stock lower-priced, ready-made garments and accessories for the fashionable Victorian woman or gentleman.

William Hemmant.

Britain's long experience with the Indian climate meant many articles of clothing were available in lighter, cooler fabrics. Even so, dressing for a day in town in Brisbane in 1864 still required an excessive amount of clothing. Underwear alone would have a modern woman sweating at the thought – a chemise, tight corset, long drawers, white cotton hosiery, several petticoats or even a hooped crinoline. Over the top they wore a full-length dress, usually with long sleeves, and an undershirt. In cooler weather a shawl or mantle was added. With a hat or bonnet, a parasol, kid gloves, a purse, and boots or shoes they were ready to go.

To attract customers, the drapers and clothing retailers were heavy advertisers, experimenting with 'puffing' – extravagant wording, offers of fantastic sales and lengthy column space in the newspapers exploiting every design trick possible with just typeface and without graphics. Inside the shops, every luxury was afforded the customer. Intricate cedar joinery concealed walls of bespoke drawers and shelves, glass cabinets held precious accessories, and brilliant chandeliers lit every corner dazzling customers in a range of ornate mirrors. Outside, goods often festooned the shop-front surrounding enormous plate glass windows.

When Stewart and Hemmant's entire stock was destroyed by the December fire along with their premises, immediately resurrecting the business was vital. They quickly moved to Refuge Row erecting a temporary structure of iron roof sheeting with a wooden door. Not surprisingly, the Council was now deeply concerned about the type of buildings constructed after the fire preferring brick, stone, iron or tin to wood.

In a city still reeling from the enormity of the fire, the edgy citizens complained that Stewart and Hemmant's flimsy business premises were unsatisfactory.

> The Act contemplated the avoidance of risk from fire, and the erection had been put up, if not within the letter of the law, at least in its spirit.[2]

They were given six months to remove the structure, but Stewart and Hemmant had already called tenders for the construction of new premises by architect James Cowlishaw. The new building would be two storeys of brick and stone on the site of the North Brisbane Hotel, which was still vacant after the fire in April. Despite the foundations for the new buildings giving way during construction and a portion of the front being torn down and rebuilt, Stewart and Hemmant were back in business in style before the end of 1865. The new building was two storeys of brick and stone with a basement and a shop area lit by a dome roof and plate glass windows. It was hailed as one of the finest buildings in Queen Street.

Alexander Stewart was always to be the front man and salesman of the business with Hemmant preferring the financial and procurement side. Hemmant was able to leave the business in his partner's hands when he sailed to England for a visit in November 1865.

In Cambridgeshire on 20 September 1866 he married 23-year-old Lucy Elizabeth Ground, a farmer's daughter. He returned to Brisbane in early 1867 and Lucy followed soon after. Their first child, Lucy Elizabeth, was born in Brisbane on 16 November 1867. With the new contacts William Hemmant had made in England, Stewart and Hemmant expanded the business to include wholesaling of drapery goods to other businesses in Queensland.

It was fashionable at the time for many prominent businessmen to become involved in public issues, some taking up positions on the Council or Parliament. After a brief period as an alderman, Hemmant was elected to the Legislative Assembly for the seat of East Moreton in a by-election in August 1871. The partnership of Stewart and Hemmant continued with Stewart in control of the day-to-day business.

From 1873 to 1876 Hemmant represented the seat of Bulimba for two years from 1874 he served as Colonial Treasurer under Premier Arthur Macalister. Hemmant is credited with the design of the badge on the state flag – a Royal crown superimposed on a Maltese cross.

As well as cementing his place in public affairs, Hemmant built a substantial residence, *Eldernell*, named after his wife's birthplace, for his growing family. Set on 11 acres of prime land overlooking the river at Hamilton, the house was designed by the same architect as for the business premises, James Cowlishaw, and completed in 1869 at a not insignificant cost at the time of £3900. His success was noted by the local media:

> A 'linen-draper bold' has ensconced himself on one of the highest hills, in a beautiful house which is said to have cost a very large sum, from which the outlook must be splendid [3]

Hemmant resigned from politics and sold the house in 1876 when he and his family returned to England. The area south east of Brisbane known as Doughboy Creek was renamed Hemmant in his honour. Today the house remains, having been the residence of Anglican Archbishops of Brisbane, and known as *Bishopsbourne* from 1962 to 2007. After its sale in 2007 the house reverted to a former name, *Farsley*, originally bestowed by Edwin and Elsie Tooth. Shortly before his return to England the retail business of Stewart and Hemmant was sold.

Once back in England with his wife and five children as the British resident partner of Stewart and Hemmant, he established a business exporting drapery products to Australia. Five more children were born. In 1881, the large and prosperous Hemmant family were living just outside London at Greenwich with five servants.

As well as his business interests, William Hemmant worked within the office of the Agent-General in London promoting Queensland as an immigration destination and encouraging trade between Britain and Queensland. While in this role he stumbled upon information which connected the then Premier of Queensland, Thomas McIlwraith, with a dodgy deal on some railway sleepers destined for Queensland. Hemmant felt compelled to expose questionable contracts via a petition which was presented to the Queensland parliament on his behalf by Sir Samuel Griffiths.

A huge furore erupted, necessitating Hemmant's temporary return to Brisbane in 1881. He gave a lengthy address in the School of Arts defending his allegations which were later accepted as the truth. His friends and colleagues had hoped to lure him back to public life in Brisbane but with his large family now London based, he returned to England. He continued in the Agent-General's office retiring in 1888.

But William Hemmant still had another great house to build. *Bulimba*, probably named after his last Brisbane parliamentary seat, was at Sevenoaks in Kent, south east of London. Completed in 1890, this lavish, ostentatious house was set in 20 acres and had a magnificent entrance hall with a huge oak staircase, several reception rooms, parquetry floors, stone pillared balconies, tall chimneys and four tennis courts. Six servants supported the Hemmant family of five small children and adult daughter Lucy. Their mother, Lucy Hemmant, only enjoyed the property for a short time, dying of pneumonia in 1897. Her youngest child, Maurice, was 11 years old.

The family remained at *Bulimba*, and after William Hemmant's death in 1916 aged 78, the house was left to Lucy. After Lucy married in 1919, the house was empty for five years. Various tenants occupied the property in the following years. It was eventually demolished in 1932.

William Hemmant had maintained links with Brisbane and Queensland all of his life. Without pressure from his English born wife, perhaps he would have remained in Brisbane and soared to greater heights. Quite properly he is remembered not as the man whose shop began the fire that destroyed the centre of Brisbane, but as an active, public-spirited citizen, an exemplary Government Minister and public servant.

Chapter 19

The flamboyant Frenchman

Emile Gaujard 1826–1870

A small number of people were quietly enjoying their early evening smoke in Gaujard's Cigar Divan in Queen Street when an agitated William McFadyean, fresh from alerting the police to the fire next door at Stewart and Hemmant's, burst through the door shouting that the whole place was on fire. Before they could reach the street, Edmund MacDonnell, the volunteer fire brigade and the police began directing the evacuation of the customers and the removal of the stock and furniture. The shocked proprietor, Monsieur Emile Gaujard, raced to secure his valuable property as willing hands began walking out with anything they could carry. Out into the street went tins of tobacco and boxes of cigars as well as furniture and numerous luxury household items that had contributed to the relaxed ambiance of the Divan.

A Frenchman of many talents – tobacco and cigar importer, restaurateur, entertainer, philanthropist, developer, champion chess player, and sometime swordsman – Gaujard was lured to Australia by the promise of an easy fortune in the Victorian gold fields in the 1850s. However it was not long before Mon. Gaujard, eschewing the grinding uncertainty of the diggings, opted for a more reliable road to riches – supplying the burgeoning population of Victoria with drapery. Even the most wretchedly poor prospector required a hat and boots, and for those who made the lucky strike, Gaujard and his wife, English-born Sarah Curtis, were there to supply the latest French fashions, fine European household linens, bonnets, hosiery and underwear. Sarah was about 10 years his senior. Their one daughter, Helen Therese, was born in Melbourne in 1857.

As the initial rush of easily-won alluvial gold slowed, Mon. Gaujard searched for new opportunities, and was beckoned by the newly separated Queensland and its booming frontier capital, Brisbane. The fashionable, male-dominated world of cigar smoking, and the attractive seclusion of the club-like atmosphere of smoking rooms and coffee houses inspired Gaujard's Cigar Divan which opened in Queen Street in about 1861.

English cigar divans evolved from coffee houses which were introduced to London with the arrival of coffee in 1652. The divans provided a place for men to enjoy a coffee or meal while smoking cigars, pipes and cigarettes. Here, reclining on comfortable sofas and divans, they also browsed the latest newspapers, discussed the politics of the day and played chess or draughts – in short an informal men's club. The 1860s version of the Divan was open to all for the cost of a coffee or cigar and became a popular addition to the cultural life of Brisbane.

Smoking cigars and pipes was extremely popular; its more sinister health effects as yet unknown. Jean Nicot (from where the word 'nicotine' originates) the French ambassador to Portugal, introduced tobacco to France in 1560. From there it spread to England and the rest of the world. Pipe smoking was the most common form of tobacco consumption in the 19th century, with leaves being imported from Brazil and North America. By the middle of the century cigars were becoming fashionable – the habit having been adopted in Spain and introduced to France and Britain by veterans of the Napoleonic Wars. Along with the habit came the paraphernalia – pipes, pipe tampers, pipe cleaners, cigar boxes, tobacco cutters, lighters, holders, ashtrays and cigarette cases. In Brisbane, the bustling atmosphere of the Divan and Mon. Gaujard's promised 'civility, attention and first class quality' ensured its success.

Gaujard revelled in the new society, contributing generously to charitable appeals, and happily displaying his many talents even on one occasion appearing on stage in 'Professor' George Parker's *Assault D'Armes* show demonstrating his prowess in swordplay. Parker travelled throughout Australia and New Zealand demonstrating his skill with weaponry. His popular displays included slicing a suspended (dead) sheep in half with a single blow of a broadsword, bisecting a lead bar with one slice of a cutlass and cutting a silken scarf thrown into the air with a scimitar. Other crowd-pleasers were the fencing matches, small sword bouts and single-stick fighting contests between volunteers from the audience

> Amongst the athletes who entered the arena, were Messrs. Drury, Hart, Caesarowicz, and Gaujard.[1]

On the night of 1 December, 1864 as flames licked the walls and burst through the floor of Gaujard's Cigar Divan, there was no shortage of patrons eager to rescue precious goods – furniture, crockery, paintings, chess and draughts sets and everything else that represented a second home for many of the prominent merchants and traders of Brisbane. Much of the contents were rescued but the building was totally destroyed. With his insurance settlement and the proceeds from the auction of salvaged stock sold at 'Prices which would be ridiculous if not so sad'[2], Emile Gaujard, anticipating the continued support of his valued patrons, began rebuilding.

Six months later, the long awaited announcement appeared in *The Brisbane Courier* heralding the business as arising 'like a second phoenix'.[3] French enthusiasm, flair and style oozed from the advertisement – an attractive, exciting change for residents of Brisbane more familiar with rough Irish pubs and dour Scots Presbyterian temperance houses.

The new Gaujard's quickly became a venue as desirable as the popular hotels and restaurants where people gathered for spirited discussions, demonstrations and public meetings. In August 1866, with Brisbane in the grip of an economic crisis, Gaujard's was the scene of fevered discussions on the prospect of gold discoveries in Enoggera Creek.

A victim of the slump, a Brisbane cattle and sheep dealer, Zachariah Skyring, had been declared insolvent and, under insolvency terms, allowed £3 per week and his clothes. After a short visit to the Nanango diggings (200 km north of Brisbane) he returned with a small amount of gold. He and others however, were convinced that they needed to find gold within 120 miles (190 kms) of Brisbane to ease the labour crisis and resolve the economic downturn. Consequently, a meeting at Gaujard's proposed funding an expedition to Enoggera Creek where Skyring was confident he would strike the jackpot. Small amounts of gold were discovered at there and mining was carried out sporadically from the 1880s through to the 1930s but the big payday never arrived.

> In the main Enoggera Creek there were nuggets found upwards of two ounces of pure gold, but the reefs that produced these are not yet discovered.[4]

The Nanango 'rush' still had the attention of the gold-digging public during 1867 but after a few disappointing months the diggers, including the soon to be celebrated James Nash, drifted away. In August 1867 James Nash dug around in Bella Creek about 170 km north of Brisbane. Finding a significant amount of gold he returned to Brisbane and sold it to Flavelle's jewellery store. Evading an excited crowd surrounding his hotel, he quietly returned to Maryborough to officially stake his claim. The Gympie gold rush was on.

Although Emile Gaujard subscribed to the Enoggera gold expedition, it was to prove a worthless effort so he continued expanding the business he knew well, opening a branch of Gaujards Cigar Divan in East Street, Rockhampton in 1870.

Chapter 19 — Emile Gaujard

By the end of 1870, the Franco-Prussian War* and its casualties were foremost in Gaujard's mind as he organised entertainments and fundraising for the widows and orphans. Although becoming a naturalised Australian in 1866, Gaujard keenly identified with the suffering of his former compatriots and worked to keep the cause in the local newspapers as well as lending his flamboyant rendition of The Marseillaise and other republican songs to numerous public events.

> A cry of anguish escapes from our hearts for our brethren in France, perishing by tens of thousands in battle, or falling mutilated, yet innocent victims, upon the field of slaughter. The wounded, the widows, the orphans, turn to us their supplicating glances.
>
> In this hour of her extreme distress we would fain render to our noble country an offering, however humble, for in her danger she requires the arms and the hearts of all her children.[5]

With continued success as a businessman and property owner, Gaujard sold the Cigar Divan to Charles Abraham in 1873 when it became known as the Old Divan. Already a popular venue for chess and draughts, Abraham further enhanced the men's club atmosphere by removing the billiard table and restaurant and replacing it with a cosy, smoke-filled back room. The divan played host every day from 4 to 6 pm to the best of Brisbane's draughts and chess players. One famous game matched Emile Gaujard himself with Charles Abraham, the local champion and instigator of the Brisbane Draughts and Chess Club. The trophy was a photograph of the two players with the loser (Mon. Gaujard) scratching his head in puzzlement.

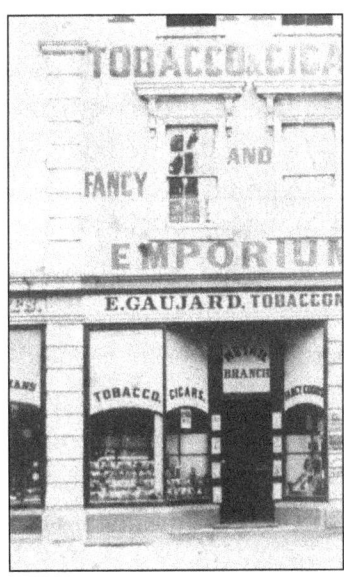

Gaujard's, 1873.

In 1874, aged 48, Gaujard expanded his real estate and wholesaling interests, erecting seven adjoining warehouses on the corner of

---

*France declared war on a Coalition of German states and the Prussian Empire on 19 July 1870. Defeated by the Coalition in January 1871, France conceded the territory of Alsace-Lorraine to the new unified German States.

Edward Street and Elizabeth Streets. Occupying the section fronting Elizabeth Street, he established the first wholesale tobacco warehouse in Brisbane and installed a new gas driven machine capable of cutting over 500 pounds of tobacco a day. The Queensland Exhibition of 1875 featured an exhibit by Emile Gaujard described as 'the preparation and finish of goods whose envelopes would do credit to a Parisian atelier'[6] (an atelier being the workshop of an artist in the fine or decorative arts). Gaujard was comfortably well off, entrenched in Brisbane society, and enjoying the rewards of business, the daily atmosphere of the Old Divan and the company of customers and friends. He ended each day at his residence in South Brisbane with his devoted wife Sarah and teenage daughter Helene.

Suddenly, in early 1876, it all started to go horribly wrong. The first hint of financial difficulty was an advertisement for an extremely desirable Villa Site (house site) between Vulture Street and River Terrace on the South Bank of the river overlooking Government house and three acres of riverfront land being used as a market garden. The auctioneer declared that Mon. Gaujard had changed plans and no longer required the site. This was not considered an unusual occurrence, as the Gaujard family was already well-established in Grey Street South Brisbane. But when in March the same year Gaujards' Buildings in Elizabeth Street went on the market as well, the warning signs went up. Immensely proud of his buildings and having finished them to an exacting standard, he had occupied three of them for his own business. The advertisement described the rental return for investors as £915 per year, a substantial yearly income.

When in May of that year the advertisements appeared for the sale of his stock and fittings it was obvious the business was in trouble. Whether Brisbane was unable to sustain a tobacco business of that size or whether he had overstretched himself is unknown. There were no insolvency proceedings but trustees were appointed and a final dividend paid to creditors in June. Gaujard and Elson, wholesalers, appeared in August of the same year as the result of James Thomas Elson, another Queen Street tobacconist, investing. Emile Gaujard retained a share in the business and continued to be associated with Gaujard and Elson until his retirement in 1884.

His beloved wife Sarah died on 27 December 1879, leaving him and daughter, Helene, 21, to fend for themselves. In early April 1882, Emile and Helene were farewelled by friends at a supper at the Café Royal Hotel before their departure for London. A summer holiday in Europe, the first time back to his native France in nearly 30 years, preceded his retirement from business.

On their return to Brisbane, Emile Gaujard left the running of the business to James Elson and concentrated on the forthcoming marriage of Helene to George Bruce Nicol, (on 31 January 1884). Originally from Glasgow and employed at the Queensland National Bank, George Bruce Nicol, with Albert Lanfear, opened the West End Brewery in 1886 at the corner of Merivale and Montague Streets, West End.

Suffering from ill health in the last few years of his life, Emile Gaujard died from a stomach complaint on 7 October 1890 aged 64 at his home in South Brisbane surrounded by his daughter Helene, son-in-law Bruce and grandchildren Corrine, Victor and Stella. He had left a lasting reminder for Brisbane with his final investment in four terrace houses in Sussex St West End named the Brighton Terraces. Completed just prior to his death, the last was leased in 1894. The houses were remodelled and split into flats over the years but have been restored to their original glory.

The Old Diva was eventually sold again in October 1897 to Mr. Hungerbuhler but around 1900 it went out of business and was replaced by a watchmaker and jeweller.

Brisbane Burns

Chapter 20

A rocky road to success

George Cutbush 1839–1913

The fire continued to rage along Queen Street away from the corner and up the hill toward George Street, fed in no small way by the dry timber shingle roofing so common at the time. For George Cutbush, the enthusiastic captain of the newly-formed Volunteer Fire Brigade and fighting his first major fire, it was this threat he had to remove first. Again, without an adequate water supply, fire fighting in the city of Brisbane was all about demolishing.

Cutbush, clutching a rope and axe, was soon, to the alarm of some of his men, scrambling onto the roof of Williams Oyster Bar, a popular establishment that was already beginning to catch alight. Smashing through the rafters then tying the rope around a roof beam and hacking away at the beam's anchor point Cutbush would signal to his men below to pull. One-by-one large sections of roof crashed down into the building as the rafters were removed, with Cutbush precariously balancing himself on the remaining structure.

But the fire was quicker. Soon the flames were reaching higher, now further fuelled by the falling timber beams and shingles. They had reached what was left of the roof and the only structure left supporting Cutbush. A weakened beam suddenly gave way and Cutbush plummeted from the roof knocking himself unconscious and sustaining a wound to his throat. Only a swift rescue by his men saved him from becoming the first victim of the fire.

A storeman at a firm of cabinetmakers, George Cutbush burst into the public life of Brisbane in June 1864 when he submitted two letters to the Citizen's Fire Committee, (tasked with organising a replacement fire brigade) stating,

> My experience gained in the London Brigade consists of being actively engaged in upwards of three thousand fires.[1]

It was by any stretch of the imagination an audacious claim that immediately attracted the attention of the committee.

Previous attempts at forming volunteer brigades had failed as members were soon discouraged after they were asked to provide not only their time, but also their own uniforms, buckets and ropes. Both business and government were unwilling to take responsibility or provide funds. A horse-drawn, steam-powered water pump purchased by the Queensland Insurance Company in 1862 was housed in a repaired Council shed in Queen Street on land now occupied by the GPO. Space was provided for volunteers to meet and practice. This had formed the basis of a Volunteer Brigade, which, though undermanned and constantly criticised, fought numerous fires throughout 1863.

Much of the negative comment from the public towards the fire brigade related to the effectiveness of the fire engine. It was heavy and awkward, consequently taking a long time to arrive at the scene. Hoses were too short, connections of joins and nozzles mismatched. Water was often only available from private tanks, soon emptied, or from the rank, slow-moving, muddy creek that ran between Adelaide and Queen Street to Creek Street.

Under the circumstances, George Cutbush's claim of up-to-date fire-fighting experience was greeted with enthusiasm in most quarters. His letters listed the required equipment, necessary training, appropriate uniforms and efficient distribution of fire stations. He offered further suggestions to combat the problem of a deficient water supply. Two more fire engines were needed and should be placed in positions such as Fortitude Valley and George Street. At night, ferry operators should be forced to leave their vessels on the north bank of the river so they could be used to transfer an engine to South Brisbane in an emergency. The Victoria Bridge was still years away from being con-

Chapter 20 — George Cutbush

structed. All the apparatus to be used with the engines should be of the same gauge. Engines would, at all times, be in full working order.

He also suggested that the Superintendent reside at the central fire station, inspect the engines daily, exercise the brigade weekly and have a full knowledge of the available water systems. A team of a dozen men with an appropriate uniform and a helmet would be required by each station. Surprisingly, these sensible and obvious suggestions were generally treated as new and radical ideas.

George Cutbush's letters were printed in full in the local newspaper, sparking interest from the reading public. Some Letters to the Editor questioned his credentials however. In reply, he detailed his London experiences, claiming he had been a member of the Hodges Distillery Fire Brigade in Lambeth, London.

The Hodges Distillery Fire Brigade was created by Fred Hodges, owner of the Hodges Gin Distillery in London in 1851. The premises were surrounded by dangerous businesses such as a fireworks factory, candle-works and tallow (rendered beef or mutton fat used for making candles) manufacturers, not to mention the alcohol stored at the Distillery. Initially formed to protect the business, the Hodges Distillery Fire Brigade consisted of about 40 employees who doubled as volunteer fire-fighters. They also began responding to local fire calls around Lambeth, often arriving before the official London Brigade.

'Captain' Hodges was a wealthy eccentric with a fascination for steam engines and he purchased the first steam powered fire engine in London and even built a lookout tower at his factory. If George Cutbush had indeed been a member of the Hodges Distillery Fire Brigade, then his fire-fighting knowledge was from a reliable source.

Incredibly though, his statement that he had been 'actively engaged in upwards of three thousand fires' was never questioned. The Hodges Brigade claimed to have attended 100 fires in a year. Cutbush, however, insisted that in the whole of London there were 1408 fires in 1860 alone. Considering that Cutbush was only aged 25 at the time of Brisbane fire, having spent time in the Royal Navy and that, in April 1861, he was an Able Seaman aboard the *HMS Ganges* in the mid-Atlantic west of Casablanca, his busy life would have left little room for fire-fighting. *HMS Ganges* was the flag ship of the Pacific Station (Vancouver Island, Canada) from 1857 until it returned to England in April 1861. Soon after, Cutbush left the navy. In 1863 he was again at sea aboard the *Comet* sailing down the east coast of Australia. Arriving in Sydney he made his way north to Brisbane. It seems his enthusiasm for fire fighting may have led to some hyperbole in his lobbying.

Cutbush had made it quite clear in Letters to the Editor that he was putting himself forward for the position of Superintendent of the new Brigade.

> My motto is, let the best man win, and if satisfied that he is more proficient, I will be the first to serve under him as a volunteer.[2]

His rhetoric must have been convincing as he was elected Captain of the Volunteer Brigade in August 1864, but missed out on the top job of Superintendent.

Cutbush had a lot riding on his performance during the December fire and was quite devastated when he finally recovered consciousness to find that he had missed the action.

The job of Captain of the Brigade vanished with a reshuffle of jobs within the Fire Brigade in 1865, replaced by just one senior position, that of Superintendent. At a new election for the Superintendent position, George Cutbush was beaten by William Watts. Cutbush, despite his apparent experience, had been a disappointment. Knowledge probably never translated to leadership, and his premature withdrawal from the action during the December fire further prevented him pursuing his own ambitions. Despite his disappointment, Cutbush was determined, forthright, and ambitious, and was not afraid to push his own agenda. His aspirations were certainly not quietened with the realisation that his dreams of a career in the fire brigade were over.

In 1866 he married Annie Murphy, sister of Peter Murphy who became a wealthy businessman and a Member of the Legislative Council for Queensland. When Cutbush's second daughter Annie Mary was born in 1871 he was still a storeman at Brabant & Co. Probably frustrated at the lack of progress and needing to feed a growing family, they moved to Tasmania later that year.

Driving trains in Deloraine in the north of Tasmania was his next wild idea. No doubt he was similarly able to convince authorities of his train driving skills as he had been to persuade the Fire Brigade that he was a fire-fighter of renown. Cutbush's train driving episode would have been lost to history had he not been in charge of a train that nearly derailed after hitting stones and timber on the track. An inquest followed, and details of George's involvement were published in the newspaper. Although the accident was not his fault, he gave up train driving and the family returned to Queensland around 1874, settling in a cottage on Kelvin Grove Road. George tried his hand at store keeping but that unravelled two years later when he was unable to repay his debts and applied for insolvency.

It wasn't until 1880, aged 41, that George Cutbush finally found his feet and launched himself into a career as a publican, helped along by his brother-in-law's contacts in the hotel industry. His first stint was as Licensee of the Royal Hotel in Beenleigh (still in existence today). In 1883 he acquired the Belfast Hotel in Queen Street, near Wharf Street. A gracious and charismatic host, he worked hard to build the reputation of the Belfast which was renowned for comfortable and welcoming interiors, superior dining facilities and an extensive collection of wines, beers and spirits.

Moving to the Palace Hotel in South Brisbane two years later, he continued his steady climb in the industry. From the Palace, which he expanded to include a billiard hall, he moved on to the Transcontinental in George Street built by his brother-in-law Peter Murphy. This hotel at one time had the largest bar trade in Brisbane. Finally, in 1887, Cutbush took over the newly built Treasury Hotel on the corner of George and Elizabeth Streets, replacing the Dunmore Arms on the corner opposite Queen's Park.

As the *Queensland and Figaro Punch* declared in July 1888,

> Altogether it would be hard to beat Cutbush's Treasury Hotel in any of its departments of service – either in their family, private, or public branches. Celerity and civility and the best of goods characterise any house ruled by Mr. Cutbush, and the Treasury Hotel forms no exception to this record.

The original Treasury Hotel building still remains today housing a popular Irish hotel.

Illustration of the Treasury Hotel, 1889.

George had finally made it to the top of his game. With his many exceptionally pretty daughters marrying influentially into the community, 'a family noted for their beauty'[3], George and Annie's place in Brisbane's society was firmly established. The extended Cutbush and Murphy families were frequently seen at many balls, card parties, weddings and engagements and were highly regarded in Irish Catholic circles.

On Christmas Eve 1913, while still proprietors of the Treasury, George and Annie journeyed to Redcliffe, visiting daughter Florrie and her husband for the holiday season. Aged 75, George had been treated for a heart condition for some time, and sadly on Christmas Day, his heart finally gave out. The funeral service was held at St. Stephen's Cathedral, attended by a large crowd. Afterwards, at the Nudgee Cemetery, Archbishop Duhig conducted the graveside service. Among the mourners were many members of George's extended family, friends, business associates and representatives of the Licensed Victuallers Association, with whom George Cutbush and Peter Murphy had both had a long association, and Perkins and Co., brewers.

With a little determination, a great deal of bravery, a touch of foolishness, and the support and influence of family and friends, George Cutbush, storeman, had fought his way up the colonial ladder of success.

Chapter 21

Dogged by disaster

Donald Dallas 1827–1867

By now the fire was well on its way to burning out the entire block surrounded by the parallel streets of Queen and Elizabeth, and George and Albert. While the Queen street frontage housed some more substantial structures, most had rough timber outbuildings behind them with small dwellings largely made of nothing more than packing case and wood scattered across the rest of the land. The whole of the interior framed by the streets was becoming a vast sheet of flame.

As George Cutbush was dragged to safety and William's Oyster Saloon consigned to the past, the 12th Regiment under Lieutenant Mair arrived resplendent in their red and blue uniforms and bayonets glinting in the flames. There was little firefighting for the barely two dozen soldiers to do however, as one after another, small wooden shops succumbed to the inferno.

Yet a crowd of nearly 6000 onlookers, many of them terrified and trying to calm screaming children, thronged the streets dodging piles of ruined furniture, rubble and crashing buildings. Mair soldiers now worked to keep the swelling crowd back from the working face of the fire.

Thompson and Sharp, a small drapery firm, which had opened just eight months earlier and, like Stewart and Hemmant, desperate to carve a position in the competitive world of drapery, disappeared in minutes, their stock having been flung out into the street.

Another new and uninsured business owned by Donald Dallas, a saddler from Victoria, was razed to the ground, although some tools and stock had also been added to the growing pile now taking up half the street.

A saddlery had stood on the Queen Street site since 1853, but Donald Dallas was new to Queensland arriving in early 1864. Dallas had travelled a long way from the fishing village of Wick in Caithness, Scotland. In 1853 his father James, owner of a previously thriving saddlery business employing six men including three of his sons, fell on hard times. Having already spent time in debtors prison, James's fear of such an outcome for his sons may have prompted his sons' move to Australia.

Thomas and Donald Dallas had arrived, like thousands of others, during the great Victorian gold rush. Often, by the time new prospectors walked to the goldfields and found a claim, the easy alluvial gold was worked out and mining was only viable by deep shaft mining requiring the combined effort of a several men. Disillusioned, they returned to their trades or secured a small farming selection.

Donald set up saddlery business in Wallan Wallan, Victoria, with a small farm on the side. He went broke in 1860 due to the failure of crops and losses in his business moving to Queensland for a fresh start with his wife, Annie Crosbie King, married in Glasgow in 1858. They had three children, Johanna, Margaret and Anne. Thomas and wife, Jane Fulton and a daughter, also named Jane, followed Donald to Queensland.

Queensland would not be kind to the Dallas brothers. After the fire, Donald Dallas applied to erect a temporary shop on his old site in Queen Street, but new regulations stipulating 'first class limits' within the city meant wooden structures were not allowed. He eventually moved his business around the corner to Albert Street.

Just two months after the fire, Thomas Dallas returned to his South Brisbane home one afternoon feeling a little unwell and promptly died. He was 36. Thomas had been visiting Donald in North Brisbane, and while sitting in Donald's yard he had felt the sun 'very hot'. He came home about 2pm and fell asleep, snoring so loudly that neighbour, Anne Blasdell, assumed he had been drinking as 'when he did he always snored tremendously'. He slept for some time, still snoring, until his wife Jane, alarmed by the change in his appearance, called the doctor at 4pm.[1]

Upon arriving, the doctor found Thomas bleeding from the mouth, his face and hands swollen and purple, his breathing difficult, and his pulse scarcely detectable. Within minutes he was dead. Without an autopsy and after a short inquest, the doctor declared he had 'died by apoplexy by the visitation of God and no other way'.[2]

Victorian apoplexy covered most forms of sudden loss of consciousness and referred to bleeding on the brain or in other organs of the body. Thomas Dallas most likely suffered a stroke. At 36 and otherwise well, this affliction did indeed seem a visitation of God. The demise of Thomas, while distressing to those around him, didn't have any apparent relationship to Donald Dallas' story until nearly three years later when it was reported the *Brisbane Courier* on 17 December 1867 that 'A well-known resident of Brisbane, named Donald Dallas, died very suddenly yesterday.' He was 40.

Donald had been apparently in robust health but was known to drink heavily, a common occurrence in Brisbane at the time. Six months previously his youngest daughter, Wilhemena, had died aged 19 months, he had lost his saddlery business once again (another victim of the 1866/67 depression in Brisbane) and had just decided to try his luck on the Gympie goldfields.

Returning home to his residence in Boundary Street, Spring Hill on the Saturday night just before midnight, he complained of a headache and went to bed. On Sunday he seemed to have an uneventful day visiting various places around the city without complaint. He went to bed as normal on the Sunday evening and woke later asking his wife Annie for some 'salts' as he felt unwell. Annie fell asleep and woke later during the night to the sound of her husband making a rattling noise beside her in bed. She shook him but he didn't wake. Fearing the worst, she went to get her landlord, Egan. She could see Donald was struggling to breathe, his eyes and mouth were open, and there was froth in his mouth. He looked like he was 'fast going'.
The landlord went for a doctor but he refused to come, assuming that Dallas was drunk. Back home, Annie watched her husband slowly slip away. 'He appeared to have died without a struggle.'[3] She and a neighbour began a lonely vigil over the body. Heavily pregnant, Annie

Dallas had good reason to be distraught. Three small children would soon be awake and requiring attention, wondering about their father. With no means of income, she was almost penniless and faced the prospect of three hungry mouths to feed. Donald's family was a world away in Scotland.

It wasn't until 11am the next day that Dr O'Doherty came to examine the body. He carried out an autopsy right away in the house, a truly horrifying experience for a new widow and three young fatherless children. Dr O'Doherty found the deceased had been 'in the prime and vigour of life' but noted that Dallas's heart and liver were enlarged and that there had been extensive bleeding in the brain. Once again, a stroke seemed to be the cause of death – officially 'serious apoplexy'[4]. Perhaps it was a genetic weakness hidden until exacerbated by stress and excessive alcohol.

Annie Dallas gave birth soon afterwards to a son, James. In May 1868, she and three of her children left in the *Queen of the Colonies* for London, never to return. Curiously, it appears that Margaret, aged seven at the time, did not return with her mother. Why would a mother leave one of her children behind? A Margaret Dallas of unknown parents died in Queensland in 1884 aged 25. An illness or disability could have meant that Margaret was unable to travel with her mother. Whatever the reason, it was one last tragedy served up by the new colonies that had promised so much to the settler.

The great fire in Queen Street had just been the start of their troubles.

In this however, the Dallas family were not alone. Other small traders, Mr. Murphy the grocer and Mr. McLeod the confectioner, were also victims of the fire, their shops close to Dallas's saddlery. They lost everything. Possibly their businesses didn't survive as there is little reference to them in newspapers after the fire. While many business quickly found new premises, those smaller and uninsured struggled to keep going. Having lost their prime position in Queen Street, and the high cost of rent on the new more substantial structures erected after the fire, smaller traders suffered. If they lasted through the next year, 1865, then the banking troubles in 1866 sealed their fate.

Chapter 22

A starry-eyed butcher

James Collins 1829–1896

Nearly an hour after flames had first been seen the fire was now an inferno consuming everything that burned in its path. The effort by the city's residents to save stock and belongings from premises yet to be destroyed continued unabated, even as the heat and smoke from the conflagration sapped the strength of the bravest. Working hard alongside the local constabulary to rescue what could be saved were the Police Magistrate as well many justices who resided nearby along with the city's prominent Bishops Tufnell and Quinn who had brought along a large number of their clergymen.

Other volunteers worked to keep up the demolition of timber structures to try and rob the fire of fuel. Shops and homes not directly at threat but nearby by were kept under close watch as embers rained down west of the fire.

But for those timber buildings already alight, there was little to be done. James Collins's butcher shop was quickly consumed while the proprietor himself was just sitting down to supper after reaching home.

At her wedding 16 years earlier, Hannah Willis 22, had stood in the ramshackle barn-like St John's Church in William Street in Brisbane wondering if she had made the right choice. Brisbane in 1848 (six years old as a free settlement) was still little more than three villages (North Brisbane, South Brisbane and Kangaroo Point) on the banks of the Brisbane River. St John's Church of England was a disused, convict-era, carpenter's workshop leased by the Bishop for a shilling per year.

As Mrs James Collins, a new life awaited. Hannah was first generation Australian, a 'currency lass' (the daughter of a convict). Stronger and taller than the 'sterlings' (those born in Britain) this first generation were brash and ambitious with the beginnings of an accent all their own. Widely agreed by their contemporaries to be less criminal than their parents, they still carried the stain of convict transportation. Hannah's father, Joseph Willis, had arrived in Sydney aboard the convict transport *General Hewitt* in 1814 from Gloucestershire, England. Aged 31, he married Mary Curtin, a free settler from Ireland in 1826 who had arrived with her sister and mother to be reunited with her convict father.

In a settlement short of respectable women, Joseph and many other like-minded single males seeking a mate was standing at the docks in Sydney the day Mary arrived on the Thames in April 1826. Permission to marry 19-year-old Mary was granted the following month. Barely a year later their daughter, Johanna (to be known as Hannah) was born. Hannah was only 11 when her father (still under convict sentencing) spent 10 days in Parramatta jail charged with drunkenness and would be 13 before her father received a Ticket of Leave, her place at the lowest rung of society well established. Marriage, a new name and new life in a distant outpost far from the stigma of her upbringing must have seemed a blessing.

James Collins' early life however is unclear. His father was Captain James Collins of the 3rd Regiment (East Kent – The Buffs). The 3rd Regiment was active in Australia during 1826 and 1827. Captain Collins may have stayed behind when the regiment went to India in 1828, and son James was born the following year. For the first years, James and Hannah worked quietly and industriously and had two children, James in 1849 and John in 1852. They witnessed the arrival of the first immigrant ship to Moreton Bay – the *Artemisa*, and the subsequent arrival of the *Fortitude*, *Chasely* and *Lima*. The settlement rapidly expanded. James saved and waited for his first big opportunity.

The Sawyer's Arms on the western side of Queen Street between Albert and Edward Street was his first target. He took over the publican's licence in April 1853. With a burgeoning population, Brisbane was also swelled with visiting squatters and stockman delivering produce to the busy wharves. Pubs providing clean, cheap accommodation, good food and drink and excellent stabling could make a good living. With the arrival of babies Charles and George, the Collins family was establishing its presence in the growing settlement.

Down at the lower end of Queen Street, an ambitious man like James Collins envied the more established hotels up the top end of Queen Street like the Victoria and Sovereign, attracting the more wealthy squatters and pastoralists. Collins craved having his name added to the list of notable citizens in Brisbane, and was always on the look-out for bigger and better, and a yearning for the big end of town. Collins seized his opportunity in 1855, taking over the long established Sovereign Hotel in upper Queen Street.

> J.C. being determined to spare no expense in his efforts to make the Hotel worthy of the Metropolis of the Northern Districts. Amongst other improvements the erection of a Billiard Room is decided upon, to be furnished with one of Thurston's best full-sized Tables. The sleeping accommodation will be largely increased, and Rooms for Families and private parties extended, and every luxury and comfort will be provided for those parties who may favour the 'Sovereign' with their presence.[1]

It was a well-known haunt for the graziers of the Darling Downs, once having been run by George McAdam, an associate of the pioneering Leslie brothers of Caning Downs Station. Perhaps during conversations with such patrons Collins formed the idea that feeding the settlement rather than 'watering' it might be more profitable. By October 1857 James Collins had left the Sovereign and was running a butchery business from a Queen Street store between Edward and Creek Street. Hannah, now aged 28, had three small children with another on the way. John, born in 1857, did not survive the year. Children failing to survive childhood, all too common in the 19th century, was to be a tragic pattern for the Collins family.

A year later Collins sold out to George Edmondstone, the largest and longest established butcher in Brisbane. James' brief foray into the meat business proved profitable as he was to return to butchery in later years. Cashed up from the sale of the butchery business, James Collins auctioned his household effects, gave up the house in George Street and shifted Hannah and the children to Ipswich, where he took over the Queen's Arms Hotel.

In a lengthy and detailed advertisement in September 1858 James Collins stated that the hotel was 'undergoing a thorough renovation and repair,' and that he was 'determined to spare neither pains nor expense' to ensure his Hotel remained in high regard.

He upgraded the billiard table, promised to secure his wines and spirits from the same suppliers to the Sovereign and declared that

> utmost attention will be paid to the supply and appointments of the table which will always be spread with the best and choicest viands to be obtained.[2]

New servants were employed and customers assured special care and attention for their horses.

Not content with the hotel business, Collins also acquired the mail contract between Brisbane and Ipswich. He purchased a four-wheeled carriage with 'seats, which are ornamented with red cushions'[3], hoping to attract passengers on the lucrative route. Unfortunately he was unable to make the business pay and it failed six months later leaving his guarantors on the contract in debt.

With the birth of two more children, William Henry and Emma Amelia, and the dissolution of yet another business partnership, the Collins family returned to Brisbane where James reopened his butchery in Queen Street. This time the business was at the big end of town, in the ill-fated Queen, George, Elizabeth and Albert Street block opposite the old convict barracks.

While undertaking improvements on the site in June 1864, the demolition of an old room revealed a swarm of rats.

> Sticks of every description were called into requisition and for about three quarters of an hour there was great fun. What with

> waddies and dogs at least fifty or sixty rats were killed while an equal number escaped.[4]

The newspaper seemed unconcerned about the health implications of such a scene in a butcher's shop, being a small indication of the accepted sanitary conditions of the time. With no refrigeration, animals being kept in nearby paddocks and killed every few days, the stench must have pervaded the town. One positive outcome of the fire in December that year was its cleansing effect.

Despite the fire, Brisbane residents still expected to be fed. Within days of the total loss of his business, James Collins had set up makeshift meat supply outlets in Albert and Edward Streets. The cattle were still in the paddocks and George Edmonstone was working from a butcher's block outside the ashes of his shop. Competition was everywhere. Eager to continue, Collins hastily moved into a temporary shop on the burned out site before building larger and more modern premises the following year.

Sometime between the failed coach run between Brisbane and Ipswich and the new butchery, James Collins hatched a plan. Ship after ship arrived in Moreton Bay almost on a daily basis. The shallow bar at the entrance to the Brisbane River forced all these large sailing ships and steamers to remain anchored in the bay. They needed reprovisioning. To be ahead of the competition, James had to be able to supply these vessels quickly and efficiently. In a bold move he commissioned his own private steamer to be built in Glasgow. Designed by his old mate and master mariner George Patullo, it was shipped to Australia in parts and reassembled at Kangaroo Point.

With a length of nearly 21 metres and a 3 metre beam, the steamer was built with wooden planking on an iron frame and fitted with two 10-horse-power steam engines. It had a cabin capable of seating 12 people. Named *Emma* after his baby daughter who had not survived to her second birthday, the steamer was launched on 2 May 1865.

The launch of *Emma* propelled James Collins quickly up the ladder of public life. For at least a decade previously he had attached his name along with other notables to election candidate notices, subscriptions and complaints. At long last he was mixing with the cream of

Brisbane's commerce and trade. George McAdam's daughter Isabella smashed the champagne bottle as *Emma* slipped into the river. Mayor Albert Hockings proposed a toast commending Mr Collins' energy, tact and business manners.

> In a young colony, nothing tended more to success than enterprising men, and the man whose health he was about to propose was such a one.[5]

Prominent solicitor Mr. Garrick praised the local ship builder. Mr. Collins regretted the absence of his respected friend Captain Patullo who had died the previous year. *Emma's* Captain Knight proposed a toast to the ladies hoping they would enjoy many excursions on the steamer. More toasts were made to the commercial and maritime interest of the port and after three cheers the party broke up. As Hannah stood beside her husband James she no doubt reflected on that day in the makeshift church where she had repeated her marriage vows pleased with her choice, despite the loss of so many of her babies.

The *Emma* took her place in the maritime business of Brisbane. She ferried cargo to the waiting ships in the bay, carried passengers between Brisbane and Ipswich and hosted many groups of holidaymakers for a day's outing to Cleveland, Sandgate and other favourite spots in the bay. In June 1865 she played a part in one of the most important episodes in the history of navigation on the Brisbane River when the hazardous Seventeen Mile Rocks were cleared. Blowing up the obstacle and removing the rocks had begun with a party of invited guests aboard the *Emma*.

The Colonial Treasurer, the Mayor, the Water Police Magistrate and others joined the foreman of works, Mr Hodges, on the trip to lay the first charge. As owner of the *Emma*, James Collins was among the distinguished group once again networking his way into society.

Never wishing to be outdone, James Collins invested heavily in a new butcher shop built on the site of the one burned the year before. Opened in October 1865, with large marble counter tops, elaborate wrought iron fittings, and papered walls the new shop 'imparted an air of cleanliness' and drew much comment from the local newspaper.

It would be difficult to find a butcher's shop in the Australian colonies fitted up with the taste, combined with the due regard to requirements of the trade. [6]

James Collins' good fortune continued and the following February he successfully stood for election in the East Ward of the Brisbane City Council. He added to his growing property portfolio with the purchase of 55 acres at Moggill in the upper reaches of the river.

In June 1866, he was still running the butcher shop in Queen Street, maintaining the steamer *Emma*, carrying out his Councillor duties and managing an impressive number of urban and rural properties. He had also begun buying large numbers of sheep and cattle for the butchery. As with many speculative business ventures in early Brisbane, finance was easily available from banks, building societies and private investors. In June that year the London bank that financed the Queensland Government collapsed and Queensland was plunged into depression. Bulging with over 20000 new immigrants reliant on public works for their wages, Brisbane became the scene of protests and widespread hardship. Like dominoes, other financial institutions called in their loans, private investors pressured their borrowers and the whole system collapsed. Those like James Collins with heavy investments suffered.

Collins began chasing small creditors in the courts and his employees brought him to court over unpaid wages. Even the Brisbane Gas Company pursued him for unpaid coke bills. His beloved *Emma* was sold to local businessman George Harris. In June 1867, in an effort to stave off bankruptcy, Collins assigned his estate for management by trustees and resigned from the City Council. His family had already moved to more modest accommodation but by July his trustees were auctioning off the entire contents of his shop and stables.

The list of shop fittings reveals rare insight into the workings of a 19th century butcher shop. Curing tanks and troughs and salting benches, tubs and casks figure largely, taking the place of modern refrigeration.

Horses were another passion of Collins'. Seventeen stable and draught horses were sold at the auction returning between £3 and £18

> **AT 11 o'CLOCK.**
>
> In the Estate of Mr. James Collins, Butcher, on the Premises, Queen-street.
>
> The Entire of the Valuable
> **SHOP FITTINGS,**
> Including Valuable Marble-Top COUNTER, Steel Rails, Gas Pendants, Scales and Weights, large Galvanized Iron Tanks, &c., &c., &c.
>
> ARTHUR MARTIN has received instructions to sell by auction, on the premises lately occupied by Mr. James Collins, Butcher, on TUESDAY, July 23, at 11 o'clock,
> The Entire of the Valuable SHOP FITTINGS, Salting Room Requisites, and Office Furniture, chiefly comprising —
>   Marble Counter
>   3 Scales and Weights
>   Steelyard and Steel Hooks
>   Steel Rail and Pillars
>   Gas Pendants
>   4 Galvanized Iron Water Tanks, 800 gallons each
>   Curing Trough
>   Curing Tank
>   Salting Benches
>   Salting Tubs and Casks
>   Large Sausage Machine with fillers complete
>   Baskets and Trays
>   1 Beef Cart
>   1 Spring Cart
>   1 Dray
>   17 Horses
>   2 Sets Cart
>   1 Set Spring-cart Harness
>   3 Saddles
>   8 Coppers
>   6 Water Casks
>   1 Wheelbarrow
>   Patent Force-pump
>   Beef Tierce
>   Choppers, and a quantity of Sundries.
> The above are for positive Unreserved Sale.
>   Terms—Cash.

per animal. Since his earliest days in Brisbane, Collins had been entering his horses in the local races, working his way up to Steward of the Brisbane Races working alongside such notables as the police commissioner David Seymour.

Now, everything was gone. The following year his infant son Albert and his teenage son John both died, leaving the family with three out of eight children. Destitute and humiliated, James Collins retreated to the Darling Downs.

Nine years later in 1877, he returned to the news as the district overseer for Ipswich supervising road repairs, rising to Foreman of Works in 1880. He and Hannah occupied a small cottage at the depot, selling the contents in 1881 as they moved back into business. In February 1884, aged 55, after scrimping and saving for nearly 20 years, James Collins bought the West Moreton Pastoral Company at Gatton and was back in the butchery business.

Only enjoying her husband's comeback for a short time, Hannah died in October of the same year aged 54 at the Brisbane Hospital. In 1877 son George had died aged 23 leaving just two boys. The eldest, James, married Margaret Ledingham in 1875 and they had three children. James worked as a Telegraph officer all over Queensland and died in 1923. Little is known of Charles Collins.

On a warm December evening in 1885 a little over a year after Hannah's death, 56 year old James Collins married widow, Mrs Sarah

Cowell. In her late thirties and mother of two, Amelia 14 and Thomas 12, Sarah brought the aging James the family he had lost. Secure in a position as Inspector of Breweries, James had retired from the racy, speculative competition that defined business in early Brisbane. James and Sarah went on to have two boys of their own, Walter born in 1888 and Arthur in 1891.

Walter Ernest Ashley Collins grew up to become a Master Mariner and died in 1938. Arthur Bennett Collins served at Gallipoli from September to December 1915 and was awarded a Meritorious Conduct medal. He returned to Australia in 1919 and a year later married Agnes Beryl MacCallum. They were divorced in 1928 and the case was highly publicised under the heading 'Married for a Day'. Arthur Collins had left on his own to work in the Solomon Islands the day after their marriage. He returned two years later to find that, unsurprisingly, Agnes no longer wished to remain married.

Their father James would not be witness to his young son's adult achievements and notoriety, dying at home aged 67 in 1896, surrounded by his adult step children and his own two boys 8 and 5. He had witnessed nearly 50 years of Brisbane's history from the very earliest days of the first land sales, the wild Darling Downs squatters racing their horses up and down Queen Street, and the riots of the mid 1860s depression through to the established, sedate and thriving streetscape of Brisbane on the eve of the 20th century.

Brisbane Burns

Chapter 23

The Café De Paris

Isaac Lenneberg 1819–1910

The flames continued to race through numerous small shops along both Queen and Albert Street, but by 8.30 pm as the fire reached an iron-roofed building in Queen Street, it seemed to pause. The soldiers of the 12th Regiment, many now having abandoned the role of crowd management after being brushed aside with the curses of proprietors and owners hell bent on saving their livelihoods, began to pull down the *Café De Paris* to create a firebreak.

No sooner had they begun the process than the shout went up that it too had caught alight, the fire once more gaining strength from the breezes and wind drafts created by the swirling inferno. Despite frantic efforts the heat soon grew too strong for the men and they retreated to watch the popular meeting spot reduce to a pile of ashes in minutes.

Isaac Lenneberg's Café De Paris had opened nine months earlier, remodelled from the former Hart's Café. George Hart, a publican with 23 years experience in Sydney, opened Hart's Café in October 1861 providing American drinks, meals at any hour and 'light and airy bedrooms'. By early 1864, George was ready to move on and newly-arrived Jewish Prussian, Isaac Lenneberg, took over. He used the already respected name of Café De Paris which also existed in Sydney, Melbourne and other Australian towns. As well as continuing the tradition of meals at any hour, the Café De Paris also served a daily set lunch from 1 until 2 pm, all kinds of wines, ales, spirits

The Lennebergs.

and liquors and offered well ventilated bedrooms for businessmen and visitors. 'Civility, promptitude, and cleanliness, are 'Household Words' at this establishment.'[1]

Isaac Hyman Lenneberg was born about 70 km east of Dusseldorf in Lenhausen, Prussia, (now Germany) in 1819. With his first wife, Sara Rosenberg, he had three sons, Hermann, Theodor and Aaron, with only Theodor surviving infancy. Sara died before Isaac left Prussia and he married Amelia Simon. The Lenneberg family began life in Australia in St. Kilda, Melbourne in about 1862, where their daughter Bertha was born. Isaac was a furniture dealer and, for a short time, an upholsterer in partnership with Michael Henger.

After the fire, Isaac Lenneberg promptly re-established the Café De Paris in temporary premises on the corner of Elizabeth and Albert Streets and gave a free supper at the official opening on 23 December 1864 to thank his friends and clients. Many of the Queen Street traders were equally quick to re-establish their businesses. Those that only required a small space were back in business within days but those like Lenneberg who had to find replacement furniture, set up kitchens and restock, took longer. Although most insurance companies were quick to pay out, the Café De Paris was only insured for about a third of its loss. Getting back to business quickly was the only option. Isaac Lenneberg was able to announce his return to Queen Street in September 1865 – nine months after the fire.

> It will be his extreme pleasure to assume his functions of 'Dispenser of all kinds of Spirituous Comforts,' and feels assured that his friends will in him, although dressed in new garments,

> find the same steady old style and hearty good will, which made him so justly the favorite of the Public.[2]

Once again Lenneberg was able to promise his clients 'airy, large and commodious rooms, furnished with every comfort', a 'good stocked cellar', 'plunge and shower baths, a superfine billiard table and good stables.'[3]

Hotels, bars and cafes became gathering places for like minds and the Café De Paris was no different. Here, the substantial German community met for meetings and parties. In early 1865, Isaac Lenneberg assisted with the catering of a Christmas picnic for over 300, featuring a 'Schutzen Fest' or shooting competition. In May the same year, the Café De Paris hosted a meeting to discuss forming a 'Deutcher Turn Verein' or German Club. Although the club continued in various premises in North Brisbane, an organisation including the German communities from all over South East Queensland was not formed until 1882. (*Turn Vererin* means 'Gymnastic Club'. These associations hark back to covert organisations formed during the Napoleonic era.)

The new Café De Paris was the Lennebergs' home as well as their business. Savina, their last child, was born there on 30 June 1866. Lenneberg would run the Café De Paris for 10 years before moving to The Exchange Hotel (which still exists today) on the north-west corner of Edward and Charlotte Streets. Although beginning his business career in furniture, Isaac Lenneberg continued in the hotel trade all his life, enjoying the challenge of starting a new hotel or re-invigorating old and tired establishments. At The Exchange he once again remodelled, this time concentrating on the accommodation side of the business providing 'Superior accommodation to Families, Commercial Travellers, Bushmen' and emphasising its proximity to the wharves and railway station.[4]

Theodor Lenneberg, Isaac's only son, married Amelia Joseph in 1873 and moved to Pimpama, between Brisbane and the Gold Coast, where he opened a general store. Within two years he had a branch store at Nerang Creek (now Southport) and was the local Postmaster. The Nerang Bridge was opened in 1878 providing faster access to Southport. Now easily accessed by coach from Brisbane, the popular seaside fishing spot of Southport became a fashionable holiday destination. Theodor acquired yet another store and, in September 1880 after extensive renovations, opened the Southport Hotel. Directly opposite the Broadwater channel, the two storey hotel had wide wrap around verandahs and offered 30 rooms with views of the sea, excellent food and a well-stocked cellar. Buggies, saddle horses and boats were provided for visitors.

> Since Southport has been settled hundreds of Invalids have been restored to perfect health by its genial and healthful sea-air. Let those indisposed try the effect of the climate, and they will soon be convinced.[5]

Isaac was so impressed by Theodor's success in Southport that in 1884 he left The Exchange Hotel in Brisbane and bought the Southport Hotel from his son, thus cementing the Lenneberg influence on holiday hotels in Southport until the turn of the century. For seven years from 1888 Isaac Lenneberg returned to Brisbane and ran the new Shakespeare Hotel in George Street. A hotel of that name had been on the site since the early 1860s. This new Shakespeare, one of the largest hotels in Brisbane, was lavishly decorated and furnished. The public rooms were fitted with Brussels carpets, velvet seating, mirrors and pianos and the windows were hung with tapestry and lace. It was three storeys high and every room opened onto a balcony. Each floor had lavatories and bathrooms.

Unable to stay away from Southport, Isaac returned aged 76 in 1895 as the licensee of the Grand Hotel. Opened in August 1886, the Grand Hotel was a spectacular addition to the holiday hotels in Southport. Situated at Deepwater Point on the Broadwater channel it boasted 'the luxury of a club with the advantages of a first class hotel.'[6]

> The hotel itself can be best described as a miniature edition of the Parliament Houses, both in appearance and in the culinary comfort to be found within. It has a central Mansard roof and terminal American gables, with projecting bays. The height from the ground to the top of the Mansard flag staff is about 80ft. The building faces the east, and has a frontage of 150ft, and its pale green and brown hues are very effective and pretty. The two balconies, which run the entire length of the building, have

ornamental iron railings, which add considerably to the general effect. The building is of pine throughout, with galvanised iron roofs.[7]

It had one of the largest dining halls in south-east Queensland, reading rooms, private suites, 50 bedrooms all with private balconies, a two storey suite of bathrooms and lavatories and a whole floor reserved for ladies. The view from its tower was extensive, spanning out across the Broadwater, Stradbroke Island and out to the ocean and South to Burleigh Heads. To the west the view extended to the Tallebudgera Mountains.[8]

Despite the healthy sea air and warm climate, Isaac's wife Amelia fell ill and died at the Grand Hotel in September 1896. Her coffin was transported to Brisbane by train and she was buried at Toowong Cemetery. Just a year later, Theodor's wife (also Amelia) died at the New Crown Hotel in George Street Brisbane, where Theodor was the publican.

In December 1900, Isaac Lenneberg was managing both the Grand Hotel and the Pacific Hotel at Southport. He once again renovated and refurnished the hotel, installed a new chef and offered first class cuisine. Theodor stayed at the New Crown Hotel, completing further improvements in 1901. Isaac continued as the manager of the Pacific Hotel until the end of 1908. Aged 89 he retired and moved to Sydney to live with his daughter Bertha and her husband Alexander Browne and their six children, where he died in January 1910.

Daughter Savina married Ernest Meyers in 1889 and they moved to Fremantle in Western Australia where Ernest died in 1905. They had two sons, Errol and Leslie. Savina died at Virginia in Brisbane on 14 May 1954 aged 88. Theodor and Amelia had seven children and he was the first chairman of the Southport Shire Council. Two of their sons served in World War 1 in France. Harry Gordon survived but Frank Benjamin tragically

The Pacific Hotel, Southport, ca.1900.

died during the influenza epidemic in 1918 before he could return to Australia. Theodor died a short time before Frank in 1918 aged 67.

Lenneberg Street in Southport is named in honour of this pioneering family.

Chapter 24

A legacy of plants, trees, parks and gardens

Albert John Hockings 1826–1890

> Further fed by the massed pile of broken boards and shingles that had been created by the previous attempts to create breaks, the fire rolled on, jumping quickly across property lines via the dry timber stabling and outhouses which featured at the back of most premises, no matter how grand their entrances. The north-easterly winds served to fan the flames from the rear of the shops toward Queen Street.
>
> Next in line was Hocking's seed and plant warehouse, an establishment that sat within a small block of adjoining shops built of brick. Again, the brick would prove only a minimal impediment to the fire, as the ubiquitous wooden roof shingles and rear stables quickly caught alight. Nothing could be done to save the structure, though most of the valuable stock previously housed within had now joined the spreading pile of rescued articles clogging the opposite of Queen Street.

From his nursery at South Brisbane and store in Queen Street, Albert John Hockings supplied the infant Queensland colony with an extensive variety of plants and seeds. The domestic market eagerly snapped up each shipment of ornamental flowers and shrubs, vegetable seeds, seed potatoes and fruit trees. Farmers could order sugar cane, coffee and tea plants, banana and pineapple suckers.

Alderman Albert J Hockings, as a member of the Brisbane City Council, was well aware of the dangers of wooden buildings, non-existing water supplies, and inadequate fire fighting equipment. The Council had been deeply involved in the coordination of a new Fire Brigade but ultimately responsible for its demise. Any new regulations regarding the type of buildings to be erected within the city centre had not yet been formalised. Finally, members of the Council were to witness first-hand the deficiencies in their civic duties.

Albert John Hockings.

Albert John Hockings' passion was horticulture. At the time of the fire he was a respected Brisbane business man and politician, having been in business for 17 years.

In December 1841, 15 year old Albert and his 12-year-old brother Henry and parents, Thomas and Jane, arrived in Sydney aboard the *William Jardine*. They were 'Bounty immigrants' from St Martin-in-the-Fields parish, London, sponsored by colonists who employed them and then claimed a bounty from the government for each immigrant employed (£30 for the parents, £5 each for the boys).

Male Bounty immigrants were required to be tradesmen and the women preferably married and employable as servants. The Hockings family supposedly fulfilled these requirements, Thomas claiming he was a carpenter and Jane a servant. Eager to leave the poverty and squalor of early Victorian London behind, many immigrants lied on their applications and there is no evidence that Thomas ever worked as a carpenter in England.

Once in Australia, trades and qualifications mattered little as employers were not fussy. Two eyes, strong legs and arms would secure employment for most immigrants. As early as August 1844, just three years after their arrival, Thomas was trading as a commission agent securing freight and passengers for coastal shippers. Barely a year later he was in partnership with son, Albert John, then aged 18.

Cashing in on a trade opportunity, in August 1845 Thomas and Albert John put together a cargo shipment for the *Sarah Wilson*, a new brigantine (sailing vessel with one mast fully square rigged and the second gaff rigged). Some of the cargo belonged to them and the rest was on consignment from other suppliers. The Hockings were trading nails, general hardware, turpentine, white lead, timber, soap, and other goods suitable for ship repair such as oakum and tar. The *Sarah Wilson* was bound for Tahiti and other South Sea ports. On board as supercargo (responsible for managing, selling and buying the trade goods) was 19 year-old Albert John. For his father to trust a young man with such a valuable task, Albert John must have already demonstrated a penchant for grass roots commerce.

The voyage to Tahiti via Auckland and home via Samoa took 10 months. On board were the captain, three crew, and Albert John. The return cargo included a ton of valuable sperm whale oil which Albert John sold on his arrival back in Sydney. Father and son continued to run a store in Prince Street Sydney selling hay, corn, flour, oatmeal, pollard and bran until February 1847 when the partnership was dissolved.

Sixteen years later Albert John Hockings would give a lecture at the South Brisbane Mechanics Institute on his 'Recollections of a Cruise among the South Sea Islands', relating entertaining observations of the 'habits, manners, and customs of the different tribes inhabiting the several groups of islands' and 'also the various vegetable productions indigenous to the several islands'. He also exhibited articles and items collected on the cruise including a cloth made from coconut bark and

> medicine, named Carva, a most peculiar powder, nauseous to the taste, but invaluable as a cure for rheumatism.[1]

Inspired by the endless possibilities of new experiences and pockets full of trading profit, Albert and his brother Henry moved to Brisbane and together they went into business. Settling in South Brisbane, they purchased three blocks of river-front land in Stanley Street between

Russell and Melbourne Streets, and leased the Stockton Store in Grey Street from Daniel Peterson. Calling themselves 'custom house agents, shipping brokers and importers of general merchandise', they began with essential supplies (buying from Sydney in cash and selling at 25% less than their competitors) branched out into wines, ales, port, groceries and eventually into clothing and footwear imported directly from England.

Within a year, Stockton Store was a successful retail and wholesale business advertising extensively and usefully listing prices (a novel advertising concept at the time). By May 1849 they were confident enough to advertise with a little jingle:

> The 'Stockton Stores,' as all must know,
> Who live in Moreton Bay,
> Contains a choice and varied stock
> Of goods, both new and gay.
>
> The quality and prices both,
> All honest people own,
> Are now the wonder and delight
> Of all who live in town.
>
> The country folks, when they arrive,
> Are silent with surprise,
> To see how cheap we sell our goods,
> While others' prices rise.
>
> The celebrated 'Stockton Store'
> In Grey Street still is standing,
> And 'HOCKINGS' with civility
> The business superintending.[2]

Chinese labourers were a secret weapon in the success of the Stockton Store. Early in 1850 the brothers engaged two Chinese men brought to Brisbane from Amoy (now Xiamen). Gan Sun was employed as the live-in cook catering to the bachelor brothers, and Kong Te had the unenviable task of breaking horses and working in the sawpit. Chinese labourers were paid £6 a year, given rations, and supplied with two suits of clothing a year. They were indentured for up to five years, the employer having paid their passage. The average wage for non-

Chinese labourers without concessions was about £20 a year. After the cessation of convict transportation and the ticket-of-leave system, cheap labour was in short supply. By this time about 200 Chinese people had been brought to Brisbane. Daniel Peterson, former owner of the Stockton Store, and agent for the importers of Chinese labour, probably introduced the idea to the Hockings brothers.

In February 1851 Henry Hockings was charged with assaulting Gan Sun. The incident and subsequent court case shed light on Henry's character. According to Gan Sun, Mr Hockings insisted that Gan Sun accompany him to church on Sundays. Gan Sun replied that he would rather go to another smaller church where he was better able to understand the minister. Enraged, Henry pushed Gan Sun from the wharf into the river. Floundering in waist deep water, Gan Sun came to no harm, but he claimed that since the beginning of his service he had been in constant dread of Mr Hockings' threats of violence. Just seven months previously Gan Sun had been sentenced to one month in jail for disobeying orders. Now it was time for Henry to face the court. His demeanour in such a position was noted at the time and described in detail.

> Defendant having seated himself, folded his arms negligently, contracted his left leg to an angle of thirty degrees, threw out his right to its full length, reclined his head gracefully on the rail behind him, and smiling with graceful nonchalance, prepared to hear the charge.[3]

Henry was confident that his superior position in society would afford him protection from such a trivial complaint. However, the court fined him £3 4s and ordered him to pay £1 16s costs. When the Stockton Store had commenced business, Albert was 21 and Henry 18. It appeared that Henry's sense of superiority, brashness and desire to remove himself from his brother's shadow would set the pattern of his later life.

Exploiting their frontage to the river, the brothers built wharves and by 1851 were able to receive bonded goods (goods requiring customs duty paid). With Albert's marriage to Elizabeth Bailey in August 1851, and the construction of *Rosaville* (the family home) on one of the blocks, the Hockings family became a fixture in South Brisbane. The following year, Thomas, the boys' father, died of pneumonia in Sydney. Henry left the business and returned to Sydney to care for his mother. The Stockton Store was closed and Albert ran the business from Hockings' Wharves. Henry worked as a broker and commercial agent in Sydney, marrying Eliza Emmes in 1853. Their first daughter, Eliza Jane Lippman, was born a year later.

Stretch of the Brisbane River from Hockings Wharf towards South Brisbane ca.1868.

Brisbane in 1855 was still split by the river. No bridge existed and all goods were transported across by slow ferry. Hockings' Wharves provided Albert Hockings with access to the river and the increasingly important North Brisbane settlement. Eager to take advantage of the growing population, and finally financially secure enough to indulge his passion, Albert opened a seed, vegetable, fruit and plant store in Queen Street, North Brisbane opposite the old convict barracks in October 1855. Taking advantage of Queensland's subtropical climate and similarity to islands he had visited in the South Pacific, he began experimenting with tropical and sub-tropical fruit growing.

By this time he was the father of two, Albert Thomas born in 1852 and Jane Elizabeth in 1854. Henry had returned to Queensland bringing his widowed mother Jane. He settled in Ipswich and opened a general store. Striking out on his own did not suit Henry and a little over a year later his business was wound up in the Insolvency Court of New South Wales. His assets included the half share he had in the three blocks of land in Stanley Street, South Brisbane. These were put up for sale and probably purchased by Albert. Henry and his family returned to live at South Brisbane renting a house from his brother.

Meanwhile Albert John Hockings had expanded his business, supplementing his imported stock with trees and plants grown and propagated in his own nursery established at South Brisbane. A visitor to Mr Albert Hockings' Rosaville Nursery in 1859 gave a glowing description:

> We expect it will be much visited by lovers of gardening during the approaching seasons. We were pleased to notice a number of different tropical fruit trees, among which is the delicious mango, and a beautiful specimen of the carica papaya, or pawpaw, loaded with fruit. The date palm, star apple, Bengal Quince, leechee, longan, coca nut, granadilla, date plum, tamarind, and others, have a most healthy appearance, and it is probable many of them will eventually be acclimatised.
>
> We were not aware that the district possessed so valuable a collection of tropical fruit trees, and much praise is certainly due to the energy displayed by Mr Hockings, who for years has been content to expend his time and means in testing the fruit producing capabilities of his adopted country.
>
> We noticed a large number of cypress pines, and other ornamental trees; hundreds of flowering plants in pots; and thousands of healthy orange and other young fruit trees.[4]

The 10 acre (four and a half hectares) nursery was situated in Montague Road South Brisbane on the river bank about 15 minutes walk from the Russell Street ferry terminal – today just past the Go-Between Bridge close to the end of Brereton Street.

In October 1859 Albert further rose to prominence when he was elected to the first Brisbane Municipal Council. Shortly afterwards his fifth child, Augustus Charles Scott, was born. Hockings Wharves, the nursery, *Rosaville* and Henry's house were the centre of the world for the eight Hockings cousins, who enjoyed the gardens and horses kept in the stables on site.

Once again Henry dabbled in store-keeping at South Brisbane, seeking to emulate his successful brother. Personal tragedies (the death of eight-month-old Ernest from bronchitis in early 1861 and another son Thornton Percy in 1862 who survived just a few days) and a drop in trade devastated Henry. By late 1863 he was again broke, his brother forgiving a debt of rent owed as the estate was placed into insolvency.

Immediately following the fire in December 1864, Hockings' Seed and Garden Tool Warehouse moved to temporary premises in Albert Street and six months later re-located to the Criterion Corner (the site of Stewart and Hemmant's shop where the December fire had begun). While busily revitalising and expanding his business, Albert also became Mayor of Brisbane and was preparing a publication which would be a summary of his horticultural experience in Queensland. In the preface to the first edition of the *Queensland Garden Manual* published in October 1865 he sought to apologise for his amateur position and expounded his reasons for venturing to nominate himself as an expert on the subject.

> On presenting this little work to the public, the Author feels that some apology is due for venturing to occupy, as a mere amateur, a position of authority on Gardening matters which could have been so much more fitly assumed by a person trained to the profession. Many reasons have combined to induce this step, among the most urgent of which is the total absence of any directions as to the cultivation and treatment of plants suited to this Colony and climate, for the guidance of the numerous class of farmers continually arriving, and anxious to adapt themselves to their new home.
>
> Seventeen years' devotion to this pursuit in Brisbane has given the writer many opportunities for observation.

Always the business man, the first edition of the *Queensland Garden Manual* contained advertising for local businesses and included a copy of Hockings' extensive catalogue. A thousand copies were printed and its popularity ensured a second edition in 1875 and a further one in 1888. In 1875 he also published *The Flower Garden in Queensland* catering for smaller allotments and householders with no interest in the cultivation of crops or fruit trees.

In February 1866 Albert Hockings was appointed one of the trustees of a new burial ground, the South Brisbane Cemetery (often today incorrectly referred to as the Dutton Park Cemetery). As development encroached upon the land previously set aside by the NSW government for burials near to the current site of West End State School, the Queensland Government decided to sell the land and purchase a greater area in a more suitable position. The cemetery opened for business in May 1870 and the first burial in August that year was Albert Hockings' mother. This first headstone, a large pillar topped with a statue of a woman dropping flowers was a spectacular start to the cemetery.

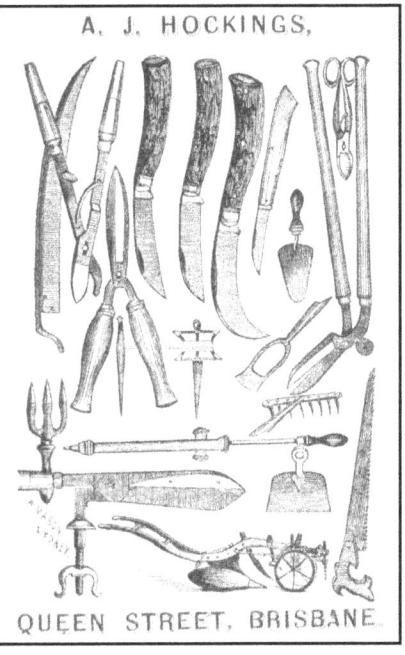

Anticipating an absorbing life in politics, Albert Hockings brought his eldest son, Albert Thomas, into the business as a partner in February 1877. After his success on the council, Albert Hockings stood for election for the seat of Wickham (Legislative Assembly) in May of the same year after the resignation of George Edmondstone. He won the by-election and remained a member until November 1878 when the seat was merged with another to form North Brisbane. Albert stood for election for North Brisbane but was defeated. His short parliamentary career was at an end. Disappointment was tempered with a sense of relief as he returned to his obsession, horticulture. A J Hockings & Son enthusiastically entered produce and exhibited equipment in local and interstate agricultural shows winning prizes, attracting plaudits for their equipment and sponsoring other awards.

By 1881 the frenzy of competition in exhibitions had slowed down. The business coasted along on its reputation still constantly searching out new products for its growing client base. Eager to contribute new and exciting ideas, Albert assisted one inventive western Queensland grazier in designing and producing a hoe especially suited to be wielded from the saddle to remove weeds from grazing runs. Now the father of eight surviving children and grandfather of three, Albert Hockings, with the help of his son, Albert Thomas, enjoyed his remaining years pottering with plants. In 1888 the third and final edition of his popular gardening manual was produced.

In 1888 the nursery, established nearly 30 years earlier at Montague Road, was still going strong. A visitor wrote enthusiastically in the newspaper of the enormous varieties of plants, describing it as "probably the oldest nursery gardens in the colony" – "a fine collection of young plants and shrubs in pots under the bush-houses, all doing well and looking healthy." There were begonias and coleus amongst poincianas and caladiums. The English hop plant was evident apparently popular as a verandah creeper. Clumps of weeping figs were clustered in a corner. Chinese fruit trees and Liberian coffee occupied another.

The nursery had some 'of the oldest mango trees in the Brisbane district growing here'[5] One tree was imported from Calcutta in 1853 and stood 37 feet (11 metres) high with a circumference of 4ft 6in (1½ metres). There were about 30 kinds of peach trees and an English oak.

The glorious 10 acre site on the river bank with many mature trees and shrubs was a haven for visitors and locals. When the nursery moved the following year, it is unknown what happened to the remaining gardens. The great flood of 1893 caused irreparable damage to the site but the large mature trees possibly survived.

Albert John Hockings' health was failing though. Early in 1890 his daughter Alice died and he followed her on 11 November 1890 aged 68. He was buried in the South Brisbane Cemetery alongside his mother. His wife Elizabeth would also be interred there 17 years later.

Hockings and Co continued as a business up until about the First World War when it disappeared from advertising on the retirement of Albert Thomas, the eldest son. In his will, Albert John left bequests to his children and the remainder of his estate to his wife and £500 to his brother Henry. He added a note stating that the money was for Henry's sole use and should he predecease Albert the bequest was cancelled.

Henry's life was never as smooth and successful as Albert's. By the early 1870s Henry was reduced to working as a telegraph line repairer, at times away from his family. During one of those periods, his fourteen-year old-daughter Lucy fell from a bolting horse and was dragged to her death. He became more estranged from his family and in 1878 took a job as a Polynesian immigration agent based in Cooktown. The government agents travelled aboard vessels transporting Polynesian (Kanaka) labour to North Queensland to ensure the men were treated properly. When his wife Eliza died in 1888 she was listed in the family notices only as the mother of Harold Hockings (no mention of Henry). A year later Henry acquired a wine merchant's licence and was living in Newtown, Sydney. In his later years he reacquainted himself with the Jewish religion, the religion of his mother's family, and became a respected member of the Jewish community in Sydney, holding many musical evenings with his niece Lucy Thornton as hostess. He died in 1912 aged 86 and is buried in Rookwood Cemetery.

The beautiful sub-tropical plants and trees in the gardens and parks of Brisbane are a legacy of the 40 years of dedicated horticultural experimentation of Albert John Hockings, his labours, and that of his pioneering family.

Brisbane Burns

Chapter 25

Pragmatic Scot and honest politician

George Edmondstone 1837–1870

By nine o'clock the three brick shops and their rear outbuildings that once included Hocking's seeds were fiercely burning, sending an immense body of flame into the hot swirling air above the entire city block. As the focus continued to be on saving the main commercial buildings of Queen Street, the conflagration amongst the cramped timber houses, shacks, sheds, and stables fronting Albert Street consumed everything in its path.

There was little anyone could do except watch in fear and dread as these flames fuelled the intensity of the fire front attacking Queen Street. The walls of George Edmondstone's building next door to Hocking's were soon glowing red. It housed his own butchery as well as other businesses. The smell of burning meat now mixed with the choking heat and smoke billowing up and around the city heart.

The sight of George Edmondstone, Brisbane's first butcher, wielding a meat cleaver on a butcher's block was a scene that had been repeated on and off in Queen Street for over 20 years. Born in Edinburgh Scotland in 1809, George was orphaned in his early teens and lived with his grandparents until he was granted permission by the colonial authorities to travel to Sydney. He arrived aboard the *Numa* in 1833. George tried his hand at various occupations finally settling on storekeeping. He ran a successful business in Sydney and married Alexandrina Tillery in 1837. His daughter Georgina was born the same year and Elizabeth two years later.

George Edmondstone 1863.

Around this time, Edmondstone moved to a large cattle station west of Ipswich called *Normanby Plains*. After an attack by aboriginals that endangered his family and injured a servant, the Edmondstone family returned to Sydney. Three years later the property was sold.

Brisbane in 1839 was winding down as a convict settlement. The majority of the Moreton Bay convicts had returned south. A few of the more cooperative were left to assist surveyors sent north from Sydney. The township and surrounding areas were to be mapped and pegged out with a view to the area being opened to free settlement, settlers and squatters having been previously prevented from coming within 50 miles (80 km) of the convict town.

News of the survey sparked interest among a few speculators hoping to cash in on the new settlement. John William, convict transport seaman, settler and trader, received permission to trade in Brisbane. Squatters on the Darling Downs were eager to ship their wool through Brisbane rather than hauling it overland to Sydney. Williams built a hut on the south side of the river near the current Russell Street and began operations. Permission was granted for a few merchants to rent rooms in the old convict barracks in Queen Street and loaded drays began transporting supplies over Cunningham's Gap to the squatters, returning with wool for export. George Edmondstone was among this small group of early traders. Two years later he was slaughtering animals and selling meat from his own shop on the eastern side of Queen Street.

An 1844 map of Brisbane shows the area west of Queen Street and up to the old windmill as 'Edmondstone's sheep for slaughter'. In the

Chapter 25 — George Edmondstone

era before refrigeration, keeping the sheep, cattle and pigs close enough to provide fresh meat meant that large paddocks within the town precincts were essential. It soon became obvious to George Edmondstone that his sheep were grazing on prime town land so he purchased 70 acres (28 hectares) at Newstead, surrounded on three sides by Breakfast Creek adjoining Patrick Leslie's *Newstead House*. (Edmonstone's property became the suburb of Mayne, with the Mayne Junction rail yards to the west and Abbotsford Rd and Burrows St the two main thoroughfares.)

In November 1846 Edmondstone was charged with allowing his pigs and a horse to roam the streets of Brisbane, evidence that animals were kept on his block in Queen Street prior to slaughter. Pigs were notoriously hard to keep confined and many disputes between pig owners occurred over the following decade.

Wickham Terrace (after George had removed his sheep) became the most desired residential area in early Brisbane and in 1847 the Edmondstone family moved up the hill amongst the fresh air and cool breezes. In an era when large families were common, George Edmondstone and his wife only had two children, both girls. His daughters Georgina and Elizabeth loved riding and were a common sight on the bridle paths between town and New Farm.

In December 1853 aged 16, Georgina Edmondstone married John Markwell (see Chapter 12 of this book) who then owned the drapers shop nearly opposite Edmonstone's butchery in Queen Street.

George, Alexandrina and daughter Elizabeth moved to a property at Newstead facing Breakfast Creek where they built a comfortable residence called *Pahroombin*. George leased out his shop in Queen Street in 1854 and concentrated on raising and slaughtering pigs, cattle and sheep to supply the local butchers and wholesale carcase market.

On 12 May 1854 the *Gazehound*, the first vessel

Pahroombin ca. 1890.

loaded at a Brisbane river wharf, set sail for London with a Captain Joseph Donald Allison at the helm. Purposely built for the Brisbane trade (shallow drafted to allow passage over the Brisbane Bar at high tide) the barque (a vessel with three or more masts, the foremasts being square-rigged) was capable of carrying 1100 bales of wool. On its return, George Edmondstone, determined to export by-products of butchering such as hides, tallow and bones directly to England met Captain Allison at the *Gazehound*'s berth in Breakfast Creek. It was the beginning of a family partnership.

Elizabeth Edmonstone 20, soon caught the Captain's eye and they were married in April 1857. George Edmondstone, a doting father, tried hard to keep the roving, restless sea captain anchored to a life on land. On their marriage, he set up a trust to administer his land in Elizabeth Street (Lot 14, Section 1, North Brisbane, where the Victoria Theatre would be built) and a block in Edward Street for the benefit of Captain Allison and his family. Less than a year later, before Elizabeth's first child was born, he also offered him a partnership in the butchery business.

The family company, Edmondstone and Co, purchased the business of James Collins (see Chapter 22 of this book) and returned to trade in Queen Street. George Edmondstone's meticulous attention to detail in business was demonstrated by a court case against James Collins soon after the purchase of the business. He claimed that Collins had removed a gun from a shed at the slaughter yards, it being a tool of the business and therefore the property of the new owner, Edmondstone. Collins was ordered to return the gun or pay £10.

In October 1859, just two months before the separation of Queensland into an independent State, Edmondstone was elected to the first Brisbane Municipal Council, heralding a political career that would last for the rest of his life. He was on the landing stage at the Botanic Gardens in December that year along with his fellow aldermen to greet Queensland's first Governor, Sir George Bowen. With the Governor in place, the election of the first Queensland parliament could go ahead and George Edmondstone, moving his career up a notch, was elected to represent the seat of East Moreton.

If George was hoping that son-in-law Captain Joseph Allison would carry the weight of the business now that he was deeply involved in politics, he was sadly mistaken. The partnership was dissolved in August 1860 and just a year, later in August 1861, Joseph left Brisbane with a party led by William Landsborough in the search for the ill-fated Burke and Wills expedition. The aim was to traverse the continent from the Gulf of Carpenteria to Melbourne. Allison provided essential navigation experience and was with the party for nearly a year before he and others returned to the central Queensland coast as Landsborough struck out for Melbourne.

George Edmondstone and his daughter Elizabeth, now a mother of two, were bitterly disappointed when Allison after a brief return to Brisbane set sail once again as the chief officer of the *Whirlwind* which left Brisbane for London in early 1863. Over a year later he returned to Brisbane but all was not well in the marriage. He had been home barely a month when Elizabeth, her sister Georgina Markwell and husband John Markwell went to Sydney for a visit. Meanwhile, Captain Allison was delivering coal down the New South Wales Coast with the voyage ending in Melbourne.

In April 1865 he left Brisbane again, this time aboard the ill-fated *Hannah More* bound for Callao in Chile where Allison fell ill. In February 1866 he left the ship, too sick to carry on. A few weeks later the *Hannah More* was lost at sea with all hands. Queensland newspapers reported the tragedy, prophetically noting the Captain Allison was not on board. On June 1, still in Callao, Allison succumbed to his illness leaving his wife Elizabeth and three children under seven, Mary, George and Fanny.

George Edmondstone continued his work with the Brisbane City Council as well as holding his seat in Parliament. During his time with the council he was involved with the acquisition of the city's ferries, town street lighting and, as Mayor in 1863, oversaw the erection of the Town Hall, the foundation stone of which was laid in January 1864. He also helped plan the first bridge across the Brisbane River which was begun in August 1864.

After his re-election to the Council in 1863 he was kept busy juggling the Council and his various committees. He also contested a general election in the seat of East Moreton. Due to electoral mismanagement, East Moreton saw three elections that year with George triumphant in September.

> We cannot but think the Government is much to blame in having twice selected incompetent Returning Officers, and owing to such mis-selection, involving the electorate in such unnecessary 'toil and trouble'

> Would that every man in the house of our Representatives was as single in his views and honest in his principles as George Edmondstone.[1]

The Town Hall construction was not without its own controversy. As Mayor, Edmondstone suggested to the council that a town hall would provide public accommodation and adorn the city. With the agreement of the council he asked architect William Coote to prepare some initial plans. He showed these to the Premier, Robert Herbert, who authorised the Council to carry out the building of a Town Hall. Mr Coote was asked to present more detailed plans. Later, after previously disagreeing with all proposals by the Council, three aldermen suddenly stopped complaining about the lack of competition in the planning process.

Though George Edmondstone as Mayor and MLA had enormous influence over the project, no allegations of mismanagement were ever laid at his door and the three aldermen were instead much condemned for their about-face. In his enthusiasm for the development of the city, he had no doubt applied his Scottish pragmatism to the problem without any thought for the possible conflict of interest.

During his time on the Council, Edmondstone actively pursued a solution to Brisbane's water supply problem and was a member of the Waterworks Board. On the night of 1 December, 1864 as fire engulfed his premises and those of his tenants it was tragic confirmation that the city desperately needed a reticulated water system.

> George Edmondstone is very thankful for the kindness of friends who put out the fire on the roof of the house which now shelters

him and his; also to the friends who so nobly assisted his family
on that fearful night when so much of our city burned down.

After the fire, Edmondstone & Co moved to Elizabeth Street and quickly re-established trading. By 1866, and in his late fifties, George was tiring. He relinquished the business in Elizabeth Street and resigned from the Council. Continuing as a Member of the Legislative Assembly he represented the seats of Brisbane and Wickham for 11 years until 1877 when he left to become a Life Member of the Legislative Council (the State upper house since abolished).

Throughout his lifetime, George Edmondstone continued to acquire land in and around Brisbane. In 1870, just prior to the tragic death of his daughter Georgina, at the age of 33, he transferred land on the corner of Queen and Edward St (David Jones today) to her husband John Markwell. When Georgina died she left eight children aged between 16 years and 15 months. Responsibility for the younger ones may have fallen to her younger sister Elizabeth, and the Markwell and Allison cousins probably spent many days together at *Pahroombin*. This closeness resulted in a further linking of the families when William Allison Markwell, John and Georgina's third child, married his cousin Mary Alexandrina, Elizabeth's eldest child, in August 1885. In November, Mary Alexandrina's child died at birth.

On his death from heart disease at 68 on 24 February 1883, George Edmondstone left his extensive estate to his wife Alexandrina. On her death in 1888, the full extent of his landholdings was revealed as Alexandrina distributed the estate between her daughter and grandchildren. Her daughter Elizabeth Allison retained *Pahroombin*, the family home, and adjacent lands. The rest of the 70 acre (28 hectares) estate went to George Edmondstone Markwell, Georgina's son. Lot 6, one of the original town lots sold in 1842, fronting Queen Street and beside the site of the original Victoria Hotel, and the land behind, lot 13, fronting Elizabeth Street went jointly to Elizabeth Allison and George Edmondstone Markwell.

Three blocks in Wickham Terrace opposite the windmill and previously known as *Dronfield* (about an acre in total) also went to Elizabeth Allison. Seven acres at Enoggera were left to Elizabeth's son, George Robert and, lastly, one block on the river at South Brisbane to George Edmondstone Markwell. Any money was divided equally amongst the grand-daughters, the contents of Pahroombin went to Elizabeth, and George's books were left to George Edmondstone Markwell.

One property remained – Lot 14, Section 1, fronting Elizabeth Street site of the Theatre Royal which had been administered by a trust since Allison's death in 1866. The other block in Edward Street similarly given to Captain Allison and Elizabeth had been sold in 1896 and the proceeds of £2000 deposited in the bank. In 1899, 11 years after the death of their mother, Elizabeth Allison's children sought to gain title to the property and access to the proceeds of the Edward Street sale. After a complicated five-months court case they were granted title as tenants in common and equal shares of the money.

Elizabeth Allison, her daughter Mary Alexandrina and Mary's husband William Allison Markwell, stayed on at *Pahroombin* until about 1890 when it was leased to James Alexander Wilson and his family. William Markwell was a surveyor and they lived all over Queensland possibly taking Elizabeth Allison with them. The Wilsons were residents until 1909. The estate was subdivided into building and industrial lots in 1913 at which time *Pahroombin* was bought by James Irving. There is a photograph of Lillian Irving in the gardens of Pahroombin about 1940 and the last photograph of the house was taken in 1963. It was later demolished. In its heyday it was built in red brick and contained drawing, sitting and dining rooms, five bedrooms, kitchen and bathroom with a cedar staircase leading to two attic rooms. In Edmondstone's time it also had a 10-room addition to the house that was demolished when Mr Irving bought the property.

Interestingly, Elizabeth Allison's daughter Fanny Georgina Peate, also called her home in Manly, Sydney, *Pahroombin* recalling the happy years she and her siblings spent at Breakfast Creek surrounded by the extended and loving Allison and Markwell clans, enjoying the legacy of the pioneering George Edmondstone. (NB. The spelling of Edmondstone varies throughout the years and I have decided to adopt this spelling as it is the most common.

Chapter 26

Scoundrel or Saint

Augustus John Kosvitz 1831–1894

Only an hour before the crowds of helpers and onlookers now witnessed the final destruction of the building housing the latest shops to fall to the fire, wealthy jeweller Augustus John Kosvitz was closing up his store. His expensive new plate-glass window display contained a dazzling array of stock headlined by an enormous pendulum clock by which passersby regularly checked their pocket watches.

That valuable stock was soon being hastily removed after a frantic hammering on the locked front door by Charles Campen, a tobacconist who had crossed the street to raise the alarm that a raging fire was only seven or eight doors away. At the rear of his shop, other frenzied neighbours had smashed a gate to access the property and were pounding on the back door.

Kosvitz would be luckier than many businessmen in Queen Street that night. By the time flames were licking at the wooden shingles of his store roof, his stock was safely removed and securely stored.

In just 18 months Augustus John Kosvitz had built a thriving business. He claimed to have had takings of £9000 (close to $1500000 in today's values) from the last four years trading with a steady 33% profit. In 1864 his rent was £1 a week and average takings for 1864 was £74 a week. Together with the value of his stock, he was worth nearly a million dollars in today's money.

Even though Queensland had only been a separate state for five years, business opportunities abounded and new residents and migrants were keen to enjoy the same quality of goods that would be available to them in a more developed, sophisticated city. Watchmakers and jewellers had been in Brisbane since 1846. While watches were of the cased pocket variety and all clocks were large and fitted with pendulums, accuracy of time was essential within the early Brisbane community.

One grumpy correspondent to the *Courier* complained of the five minutes discrepancy between Kosvitz's time on his regulator clock and the Time Ball at the Windmill on Wickham Terrace – 'time is money, I say a good deal must be lost in Brisbane, for no two men set their watches alike'[1]. (The Time Ball was a large black wicker ball dropped from the pole on top of the Windmill at 1pm signalling sailors and citizens to set their time pieces).

Until 1846, any timepiece repairs were carried out in Sydney. Similarly, purchases of new watches and clocks were made by post and shipped from Sydney on steamers. A constant stream of watchmakers and jewellers arrived in Brisbane in the following decades, but Augustus John Kosvitz stood out for his unique style learnt and practised in Sydney using colonial gold and specialising in Australian emblems and motifs.

Kosvitz was born in Prussia in 1831. The Kingdom of Prussia encompassed present day Germany, Northern Poland and the Czech Republic. His birthplace was listed as Yauer, difficult to locate on today's maps but probably within modern Poland. He worked as a watchmaker in London at the firm of Edward Dent before arriving in Sydney in 1855. The following year Kosvitz was employed at Hogarth, Erichsen & Co in Sydney, respected for their high quality work and instrumental in introducing the 'Australiana' theme into jewellery using colonial gold and motifs of Australian fauna and flora.

Kosvitz moved to Brisbane in 1859, setting up his own establishment in Queen Street, further north than his location at the time of the fire. He described himself as a 'Practical jeweller, chronometer, watch and clock maker' who:

has on sale a large assortment of Jewellery, of English and Colonial manufacture. English and Foreign Watches. A great variety of opera and stock glasses, fancy goods, etc., etc. All kinds of watches, clocks, and jewellery repaired.[2]

Jewellery shops also carried spectacles, other eyeglasses and some navigational and surveying equipment. Local watchmakers branched out into the sale of jewellery and fancy goods, importing items from England, Germany and America.

Published descriptions of commissions Kosvitz received in Brisbane reveal the distinctly Australian elements which identified his work. His known commissions include a silver medal manufactured for the Rifle Prize of the Volunteer Regiment in 1861 with a laurel wreath and Australian Coat of Arms and the Drum Major's staff for the Queensland Volunteer Regiment – a wooden rod topped with a silver decoration, again with the Coat of Arms, and supported by a kangaroo and emu. A new set of insignia for the Prince of Wales Masonic Lodge attracted the attention of the press.

> The articles in question have been manufactured from silver by Mr.Kosvitz, and they demonstrate that the colony already presents attraction to those skilled in a branch of art which it might naturally be imagined would meet with adequate support only in the more refined and populous cities of older countries.[3]

To celebrate the turning of the sod for the first railway line in Queensland, the Governor's wife Lady Bowen used a silver spade decorated with Australian emblems designed and manufactured by Augustus Kosvitz. A silver mount for a cricket bat presented at an Intercolonial cricket match between Queensland and New South Wales and a 22 ct gold mount for a whip and pair of spurs featuring kangaroos and possums were also among his creations.

On the night of the 1864 fire Kosvitz had more at stake than many of Queen Street's other traders – a dazzling display of watches, clocks, precious stones, rings, chains, brooches

```
A. KOSVITZ,
PRACTICAL WATCHMAKER & OPTICIAN,
QUEEN STREET,
(NEXT TO THE VICTORIA HOTEL),
NORTH BRISBANE.
```

and gold and silver items housed in exquisite, bespoke glass and cedar cabinets. Along one wall was a curious, but valuable, collection of carved and decorated emu eggs unique in Brisbane. Upon realising the fire was approaching Augustus had immediately enlisted the aid of his uninvited visitors to pack and carrying this stock to safety. Unlike some other Queen Street proprietors, Kosvitz's stock was highly portable. However, this was to also prove a liability as small valuable items went astray – dropped, left behind, absent-mindedly slipped into a pocket or stolen in the confusion.

Augustus had hastily prioritised items left for repair and packed them carefully into small drawers and boxes, and locked glass cases for the valuable pieces. These were all able to be transported out of the shop. Some went across the road to Mr. Campen's tobacconist shop, some to Richard Warry's grocery shop about a block and a half further north along the opposite side of Queen Street, and the rest was dropped in premises between the Supreme Court Building, Mason's Concert Hall and the street.

Although locked, the glass cases broke and cracked as they were carried through the mayhem and confusion on Queen Street. Arriving at Warry's grocery shop they were stacked on the floor and benches joining the myriad other items belonging to similarly threatened Queen Street traders. (Richard Warry started his wine, spirit and grocery business in Queen Street in 1853. In 1862 he erected what was then the best building in Queensland, later the first office of the Queensland National Bank.) As the fire raged, another jeweller, Mr. Cochrane, took Kosvitz's well-known regulator clock to pieces ready for transportation and Mr. Campen rescued the account books and invoices.

The jewellery shop was therefore almost empty before it was consumed by the fire but the valuable front shop plate glass window, awning and iron shutters were destroyed. (The shop window had been fitted at a cost of £150, equivalent to almost $20,000 today).

While the fire brigade, the 12th Regiment and other weary firefighters battled the blaze, Kosvitz and his band of helpers took off down the street to Richard Warry's shop, supposedly to guard the jewellery stock which he later claimed was worth approximately £3400 (equivalent to about $400,000 today). Pleased that all his goods had been safely rescued from the shop, Augustus Kosvitz checked that the back door of Warry's was locked then settled down with his mates. To pass the time, he borrowed a few bottles of champagne from Mr. Warry's supply. Months later in a protracted court case between Kosvitz and his insurers, one of his helpers, John Simmonds, complained that

> Warry's shop was so crowded with plaintiff's goods that we had scarcely room to stand and drink our champagne. [4]

Just a block away on that night, 50 buildings would be destroyed, 6000 people were on the streets and hundreds were fighting the worst fire in Brisbane's history. Meanwhile Mr. Kosvitz and his crew were hunkered down with a few glasses of champagne in a quiet grocery store. Purportedly protecting valuable stock, a passing constable checking on the security of other premises in the city that night reported that Kosvitz's 'men were guarding the goods (one with a drawn sword and very drunk).'[5]

Escaping the worst of the fire, wealthy, respected and mixing with the notables of Brisbane, Augustus Kosvitz was at the peak of his creative career. When the foundations were finally laid in 1866 for the new Brisbane Bridge, (on the site of today's Victoria Bridge) the Minister of Works used a silver trowel, square and plumb made by Kosvitz.[6]

However, his life was about to change forever. In October 1868, aged 37, he married 21-year-old Elizabeth Mary Josephine Doyle, eldest daughter of James Doyle Esq. of Albermarle Street London at St. Stephens Church in Brisbane. The term 'Esq.' defined James Doyle as a gentleman – in the English class system a man of position and education. Albermarle Street, in Mayfair just off Piccadilly, is today home to many prestigious art galleries. James Doyle was a man of substance with a fancy address.

Despite her upbringing, it turned out that Mrs. Kosvitz was no shrinking violet. Shortly after the birth of their only child, Augustus James in December 1869, Kosvitz summoned his wife to court on a charge of assault. The court case was postponed as Augustus was 'in an excited state and not fit to appear.'[7] 'Excited' was a polite term for drunk. Did his wife hit him because he was drunk or was he drunk because his wife hit him? Either way, in the following years he became a seriously ill alcoholic.

After spending over a month in jail on remand, Elizabeth had her say. In reply to her husband's claim that she 'was in the habit of assaulting him from Sunday morning to Saturday night'[8], she brought similar charges against him. Furious at her behaviour, he cut off her line of credit with a public notice in the newspaper, offering her £2 per week if she would live somewhere else. Elizabeth refused unless she could have custody of their child (then two years old), and she was bound to keep the peace for six months.

Whether Elizabeth left with the child is not known, but just three weeks later Kosvitz had auctioned off the entire valuable contents of the Queen Street house expressing a wish to 'relinquish housekeeping.'[9] The level of comfort this wealthy man provided for himself and his family is revealed by the list of household contents: Axminster carpets, bronze figures, extensive silver plate, musical boxes, an elegant cedar dining suite, mahogany wardrobes, a four poster bed, cedar washstands, silver tea and coffee pots, expensive china, and even an up-to-date American Cooking stove in the kitchen.

Eventually Kosvitz moved to a small cottage in Ann Street, but there was no peace. Often he was unable to open the shop because of his wife's behaviour. In November 1872 Elizabeth Kosvitz went to Sydney providing her husband with a much needed break during which he tried to revive the business. She returned in May the following year and immediately Kosvitz's business and health began to suffer. During the latter half of 1873 Elizabeth Kosvitz was committed to the Woogaroo Lunatic Asylum (later renamed Wolston Park Hospital).

Built in 1865 to house the mentally ill, violent patients could expect to be restrained in a straitjacket or tied to a chair and blindfolded for long periods. An official government enquiry in 1869 confirmed rumours of maltreatment and sexual abuse of inmates. This resulted in improved accommodation, management and treatment. Brutal and tortuous restraint gave way to more gentle treatments, but loss of reason, exacerbated by excessive drinking, was not distinguished from mental illness and, as a consequence, without the proper treatment many an alcoholic was committed to Woogaroo to join the insane.

Kosvitz's love of the odd glass of champagne became a serious illness. By September 1873, customers and friends described Kosvitz as often being in a state of confusion, excited, boisterous, pale and trembling. The store was still trading and there was a substantial quantity of valuable stock, but debts were mounting and the commissions had disappeared. Elizabeth Kosvitz's erratic behaviour, Augustus' wild and incoherent ramblings and irregular shop hours frightened away the customers.

On 13 September 1873 Kosvitz fell ill. Isaac Lenneberg, a fellow Queen Street trader and proprietor of the Café De Paris (See Chapter 23 this book), became concerned for his friend and summoned Dr. Emmelhains who diagnosed delirium tremens (or the D.T's, acute delirium caused by the withdrawal from alcohol). The following day, Dr. William Hobbs (visiting surgeon for the Asylum) called on Kosvitz to inform him of the impending release of his wife from Woogaroo Lunatic Asylum. He found him 'like a man on the verge of insanity.'[10] Fearing for Kosvitz's safety, Isaac Lenneberg took him in and assigned an employee, William Fetherstone, to watch over him. As a witness in the insolvency case of Augustus Kosvitz just two months later, William Fetherstone would depose that he watched over Kosvitz for three nights, listening to his mad ramblings and described Kosvitz as 'not in his proper senses.'[11]

One night Kosvitz broke open the back door of Lenneberg's and tried to jump over the back gate. It took two men to bring him down, breaking the fence in the process. Kosvitz lurched straight back into the building, through the bar, out the front door and returned to his own shop. At this point Lenneberg gave up on his friend and sent William Fetherstone home. Dr Emmelhains visited Kosvitz, sometimes twice a day, for ten days after which, in his opinion, he had recovered from his delirium.

At the beginning of November, Kosvitz applied for insolvency. An intricate story emerged during the insolvency hearings over the following months as his creditors sought to set aside the sale of Kosvitz's business allegedly undertaken on 26 September 1873 just days after his supposed recovery from his delirium. According to Samuel Lesser (importer and general wheeler-dealer) as he passed Kosvitz's door on the morning of 23 September he was invited in and told that due to troubles with his wife, the business had suffered and Kosvitz was anxious to sell out. Kosvitz vaguely recalled Isaac Lenneberg and Samuel Lesser discussing the sale of the stock while he was resting in another room about 24 September. Of the night of 26 September he remembered very little only recalling that a few people were in his shop. He later admitted that, despite his apparent recovery, he had been drinking continuously for the previous two days.

Lesser maintained that Kosvitz was 'sober and rational'[12] as they discussed the drawing up of a stock list and the subsequent sale of the business. Initially Lesser agreed to pay Kosvitz £1650 for the business and handed over a deposit of £100 on 24 September. The following day, after perusing the stock and making his own valuations, he realised that he had offered too much. After approaching Kosvitz and requesting a return of the deposit, he found that Kosvitz had already spent the money. As a consequence, Kosvitz agreed to sell the business for £1500 and on the night of 26 September Lesser paid the remaining amount in Bank of New South Wales notes and the deal was signed off in the presence of a solicitor's clerk.

Kosvitz even signed permission for a notice in the newspaper announcing the sale of the business. Lesser described Kosvitz as 'perfectly sane and sober'[13], yet Kosvitz, in his evidence to the insolvency hearing, declared 'I don't recollect anything that took place.'[14] When Dr. Emmelhains visited him on the night of the sale, Kosvitz told him the sale was concluded and that he was taking a steamer to Sydney the following day and then returning to Germany, abandoning his young son and troubled wife ('a cause of much vexation and annoyance'[15]). Running away was to become a theme in the life of Augustus Kosvitz.

Even in 1873 bad news travelled fast and as the *Kembla* docked in Sydney, detectives were waiting at the wharf. Kosvitz's Sydney creditors, eager not to let their quarry (now flushed with funds from the sale) escape, had sought backup from the law. Kosvitz spent two nights in Darlinghurst jail, and £1325 was recovered and put in trust for the creditors to fight over.

After his release he stayed at the German Club where he was found by Henry Morwitch, a pawnbroker, auctioneer and moneylender, to whom Kosvitz owed £200. Morwitch said Kosvitz was 'in a very stupid state, raving about being in gaol and about fishes and snakes.'[16] Morwitch accompanied Kosvitz on the steamer back to Brisbane, leaving him in the care of the steward for the trip as he was 'not fit to be at large' and 'his mind was wandering during the whole of the voyage up.'[17]

The D.T.'s had returned. (Or perhaps they had never left – Kosvitz may have been suffering more from the effects of continued alcohol consumption rather than withdrawal.) On his return to Brisbane he was detained for his own protection. On the advice of Dr. Hobbs he was admitted to the Lunatic Reception House. This was a temporary facility where a person could be sent for up to 30 days on the certificate of one doctor. Patients in the Reception house were carefully observed and given some treatment. Many, particularly alcoholics, were able to avoid Woogaroo Lunatic Asylum and return to their normal lives.

On October 10, 1873, before Kosvitz was discharged from the Reception house, where he had quickly recovered, Samuel Lesser sold the business to James Martin, owner of the Civit Cat toy shop in Queen Street. In July 1874, Kosvitz's financial woes were settled with a Certificate of Discharge (all the conditions of his insolvency had been met), his creditors being paid a final dividend of one shilling and ninepence.

Broke and unemployed and unable to comply with the order to support his wife, Kosvitz bolted again. Elizabeth Kosvitz tracked him to Rockhampton where she summoned him to court for neglecting to support her. He agreed to pay 10 shillings a week. A year later she was still pursuing him for desertion, this time claiming 30 shillings a week. A Rockhampton court imposed maintenance of 15 shillings a week with a penalty of six months in jail if he did not comply.

Kosvitz went on the run again. In March 1876, the Townsville Bench issued a warrant charging him with leaving his son, Augustus

James, without any means of support. Described as an offender well-known in Brisbane and other coast towns, it was thought he had gone to Sydney. Finally arrested in Newcastle, he was remanded to Sydney and in May 1876 was charged with:

> having unlawfully deserted Eliza his wife, and, being found guilty, was ordered to pay £2 a week for her separate maintenance, to give security for one year's payments.[18]

Elizabeth Kosvitz remained in Rockhampton and by 1879 was working as a ladies nurse. Kosvitz disappeared from the records until 1884 when he reappeared as a jeweller in Brisbane operating from a shop on the north east corner of Albert and Elizabeth Streets.

One night, 20 years after her unfortunate marriage to Augustus Kosvitz, Elizabeth was found in Footscray, Victoria having been assaulted by a man she had met on the train who offered to help her find lodgings. She was knocked down and injured, but refused to press charges. Accused of having no lawful visible means of support, she claimed she was a nurse from Fitzroy. At this point Elizabeth Kosvitz disappeared from the records. No trace remains of her or her son. Augustus Kosvitz's career never returned to the dizzying days of the early 1860s and he continued working as a jeweller in Brisbane until his death on 10 July 1894 aged 63.

Chapter 27

A chequered history

The Victoria Hotel 1843–1880

As the brick walls of Edmondstone's block of shops collapsed amidst a pile of burning timber, the Victoria Hotel was obviously going to be the next consumed in short order. It was a timber construction and its front verandahs quickly caught alight, transferring the flames to the shingle roof and rafters and spreading the fire rapidly toward the rear outbuildings.

Behind the hotel was also the adjoining billiard room complete with an impressive and expensive Thurston table shipped from England by the owner George Mason to replace one he had lost in a small fire a few years previous. This second table would not succumb to any new fire. Before the fire burst through the roof of the billiard room, a large group of sweating straining workers and volunteers were seen hauling the table down Queen Street to safety.

As the fire engulfed the billiard hall a furious fight was also being waged to prevent the destruction of the newly completed Music Hall which sat to the rear of the billiard hall and fronted onto Elizabeth street. A robust structure with a tin roof and large skylight, the rear and side of the hall were perilously close to the flames. A team of workers from the nearby Town Hall under able direction managed to keep the building from catching alight, though several men suffered injuries from the flames and heat. The successful battle was not a long one however, the fire front, having made short work of the Victoria Hotel, moved on toward George Street.

The Victoria Hotel stood on the site later occupied by the New York Hotel, whose façade is still visible today above the bustling entrance to the Myer Centre in the Queen Street Mall. Built of weatherboards, the Victoria Hotel had evolved over the previous 20 years into a series of sprawling, hastily erected service buildings extending all the way through to Elizabeth Street. It was the first hotel north of the river, established in 1843 by David Bow and was affectionately known as Bow's and the Old Vic. It featured on an 1844 map of Brisbane as one of the few buildings on the sparsely populated block later to be bounded by Albert, Queen, George and Elizabeth Streets

David Bow married Elizabeth Rowland in Tasmania and their first child, Elizabeth Matilda, was born on 7 Dec 1835 in general store in Liverpool Street, Hobart. Within two years the business had failed and the family moved to Sydney where their sons David, Rolland and William Rolland (a misspelling of Rowland by the clerk who registered their births) were born. After a steamer trip to the newly opened settlement of Brisbane in 1842, David Bow recognised a business opportunity and brought his family north. From mid 1843 the Victoria Hotel was the social centre of Brisbane, hosting dinners and meetings and providing food, drink and accommodation.

> **VICTORIA HOTEL,**
> QUEEN STREET, BRISBANE.
> **G. B. MASON,**
> PROPRIETOR.
> EXTENSIVE alterations have recently been made in this Hotel, and there is also on the premises, a spacious
> **BILLIARD ROOM,**
> Fitted with an excellent Table by a first-class maker.
> ORDINARY EVERY DAY AT ONE O'CLOCK.

A farewell dinner for explorer Ludwig Leichhardt was hosted by Bow at the Victoria Hotel in 1844 before Leichhardt set out on his Port Essington expedition.[1]

First described by Thomas Dowse (ex-convict and diarist) as 'a hotel of grand scale'[2], and by Henry Stuart Russell (explorer and pastoralist) as 'The only hotel in Brisbane! Always full of squatters' and 'disagreeably notable'[3], the Victoria was later to be the hot-bed of radical meetings urging separation from New South Wales. To Mary McConnell (founder of Brisbane Children's Hospital, now the Royal Children's Hospital) though, in 1850, it was a place where she 'could not tolerate its lack of privacy, without any sitting room, door handle, lock or blind.[4]'

Every day promptly at 1pm the meal of the day was served to patrons gathered at the long table in the front room. Mostly it was plain solid fare, roasted or boiled meat and vegetables, but occasionally, due to the hunting skills of the local indigenous population, there were specialties such as turtle soup.

Yet the plain food was not to everyone's' taste. Henry Stuart Russell, an explorer, pastoralist and politician on a visit in 1843 described the midday meal.

> Chops of mutton, or steaks of beef, just killed, shot out of a frying pan in company with potent onions and floods of boiling grease.
>
> What wonder that such solids sorely tried the complacencies of degustation, deglutition, and digestion, and too often drove the Queen Street diners from disgusting diet to disgust-drowning decoction.[5]

One morning, aroused from sleep in his 'flea-branded blanket of a stretcher' by the clatter of cups and plates, the click of spoons and a breakfast bell, Henry Russell arrived at the Victoria Hotel dining room to find noted Darling Downs squatter Arthur Hodgson, still wearing his cotton-tasselled nightcap, carefully pencilling dates on boiled eggs in a huge bowl. After asking Arthur what he was doing, Henry received the reply, 'these eggs, at least can't be dirty in their innards, whatever they have been boiled in.' To Henry's continued puzzled look, Arthur added, 'Don't you see? I've marked them all with a date two, three and four months ago: Who'll eat them?' He and Arthur enjoyed 'the gratification of rejected eggs – to which no one, on inspection, addressed himself.'[6]

Licensed until 2am, the Victoria was the scene of many rowdy evenings much to the despair of any residents wanting a quiet night's sleep. In 1846 *HMS Bramble*, the first naval vessel of war to anchor in Moreton Bay, arrived on its way to a surveying expedition in the Torres Strait. John Sweatman, the ship's clerk, kept a journal which detailed his adventures including his visit to the Victoria Hotel in Brisbane describing it as a 'plain unpretending wooden house, but roomy and kept very clean'[7] The squatters also staying at the hotel greeted the sailors warmly and the *Bramble*'s commander Lt. Yule and his crew settled in for an evening's drinking. Sweatman recalls his commander apologising for his age and rank then retiring early. So noisy were the patrons and so thin the walls, that by late evening Lt. Yule was pleading to be taken somewhere quieter. His appeal was in vain. Thwarted by a locked door, the rowdy squatters climbed into the open rafters of the hotel and along to Yule's room laughing and loudly cheering his health. It was 3am before the drinkers retired, some of them already snoring on the floor of Yule's room after falling from the rafters. On a return visit a week later the squatters were not sorry that Mr Sweatman had returned to the Victoria with Yule declaring, 'there was no fun in him'.[8]

Despite the steady stream of immigrants and squatters passing through Brisbane, trade was difficult and patchy with competing hotels opening on both sides of the river. By 1848 David Bow's finances were in such a desperate state that he travelled to Sydney to visit the solicitors handling the affairs of the Victoria Hotel to discuss his impending insolvency. While there he was assaulted and robbed by three men. They stole a pocket book with some cheques, orders, promissory notes, seven sovereigns and £120 in bank notes. The following day the pocket book was recovered but the money was gone. On 27 May 1848, a meeting of creditors was called and over £500 in debts were proved.

Three days later at the Victoria, his wife Elizabeth collapsed and died after hitting her head. According to her son, eight-year-old William Rolland Bow, Elizabeth went to get a drink of water and fainted, hitting her head on some boxes. A servant picked her up and put her on the sofa and a doctor was called. He found her unconscious with a flushed and swollen face and a red mark on her neck. 'She was unable to speak, and appeared quite insensible.'[9] She died about a half an hour later.

Rumours of a serious domestic incident in the Bow household were already spreading before Elizabeth's death. She still had bruises from another undetermined cause and two days before her death had complained of headaches. A Coronial Jury was called. One of the jurors at the inquest was later criticised for asking the witnesses if Mrs Bow had complained of any illness. Both the witnesses replied, 'Yes. Since the assault and the row in the house.' [10]

George S Le Breton, the aggrieved Juryman, replied:

> I was bound to put such questions on the fact of the sudden death, coupled with the notoriously public report of an assault having previously taken place; and I must say that, instead of offence, had I been one of the parties implicated – however unjustly – I should have felt my mind much relieved at the unanimous verdict, coupled with medical evidence, that death occurred through the visitation of God. [11]

With that verdict David Bow was cleared of any involvement in his wife's death but the rumours remained. In November of the same year he become insolvent and his household furniture, bar fittings and tools of trade were auctioned off and he returned to New South Wales.

John Smith and his wife took over the license from David Bow and within a year the coroner had returned to the hotel when the Smith's cook, Andrew Purfitt, died suddenly in the Victoria's kitchen. He had only been ill a short time and hadn't been drinking. His death was attributed to natural causes. In May 1852, John Smith leased the Victoria Hotel after illness forced his retirement. In the advertisement the hotel was described as having 18 recently renovated rooms, and a six-stall horse stable. The lease was taken over by James Greenwood who, two years later, was also forced to retire due to illness and died in 1857 aged 42. John Campbell ran the hotel for a short time until it was taken over by Thomas Cowell in April 1858. The Victoria Hotel, it seemed, was plagued by misfortune and ill health. There were six license changes between David Bow in 1848 and Cowell's successor George Birkbeck Mason in April 1863.

Artist and music teacher George Birkbeck Mason was to have a profound effect upon the infant Brisbane town. Arriving in Sydney from San Francisco in about 1850, George belonged to a family of well respected wood engravers. His father Abraham John Mason was a well-known engraver and artist who had worked in London and New York and his brother Walter Mason was also a noted artist and engraver in Sydney from 1850 to his death in 1866.

With the advent of photography and the demise of wood engraving, George brought his family to Brisbane in 1861 where he began as a music teacher and proprietor of a music store before taking over the license of the Victoria Hotel. With no previous experience, becoming a publican seemed like a wild idea, and a little ironic as George's primary employer in Sydney had been the temperance publication *Band of Hope Journal*, but George had bigger, better plans. He immediately started work on Mason's Concert Hall, on a site behind the existing hotel and fronting Elizabeth Street.

A dedicated entertainment hall capable of seating 500 people with a flat floor that could be cleared for balls and meetings was a revelation for the people of Brisbane. Until Mason's Concert Hall the School of Arts on Creek Street, a small stuffy building was used for public meetings, lectures and the occasional musical concert – certainly not a place suitable to entertain Governor and Lady Bowen. Designed by architect William Coote, the auditorium was 22m by 11.5m (about the size of a 25m pool) with a 6m by 5m stage, 5.5m high at the centre. The interior was varnished wood with a highly decorated proscenium (stage arch) featuring the Royal Arms. Seating was provided by benches with comfortable backs. The roof was largely a skylight and most importantly, the rest of the roof was iron. This and the walls of brick and stone played a big part in the building's survival in the December fire.

George Birkbeck Mason was to introduce the first regular theatrical performances to Brisbane, presenting local and overseas talent and providing dance, band performances, singing, drama, comedy and farce all for 4 shillings down the front and 2 shillings and sixpence up the back.

About two months after George Mason had taken over the Victoria, a small fire broke out in the stables. A servant, with the help of some residents of the hotel, rescued the horses. The police arrived and the Volunteer Fire Brigade engine was dragged to the stables. A hose was attached to a large tank at the Sovereign Hotel. That time there was plenty of water, but even with the engine pump and numerous bystanders tossing buckets of water in all directions, the stables and billiard room and its valuable table were lost. It is not surprising then that during the December fire there were numerous willing helpers to carry away the Victoria's replacement table to safety. The good citizens of Brisbane did not want to lose another billiard table.

George Mason had also faced the prospect of damage to his new Concert Hall only days away from the opening, for which a grand ball had been organised on 9 December at the Victoria Hotel. Thanks to the efforts of the building crew from the also nearly completed Town Hall across the street from the Victoria Hotel, the iron roofed, brick and stone building was saved. For a short time after the fire, it was used as a temporary hotel for the victims of the fire, eventually opening on 25 January 1865 with a spectacular program of vocal, pianoforte and dramatic performances. Many of the piano accompaniments were played by George himself.

In the months following the destruction of the Victoria a hastily erected, smaller, structure facing Elizabeth Street named Mason's Victoria Hotel, continued trading, as did the untouched Concert Hall.

But while these establishments remained active, the devastated land of rubble, discarded tanks and ash fronting Queen Street upon which the Hotel had stood went untouched for a year, causing some consternation amongst those eager to see the city rebuilt.

> Really it is a disgrace to the city that a quantity of stagnant holes of a most unsavoury character should be allowed to remain open in the centre of the principal street for upwards of twelve months. Time has to a certain extent exercised its deodorising influence, but who can tell what amount of fatal miasma is still lurking in those abominations.[12]

After the fire, the life of George Birkbeck Mason spiralled into disaster. Was it bad luck, bad management, or personal tragedy? By the close of 1865 he had given up the licence on his hotel. He also gave up the bright lights of the stage at his concert hall when, in April 1866, he applied for a license for the Brighton Hotel at Sandgate, 16 kms north of Brisbane, where he then lived. But with the downturn in the Queensland economy, George abandoned the license at the Brighton Hotel just 10 months later and took up a license for the Kelvin Grove Hotel. Back closer to the centre of the town he advertised dancing instruction.

In November of 1867 he abandoned the Kelvin Grove Hotel after his newborn daughter Frances Blanche died. Sometime later he returned to Sydney, briefly dallying with the hotel industry again, going broke in 1874. By Christmas 1878, he was advertising himself as a Quadrille (traditional dance performed by four couples) pianist for Christmas parties. He never returned to the theatre, found employment as an engraver difficult, and ultimately returned to music teaching. Financial woes came to a head in 1886 when, to pay his debts, all his household belongings, down to the kitchen utensils, were sold at auction.

Margaret, his beloved wife of 44 years, died in 1896, leaving George with four surviving adult children out of ten. (George's son Arthur Mason inherited his father's musical skills and was appointed the City of Sydney organist in 1901 and later organist at St James's in Piccadilly, London. He was also London correspondent for the *Sydney Morning Herald* and the Australian Broadcasting Commission.)

Official records and newspaper reports for George Birkbeck Mason disappear until his death in Thargomindah Queensland in 1899 aged 72. How he had ended up back in Queensland yet far out in a bush town is unknown. Perhaps it was to escape the tragedies that had plagued him since owning the accursed Victoria Hotel.

Meanwhile the hotel itself, now trading out of its Elizabeth Street address, was a ghost of its former self, with a reputation that continued to decline.

In 1874 the then publican of the Victoria Hotel, William Drummond, had his license cancelled after being charged with 'allowing women of loose character to assemble in his public house.'

Lambert Gallagher, newly arrived in Brisbane from Victoria, had been staying at the hotel. Little did the landlord know, but Gallagher was a police detective. So appalled was Gallagher by the activities in the hotel that he kept a detailed notebook of the nightly, 'pandemonious' goings on, the contents of which were described as being 'totally unfit for publication.' On one night alone, the publican, William Drummond had served drinks to customers entertaining 'no fewer than thirteen unfortunates.' Drummond was fined £10 and his license cancelled. [13]

The hotel, along with the original Mason's Concert Hall, were eventually demolished in 1880 to make way for the Theatre Royal.

The vacant land fronting Queen Street had finally been redeveloped in 1866 when a former publican of the Victoria, Thomas Cowell, erected a building large enough for three shops with dwellings above. The building was leased by the enterprising James Collins whose butchery business was also a victim of the fire and for 36 years it operated as the European Hotel. After major renovations in 1902 it was renamed the York Hotel, renamed again in the 1970s the New York Hotel. It was finally demolished to make way for today's shopping mall, the Myer Centre, in 1986 by which time, except for a short period after the fire, a hotel on this site had watered, fed and accommodated travellers for over 143 years.

Brisbane Burns

Chapter 28

Dispensing utmost civility and attention

The Sovereign Hotel 1846-1926

With the Victoria Hotel reduced to a lone brick chimney left standing amid glowing ashes, the fire quickly consumed a short row of wooden structures that sat in front of the Australasian Bank before latching firmly onto George McAdam's Sovereign Hotel.

It was clear to all that, like the Victoria, the Sovereign could not be saved. It was constructed along the lines of a typical bush pub of the day – long, low, pit-sawn weatherboard with a shingle roof and shady verandah. McAdam and as many employees and volunteers as he could muster dragged clear horses and vehicles from around the back and precious few contents from the hotel itself. Its brick chimney too would soon be standing alone amongst burning wreckage. The bank meanwhile, while built of brick, was caught between two fierce blazes and soon was totally burnt out, its walls remaining but fatally weakened.

Sparks and embers continued to rain down on the flammable rooftops around the burning hotel. It was clear the raging inferno would overtake the motley band of hundreds of citizens desperately trying to delay the path of the fire. There was an unspoken understanding between fire-fighters, police, military and volunteers that there was now no hope of saving anything left in the Queen Street block until the brick and stone Bank of New South Wales building on the corner of George and Queen Streets.

Two doors up Queen Street towards George Street from the Victoria Hotel James Powers, one of the earliest free settlers in Brisbane, built the Sovereign Hotel. It was 'a house of accommodation for the better classes only' and occupied the land through to Elizabeth Street.[1] Stables, yards, ancillary buildings and a billiard hall eventually completed the site.

The first publican was George McAdam who would, for decades afterwards always be associated with the hotel. Amongst the locals it was referred to as McAdam's. George McAdam was a Scot from Aberdeen, one of a group of settlers who arrived with George and Patrick Leslie on the Darling Downs in the early 1840s. For some years George McAdam worked as a groom for the Leslies on Canning Downs Station and then moved to Brisbane to run the hotel. George was more of a wheeler-dealer than a grazier. He quickly established a horse trading business as well as running the hotel and frequently advertised the Leslie's prize horses for stud. Initially he spent only two years behind the bar at the Sovereign, but would return twice in later years cementing his association with the hotel. In 1846, when George McAdam took a break to concentrate on horse trading and breeding, the licence passed to Benjamin Lee.

Arriving in Sydney on the *Esther* in July 1833 with his family, Benjamin Lee, a hat manufacturer, began his commercial career in Sydney with a market stall, eventually settling into the hotel trade running the Harp & Shamrock and the Flower Pot before coming to Brisbane in 1842. Prior to taking over the Sovereign, he was publican at the Shepherd and Flock Inn also in Queen Street. In June 1846, the Lee family returned to Sydney and the licence for the Sovereign passed to Robert Edmund Dix.

Dix was a versatile man with a tendency to exaggerate. When he became the publican of the Sovereign Hotel he was also first mate on the *Experiment*, a steamer plying its trade between Brisbane and Ipswich. He later ran the Bush Inn at Bigge's Camp (now Grandchester) 76 km west of Brisbane where he was wont to spin a tale to the locals.

Chapter 28 — The Sovereign Hotel

In 1847 the steamer *Sovereign* was wrecked on the Amity Banks off North Stradbroke Island. Only 10 people survived and, according to Dix, among them were himself and his future wife. He claimed that in celebration of their survival he had named the hotel in Queen Street the Sovereign. Given that the hotel was already well-established by 1847, and the fact he had married in 1844, it was obviously false.

The true story was that Robert Dix was the chief officer of the *Sovereign* steamer during its runs from Sydney to Brisbane in the early 1840s. In July 1844 he married Anna Marie Elliot, a 17-year-old Sovereign stewardess and in September that year they left the steamer to settle in Brisbane – three years before the wreck of the *Sovereign*. The busy, somewhat imaginary, life of Mr. Dix unravelled and the license for the Sovereign passed to James Powers, the original builder, in March 1847.

In November 1849, George McAdam and his bride Mary McDonald reacquired the license and extensively renovated the premises where his guests could

> depend upon receiving the utmost civility and attention, and every care will be taken to have the Wines, Spirits etc, of the very best quality. The Feeding department will be under the especial care of the Hostess, who will use her best endeavours.[2]

Hotels in North Brisbane were at a disadvantage. The only river crossing was by punt. Squatters, explorers and travellers entering the settlement from Ipswich or the Darling Downs first encountered the hostelries of South Brisbane so it took some time and effort to move horses and drays across the river. The Sovereign, however, with its host's ties to the squattocracy of the Downs and his former employers the Leslies, was the fashionable place to be seen in North Brisbane.

> McAdam's hotel, nearly opposite the present Town Hall, was, from the fact of its boniface having been an old employee of the Cannings Downs Leslies, as fashionable on the north side as Grenier's was on the south side.[3]

George McAdam settled into the life of a publican and horse dealer although his fortunes waxed and waned. In addition to the horse bazaar (trading in horses, mules, dogs and ponies) and renting out carriages and drays, in 1858 he went into partnership with James Bolger in a grocery, wine and spirit store in Elizabeth Street behind the hotel.

With the hotel and horse trading keeping him busy, he tended to leave the grocery business to James but just a year later it was in trouble. McAdam admitted to his creditors he had paid little attention to the shop and as a consequence, the Sovereign and its contents were put up for sale and the license passed into other hands.

Whether the sale never went through, or McAdam managed to make enough from horse trading to retrieve it, or whether his influential friends on the Downs supported him, he was back in business at the Sovereign a little over two years later. In April 1864 just eight months before the December fire, he announced grand plans to erect a magnificent new Sovereign Hotel on the site of the old one in Queen Street.

> A grand hotel is to be erected in Queen Street, Brisbane, on the site of the Sovereign Hotel, now occupied by Mr. McAdam. It will form an appropriate vis a vis to the new Town Hall, for its architectural merits will rank high.[4]

George McAdam's fortunes were again on the up, until the fire. There was some insurance, but McAdam suffered heavy losses both financial and personal. A new hotel was duly built, called the New Sovereign Hotel, on the back of the land fronting Elizabeth Street (It was still standing in 1926.) but life for George McAdam had become a struggle.

It reached a turning point when his wife Mary died in December 1865. Mary McAdam had been a key figure in the life of the hotel, being responsible for all the catering, housekeeping of the many bedrooms for residents and visitors and supervising the staff. After her death, George McAdam was left to look after John Thomas 15, Isabella 12, Ann 10, Flora 8 and baby, Mary Margaret, who died a month later.

Worsening economic conditions within the colony meant that loans were being called in including George's £4000. The banks were finding money tight and private lenders needed to consolidate. Economic conditions eventually caught up with him and he filed for insolvency once again in 1867. George briefly returned the hotel trade again, using his name as publicity – McAdams Hotel in George Street, but failed. He took to the country, tin mining on the Severn River, south of Warwick, accompanied by his children. John Thomas eventually moved further up the Severn River to Emmaville in New South Wales still chasing tin. Isabella married Thomas Cumings in Whetstone, not far from Warwick.

In 1879 at Beauraba, later renamed Pittsworth, south west of Toowoomba, George leased 160 acres. He remained there for six years, running cattle and horses. By 1888, he was living near Warwick, where he had first settled in Queensland with the Leslies 50 years earlier working as road Inspector for the Inglewood Divisional Board (now the Inglewood Shire, south west of Warwick close to the border with New South Wales).

Looking forward to a restful later life with his horses, George was accidentally killed at the end of 1888 when his horse bolted and slammed him into a tree on the road to Leyburn, 60km north-west of Warwick. He died at the scene without regaining consciousness. At the inquest it was claimed that he was under the influence of liquor. He was 62. George McAdam was remembered as 'one of Leslie's mob', a popular and successful publican, and a pioneer of cattle-raising on the Darling Downs.

Brisbane Burns

Chapter 29

Shadowed by misfortune

Benjamin Henry Palmer 1834–1894

With only chimneys, collapsed brick walls, piles of charred timbers and the odd tin capped stump left to delineate where many of the city's drinkers had stood just hours before, Queen Street now resembled a chaotic goods market. Stock and belongings piled up in teetering stacks lined the opposite side of the road to the fire.

The stock from Mr Palmer's colourful and popular drapery store was soon added as his timber premises caught alight and burned to the ground in a matter of minutes. Skirts, crinolines, hats and suits were saved along with a smattering of furniture and fittings. The small but eager army of volunteers helping Mr Palmer even included the newly minted politician William Brooks MLA, himself a former draper's apprentice and now a radical liberal humanitarian. It seemed that all of Brisbane was on hand to witness the final stages of the fire.

The earliest records of Benjamin Palmer, a tailor by trade, show him in partnership in Sydney in 1858 with another tailor, John Sturday Jones. The partnership failed in a spectacular insolvency with a deficit of over £5000 in 1859 ($800,000 in today's money).

Bad luck (or more likely bad management) seemingly dogged Benjamin Henry Palmer's steps wherever he strode. Just three years before that fateful December evening of 1864, still recovering from the spectacular business failure in Sydney, Benjamin, and his young bride Mary (they were married on 2 March 1861), had set up shop in Ipswich.

Mary and her sister, Selina were born in Sydney, the daughters of convict Phillip Bourke who had arrived in 1823 aboard the *Medina*, transported for life from Tipperary, Ireland. In 1831 he married a free woman, Harriet Downer. After serving his sentence he returned to his trade of tailoring and died in 1853 when Mary was 15.

Almost immediately upon settling in Ipswich, and within weeks of his marriage, Palmer was still struggling to make a viable business. Hoping to continue in the tailoring trade, he had brought with him from Sydney woollen cloth, ready-made clothes and some sewing machines.

By the 1860s sewing machines were becoming popular in the home, while tailors and dressmakers were using them to manufacture ready-made goods for sale in their stores. The time taken to sew a garment dropped from days to hours, significantly reducing the price of tailor-made clothes. In 1865 in Brisbane a second-hand Singer sewing machine cost £8. By comparison, the cheapest ticket (steerage) from London to Australia was £15, a bullock driver earned £65 a year and a female servant £26 a year.

In immediate need of funds, Benjamin Palmer sold the goods he had brought from Sydney to his sister-in-law Selina Burke for £450. At a meeting to discuss a partnership with Thomas Kenyon, another Ipswich draper, it was agreed each party would invest £300. Palmer brazenly offered the goods in Selina's possession as his share of the £300 investment, but Kenyon refused to accept them. Nevertheless, a partnership agreement was drawn up and Palmer immediately departed for Sydney where he purchased £1000 worth of stock on credit in the name of Palmer and Kenyon. In a detailed advertisement in *Queensland Times, Ipswich Herald* and *General Advertiser* on 3 January 1862 they announced the opening of Palmer and Kenyon Drapers and Mantle Makers (a mantle was a long cape-like cloak worn outdoors over women's dresses).

> Every article of female attire will be made in the latest style and design, and all orders executed in the shortest notice, from the facilities afforded by the large amount of machinery brought to bear on its production, which will have the effect of giving a superior article at a lower price.

But there was a problem. Selina Burke owned the sewing machines. Benjamin Palmer bought the sewing machines back off her with a £300 promissory note in the name of Palmer and Kenyon (without Kenyon's agreement). The shop opened for business on 10 January, 1862. Eleven days later Kenyon, furious at what he saw as collusion between Selina and Palmer to defraud the partnership, and incensed that Palmer had neglected to invest his half of the money, gathered together some friends and stormed the shop. Shoving Palmer out of the way and ripping off his shirt sleeves when he refused to budge from the doorway, Kenyon and his mates seized boxes of stock and carried them outside to the waiting dray. Palmer brought charges against Kenyon and his friends of unlawful assemblage and violence or terror to Her Majesty's subjects which the court threw out. In a further court case Selina Burke successfully recovered the £300 owed by Palmer and Kenyon. The business was over, again.

Setting up anew was to be a feature of Palmer's business life though it has been noted that he had other talents – 'a splendid platform speaker', he 'wielded a capable pen'[1], he 'was a great reader and classical student'[2] and was to be a driving force in the North Queensland town of Cooktown.

Somerset House in Brisbane's Queen Street close to the George Street corner became Ben Palmer & Co's 'Cheapest Drapery Emporium in Brisbane' in 1863 but was unfortunately right in the path of the December 1864 fire. Thanks to the enthusiastic assistance of onlookers on the night of the fire, most of his stock was saved and he was able to hold a monster 'fire sale' at his temporary shop in George Street. He returned to Queen Street in June 1865 when new first class brick and metal buildings were constructed on the old site.

Ben Palmer and Co soon expanded, hiring tailors and young people who understood how to use the new sewing machines. With the help of the machines, he was able to offer a reasonably priced made-to-order service for men and women. Drapery and tailoring was however a fiercely competitive business. Constant advertising, continual sales and new and exciting goods were needed to beat the competition. Mary and Benjamin Palmer, along with Selina, and three children (with names that reflected Benjamin's devotion to the classics) Demosthenes 4, Atalanta 3 and Archimedes 11 months, settled into a busy working life, living above the new shop in Queen Street.

On 23 September 1868, fire once again threatened his store. Trading was over for the day and Benjamin was out. Selina was tidying up the shop, Mary was upstairs with the children. Selina picked up a kerosene lamp, burnt her hands on the hot base, screamed and dropped the lamp. It fell into a pile of muslin which quickly caught alight. Panicking, she called 'Fire' to alert Mary, grabbed one of the children and fled the shop followed by Mary and the other two children. By the time they were able to extinguish the flames with a nearby water supply, half the store was damaged.

Ben Palmer & Co's newly arrived stock of summer garments was destroyed and he was only insured for half the value of his losses. Palmer was in trouble again. New shipments of stock would take many months. Although he informed the insurance company and supplied all the necessary documents, he lodged a claim for £1863 which inadvertently included an exempt £118 worth of book debt. This was enough to delay the claim, the Pacific Fire and Marine Insurance Company saying it was fraudulent, eventually taking the case to court in May the following year.

It was too late. Ben Palmer closed the business and the family moved to Margaret Street where their fourth child, Cicero was born in May, 1869. Unable to pay the rent on the store, his landlord Mr Sutherland seized goods from Palmer's home to recoup the debt.

Outraged, Palmer sued him for £1000 pounds for trespass and excessive distress. The court found in favour of Palmer but awarded him only 35 shillings.

In June 1869 Selina Burke married John Watson, a successful photographer and future partner in Watson Ferguson & Co (printers and stationers who still exist today) – and the Palmer family lost its free live-in help. Brisbane now held no future for Benjamin Palmer. Over the past two years he had watched the town empty as an economic downturn hit. He would have to chase a new dream.

James Nash's 1867 discovery of gold in Gympie north of Brisbane in 1867 had already drawn thousands of prospectors from Brisbane and all over Australia. Many merchants had already exploited the opportunity of providing goods to the isolated settlements. Having hung on in Brisbane, Palmer now realised that his best chance lay with the goldfields. Gympie was already oversupplied with stores and traders, so North Queensland and the rich fields of the Cape River beckoned. In 1869, Ravenswood, 129 km south west of Townsville, already had a population over 2000 and was one of the largest goldfields in the North and although only three years old, Townsville was already established as a major northern port.

Leaving his family to pack up the house and settle their debts, Palmer left Brisbane for Townsville in August 1869, where he quickly set up shop with a branch store in Ravenswood. In April the following year Mary and the children left Brisbane aboard the steamer *Boomerang* on one of the first voyages directly from Brisbane to Bowen and Townsville. The day after they left there was an auction of their household goods in Brisbane. They included an extensive collection of books described as 'a large assortment of valuable literary works'[3], which classical scholar Benjamin must have regretted leaving behind.

Townsville in 1870 was 'host to all the lawlessness of the goldfields' and reports of 'drunkenness, violence and vagrancy'[4] were common. This was the new settlement that Benjamin Palmer had chosen for his family. Sometime in 1870 his store at Ravenswood was robbed of £700 (a considerable sum of money, more than $100,000 today) and an indication of the money to be made on the gold fields. Unable to pay his creditors, Palmer reached a gentlemen's agreement which wasn't legally binding repaying a small percentage of the debts in cash and providing promissory notes for the remainder. As a debt of honour, the balance was not to be claimed for at least seven years. This resolved the immediate financial difficulty and avoided insolvency but he was unable to continue in business and was forced to seek work as a tailor in Townsville. Meanwhile the family was still growing; a fifth child, Horace, was born in 1871 followed by Cleopatra in 1873.

In 1873, gold was discovered on the Palmer River, west of Cooktown and the first major settlement was Edward's Camp (later named Maytown). Here, in December 1874, Benjamin Palmer arrived with six tons of merchandise ready to try his hand at trading once again. Having no shop front and the settlement being rudimentary at best, he stored the goods with a casual acquaintance, John Edwards. The following February he took some of the stores to sell at another camp and when he returned for the rest, discovered Edwards had sold the remaining goods. Edwards claimed never to have received them. A case to recover the goods or money was never resolved as Palmer didn't have the funds to pay the solicitor.

Palmer continued working for wages as a tailor in Townsville until 1877 when the gentlemen's agreements came due and he sought the protection of the law, pleading insolvency once again. The only debt proved was that of his son-in-law, John Watson. Nevertheless, a certificate was issued and Benjamin Palmer was free to try again.

With the births of Ethel and Socrates the family was complete and the Palmers moved to Cooktown 'he has a large family and it is no joke to "shift camp", when they are about.'[5] Here they established another drapery and tailoring business in Charlotte Street. As teenagers, Horace and Archimedes became involved in the business, taking on the name Palmer Bros. Shrewd Benjamin began acquiring assets once again, but ensured that the furniture and household belongings were in Mary's name. Appearing financially secure, with his large family around him, he described himself as a gentleman and quickly became involved in the intricate politics of the northern outpost.

> He was the leader of democratic thought in the town, he was a fluent and effective speaker, he was solid, active and wore a long brown beard. There was much in him that was reminiscent of Henry Parkes.[6]

(Henry Parkes was known as the 'Father of Federation' and was renowned for his speeches).

> He[Palmer] is a tailor, but he is one who has more than the average share of intelligence, has a ready pen, and as a stage orator, there are few his equal in the North.[7]

In 1878 he stood for election for the seat of Cook in the State parliament but was unsuccessful.

North Queensland in 1884/85 was the setting for many acrimonious and violent meetings between Separationists and opponents. Many believed that the economic problems of the north, the government's refusal to build infrastructure and the debate over Kanaka labour (Pacific Islanders exploited for their cheap labour) could only be solved by separating into another colony. Ben Palmer saw separation as the only panacea for the evils he saw in a lack of citizenship rights.

The drapery business was largely left to his sons to run and, in 1884, Palmer received an auctioneer's licence.

The state election of 1888 saw Palmer nominate once again for the seat of Cook. Commentators often stressed that Ben Palmer was only a dummy candidate and that at the last minute another would be substituted but he carried through and was defeated yet again, the local newspapers quick to announce the fact that 'poor old Ben Palmer was sent back to Ocean Retreat'.[8] *Ocean Retreat* was the name of the small cottage he shared with his large family on Grassy Hill, the same hill climbed by Captain Cook and his crew looking for a safe passage through the reef for the repaired Endeavour.

On the night of 28 February 1890 in Far North Queensland waters, the steamship *Quetta* was wrecked and sank drowning 134 passengers and crew. Among them were John Watson and his wife Selina, Mary's sister. John and Selina Watson had no children and under the terms of Selina's will, Mary was to be left £3000. This could have saved the Palmers from further financial embarrassment but because they died together, John and Selina Watson were declared as having died intestate (without a will) and Mary's inheritance vanished as the estate was divided amongst John Watson's siblings.

Later the same year Palmer's eldest son, Demosthenes, married Laura Blanchard. Palmer had seven children still at home aged between 12 and 25. Horace and Archimedes worked in the shop and Cicero with the railways. Perhaps seeing the inevitable failure of yet another business, in January 1892 Palmer sold the shop to Horace and Archimedes for £8500 to be paid in instalments over four years. The brothers distributed a flyer to the residents of Cooktown explaining the new arrangements and requested 'Come, kindly send your orders in, and give the young Cooktownites a loyal and generous start.'[9]

In March, with the creditors owed over £2000, the receiver entered the shop and took control unaware of the change in ownership. Further investigation by the receiver showed that Mary Palmer owned all the household goods and was in fact, the largest creditor. As the insolvency proceeded, the ownership of various blocks of land and the leasehold on the shop were questioned. Land often belonged to one person while another owned the building. Palmer's landlord at Grassy Hill threatened to evict the family if he was not counted among the creditors.

Even with the business in his sons' names, it was time for the Palmer family to move on. On the morning of 9 August 1892, Benjamin 58, Mary 54 and seven of their children aged between 14 and 27 departed in the *Arrawatta* for Perth. 'We wish them bon voyage, and abundant prosperity in their new field of operation.'[10] Eldest son Demosthenes and his wife, Laura, remained behind. Horace and Archimedes's debt was forgotten and they could all start again.

The family settled into a purpose built boarding house called *Tower House* in Russell Square, Perth, now the suburb of Northbridge. The Victorian Italianate style building still exists today. Within a year Mary Palmer was listed as the contact for all tenancy inquiries. Benjamin Palmer retired from business and Horace and Archimedes found jobs as drapers and tailors. Cicero headed east to work as an assistant surveyor with the Railways eventually ending up in the goldfields of Kalgoorlie.

On 2 May 1894, aged 60, Benjamin Henry Palmer died at his home *Tower House*. *The Queensland Times*, *Ipswich Herald* and *General Advertiser* ran an obituary on 15 May 1894 which concluded

> Altogether, Ben Palmer was a worthy resident of Queensland, and his many friends will learn with regret of his death.

Mary and her daughters remained at *Tower House* until the death of Cleopatra in February 1895. Atalanta and Ethel May, still spinsters, started the Brisbane Street Day School, Perth, which eventually became the Brisbane Academy in William St, Mt Lawley, Perth. Ethel May died in 1912, but Atalanta continued her association with the school well into the 1930s. She died, still unmarried, in 1954 aged 88.

Mrs Mary Palmer (nee Burke) daughter of a convict, died aged 88 in May 1926 at home with Atalanta, her sole surviving daughter. Harold, Horace and Demosthenes and their wives attended the funeral along with granddaughters Tess and Lillian.

Queensland Figaro and *Punch* of 11 Sep 1886 summed up the life of Benjamin Henry Palmer.

> He experienced a great deal of the bitters when compared to the sweets of a wandering life.
>
> And – here's good luck to your ould soul, Ben Palmer!

Brisbane Burns

Chapter 30

A tragic tale

Nathaniel Lade 1835–1895

As the frantic work of emptying the few remaining structures left fronting Queen Street continued, behind and further to the centre of the block the densely packed flimsy cottages, stables and sheds added the final fuel to push the fire onward to the George Street corner.

Arguing his way past the soldiers holding a crowd containment line at the top end of Queen Street an exhausted Nathaniel Lade, master saddler, reached his shopfront to find it ablaze, with most of his stock and furniture piled on the footpath opposite, saved by bystanders.

He had just run five blocks after catching the crowded ferry to Queen's Wharf, his only way of getting across the Brisbane River once he had spotted the ominous red glow from his house in Raymond Terrace South Brisbane.

Only an hour before he had been settling down with his family to an early dinner and looking forward to a cooling stroll afterwards.

Nathaniel Lade's successful business was situated opposite the old convict barracks in Queen Street. He supplied saddles for every kind of horse, from children's ponies to racehorses, and harnesses for all types of transport including horse-drawn, bullock drays, goat and dog carts.

Saddleries were an essential service in 19th century Brisbane. In 1864 there were no sealed roads, the railway to Ipswich was still under construction and Cobb & Co had yet to begin regular coach services in Queensland. People moved by foot, horseback and horse-drawn vehicles. Two-wheeled wagonettes and four-wheeled hansom cabs were available for hired transport. Heavy drays pulled by teams of bullocks hauled goods between the settlements.

Horses of all types and sizes kept the city moving and their care and equipment represented a major segment of the settlement's economy. A first class saddle horse or draughthorse cost between £17 and £24 – a year's wage for a labourer – while the cost of a carriage was upwards of £70. Most businesses kept horses for transporting goods. Stables and horse-trading bazaars were common in the city. Ballantyne and McNab, manufacturers of the first hansom cab in Queensland, built carriages at their large workshop on the corner of Albert and Elizabeth Streets in central Brisbane. Regular auctions ensured a quick turnover for new and imported vehicles, saddlery and harnessing. Licensing laws not only regulated hotels' opening hours and accommodation, but also required them to provide stabling for at least six horses. An award-winning experienced saddler with good business sense in a growing city would prosper.

At the age of 15, Nathaniel Lade had left his birthplace in Kent England and arrived in Melbourne aboard the *Clifton* with his parents and siblings in 1850. The family initially settled in central Melbourne and later moved to Brunswick, 6km to the north, where Nathaniel Lade learned the saddler trade from his father, winning medals for his work in the 1862 International Exhibition in London.

In 1859, Nathaniel married 18-year-old Elizabeth Helen Bridges from Cornwall. They moved to Brisbane in May 1863 with children Frank and Mary. His uncle, Thomas Lade, was already settled on a farm in Upper Kedron Brook, now the suburbs of Gaythorne and Mitchelton. Lade's farm *Surrenden*, famous for its grapes, poultry, honeycomb and butter, was a favoured destination of the Brisbane social set (or the 'upper ten' as they were called) for riding parties and picnics. With a guaranteed introduction to the wealthy and notable of Brisbane, young Nathaniel purchased the saddlery business of Caspar Burdoff in Queen Street.

> N. L. has brought with him from Melbourne a large and well-assorted stock of goods, and hopes from the experience gained there, should the public favour him with their commands, to execute all orders to their entire satisfaction.[1]

The family settled into *Brunswick Villa*, a two-storey wooden house on a leafy hill at Raymond Terrace South Brisbane (the area now occupied by the Mater Hospital complex). Later renamed *Hillside*, the house was still standing in 1932 and surrounded by pine trees planted by Nathaniel Lade.

While Nathaniel's shop was destroyed in the December fire, just two days later he was open for business in temporary premises in George Street. Three months later he settled into a new building back in the commercial heart of Queen Street. Business expanded rapidly, as did the Lade family with the birth of their sixth child Lucy in 1867. Eventually there would be 15 children born in 22 years, six of whom died in childhood.

On 25 February 1868 the ear-splitting blast of three cannon announced the arrival in Brisbane of Australia's first royal visitor to Australia, Prince Alfred, Duke of Edinburgh, the second son of Queen Victoria. The Prince was transported up river by the steamer *Kate* to a specially constructed carpeted landing stage crowned by a triumphal arch decorated in natural foliage from the city's new Botanical Gardens. After a greeting from the judiciary, members of Parliament, bishops, consuls and the Mayor, the Prince was seated in an open carriage pulled by four magnificent iron-grey horses for the grand procession to Government House.

Nearly the whole population of Brisbane turned out, particularly the beautifully dressed and coiffured young women who rushed the Prince on his arrival. (The Prince's view of the colonies would be soured just weeks later by his attempted assassination in Sydney. Shot close to his spine by Henry O'Farrell, an alcoholic newly released from the lunatic asylum, the Prince quickly recovered from his injuries and returned to England).

The intricate harnessing for the Prince's carriage used in the procession as part of the meticulous and lavish preparations for the visit, had been crafted by saddler Nathaniel Lade, but while considered the best in his trade, Nathaniel struggled to gain recognition for his effort. Prior to the Prince's visit, Nathaniel had sent a letter to the editor of the *Brisbane Courier* correcting a statement stating that the harnessing for the Prince's carriage had come from Sydney. 'Permit me to inform you that I had the honour of supplying the Government with the Prince's harness'[2], adding that the harness had in fact been on display in his store for the month leading up to the visit. Inexplicably, he was nevertheless left off the guest list for the reception held in the Prince's honour at Government House which was attended by many of his fellow Queen Street traders.

Despite the lack of recognition for his work, Nathaniel Lade's business continued to grow. By 1869 Lade's Saddlery was the largest of its kind in Brisbane, employing 10 people. Nathaniel was a regular prize-winning exhibitor at the Brisbane Exhibition and, in 1874, his advertisements proudly announced 'By Appointment to His Excellency the Most Honorable the Marquis of Normanby,'[3] who, at that time, was the Governor of Queensland. Experts in the manufacture of all types of leather goods, Lade's increased its range to include portmanteaus and travelling bags in the late 1870s.

By 1875 Nathaniel and his large and prosperous family had outgrown the cottage at Raymond Terrace, and moved out of town to the new suburb of Coorparoo, about a 20-minute carriage ride away. *St Leonards*, their new home, was a large, lowset Queenslander-style with bull-nose verandahs on three sides set in 13 acres situated between Old Cleveland Road, Norman Creek and St Leonards Street Coorparoo.

The euphoria of success, however, was short-lived In May 1875, not long after the move to *St Leonards*, Nathaniel and his eldest son Frank, 14, set out for town in an old, work-worn borrowed buggy while his own was being repaired. After a short distance, a pin in the axle came loose and the buggy collapsed dragging dangerously on the ground. As Nathaniel instinctively pulled on the reins, the pace slowed, but the momentum rammed the buggy into the back of the horse which took fright and bolted. Nathaniel was thrown clear unhurt but Frank stayed trapped in the buggy as it careered onwards, eventually being tossed out fracturing his skull. He died at the scene.

Tragedy, it seemed, had continued to stalk the family. Since coming to Brisbane the Lade family had already lost six-year-old Mary, nine-year-old Anne, an infant son, and a month after Frank's death, the infant Rachel. When the Coorparoo State School opened in 1876 the remaining school-age Lade children were on the first roll. Nathaniel Lade was a member of the Coorparoo School Committee and later trustee of the Coorparoo Methodist Church and Superintendent of the Sunday school.

Between 1876 and 1883, five more children were born: Benjamin, Athole, Hugh, Ruth and George. Hugh died in 1881 aged 11 months and the last child, George Reginald Vincent, died aged 7 months in 1884 at St Leonards of marasmus – malnutrition. Today it is a disease of developing countries but in 19th century Australia, it was common in babies under twelve months even among wealthy families, caused by unsuitable food, chronic vomiting and diarrhoea or other undiagnosed serious illnesses.

Nine of the Lade children lived to adulthood and shortly after George's death, the family moved to *Eastwell*, a larger house further up the hill in Cavendish Road Coorparoo. The new house, set in 10 acres of gardens, had six bedrooms, a bathroom, two kitchens, servants' quarters, a large drawing room, a huge breakfast area, a coach house, stable and outhouses. Furnishings included Brussels carpets, chandeliers, a walnut drawing room upholstered in silk and tapestries, Dresden figurines, and an 11-piece mahogany dining suite.

In March 1888, the saddlery business moved to larger premises at 53 Queen Street.

> Nothing has been spared in the general arrangement of the establishment to a make it one of the best of its kind in Queensland.[4]

Barely a year later, *Eastwell* was on the market. The economic downturn that became the deep depression of the 1890s was just beginning. A major cause of the crash in Brisbane was the collapse of the building industry along with the demise of many building societies. In 1892, 12% of houses in South Brisbane[5] were empty.

Despite being just 54, Nathaniel Lade's health was deteriorating. This, together with costly business expansion, the lavish expense and inability to sell *Eastwell*, forced the Lade family to face some tough decisions. In 1893 the house was unsuccessfully offered for sale once again, this time when rent, land and house values had fallen to their lowest level. Nathaniel Lade's world crumbled around him. In 1895, with liabilities of over £4,000, he went into liquidation. The splendid contents of his fine house had dwindled to pay off debts, finally being valued at only £160. Desperately ill and broke, Nathaniel auctioned off the final contents of *Eastwell* in June 1895 and the family moved to a small house in West End. The business was wound up by arrangement instead of insolvency and Nathaniel Lade died a month later on 17 July 1895 aged 60.

As a trustee of the Brisbane Cemetery at Toowong, he had chosen his plot well, and Nathaniel Lade today rests high on the hill at Toowong, overlooking modern Brisbane. The Lade family remained a fixture in Grey Road, West End until the death of daughter Lucy in 1949, aged 82. The eldest surviving son, Nathaniel Bridges Lade, continued with his father's leather trade. The other Lade children took up professions rather than trades, becoming civil servants, nurses and teachers. Lade, St Leonards and Eastwell Streets in Coorparoo are a reminder of the suburb's past pioneers.

Moderately successful, the younger Nathaniel Lade continued to ensure his father's legacy contributed to the transport needs of the city until his death in 1900 at the age of only 36. He was buried alongside his father and mother. Soon after, in 1901 the first motor car arrived on Queen Street. It signalled the decline in horses as a major form of transport. Harnessing and saddles would be relegated to recreation and sport as the benefits of the motor car were soon available to all:

> It can be propelled with perfect safety up to twenty-five miles per hour. It carries sufficient fuel to cover 250 miles without replenishment, and its cost of running amounts to less than a penny per mile. [6]

Chapter 31

A most extraordinary citizen

James Robert Dickson 1832–1901

The fire had reached its peak and begun to subside in intensity as it consumed the final shopfronts adjoining the strong stone walls of the Bank of New South Wales. Elsewhere, amidst the burning and smouldering wreckage of the entire city block, exhausted fireman, police, soldiers, storekeepers and volunteers wound down their individual efforts. Nothing more could be saved, nothing more could be pulled down to starve the fire.

For the staff at Dickson and Duncan auctioneers it was the end of a long day of rapid-fire bidding, heckling and raucous bantering, then frantic activity as it became clear the fire at the end of the street was moving inexorably in their direction. Horses and wagons had already removed many of the 'sold' items of the day's trading but a large inventory of goods being prepared for the next big auction were still stored on site. Staff quickly shifted into organising its removal.

Bystanders and fire fighters dragged boxes of rifles, bags of flour, sides of bacon, casks of sherry, saddlery equipment, sacks of potatoes, office furniture and documents onto the street. The quick action saved most of the contents, but by 11.30pm Dickson and Duncan's bustling auction house was a pile of ashes.

Dickson and Duncan, auctioneers and agents, was established in Queen Street Brisbane on 1 July 1864. James Duncan and his family arrived in Brisbane aboard the *Helenslee* in 1862. The same year James Robert Dickson had moved to Brisbane after eight years in business in Victoria, having emigrated in 1855. They were one of the foremost traders in real estate and the myriad of goods required by the growing city. Their partnership lasted 15 years, after which James Duncan suffered several financial collapses. In contrast James Robert Dickson achieved financial and political success, eventually becoming Premier of Queensland and Australia's first Minister of Defence.

James Robert Dickson.

Born in 1832 in Plymouth, Devon, England to Scottish parents, Dickson was educated at Glasgow High School and was a clerk with the City of Glasgow Bank. In 1854, at the height of the Victorian gold rush when up to 300 ships at once were anchored in Port Phillip Bay, James Robert Dickson left his homeland for Australia. His cousins, Thomas Rae and John Dickson, were already operating a thriving business as soap and candle makers and general merchants in Melbourne. Aged 22, James Dickson arrived eager to grab every opportunity offered by the bustling, gold-fevered state. Beginning as a banking clerk, within three years he was a partner in his cousins' business, Rae Dickson & Co.

Arriving a year earlier in 1853, 16-year-old Annie Ely, daughter of a boot-maker from Suffolk England, settled with her parents and siblings in the marshy fields of Collingwood Victoria in a small wooden shanty along with thousands of other immigrants also determined to exploit Victoria's gold rush. On 8 November 1855 she married James Robert Dickson at St Mark's Church Collingwood. By the end of the following year, James and Annie celebrated the birth of the first of their 15 children. The infant, James Robert, only survived a month but was quickly followed by another son. When the Dickson family moved to Brisbane in 1862 and settled in Gregory Terrace, there were four children – James Robert, Frederick William, Alice Myra and Annie Maud.

Securing an auctioneer's licence in 1863, Dickson began his career in Brisbane with established agent Arthur Martin before setting up Dickson and Duncan in Queen Street in mid 1864. The disastrous fire of December 1864 barely caused a ripple in the auctioneering trade because secure storage and space to hold an auction were all that was required to recommence trading. Dickson invested his profits in land and continued building the business and, soon after the fire, began construction on a new residence for his growing family on Hamilton Hill about five kilometres north east of the city.

The stately, gabled-roofed, sandstone house called *Toorak* with its prominent central stone tower still exists today. With an iron-roofed verandah the width of the front, the house was originally built as a single storey with the tower extended in 1898 and a second storey added a few years later. Inspired by Italian architecture after a visit to Europe in the early 1890s, Dickson commissioned artist and builders to construct new windows and decorate the house with colourful paintings.

> There are flowers in urns and goblets, and bunches of fruit in rich, warm Southern tones, and trailing vines. The painting on the glass panels are done in small sections, and represent old-time scenes.[1]

Although close to the city of Brisbane, the 22-acre (9 hectares) *Toorak* estate was isolated bush, sheltering local aboriginals, misfits and petty criminals. At night the only lights were those of similar houses perched on the surrounding hills of Hamilton and Breakfast Creek. Writing in 1930, F. E. Lord described how the eldest of the Dickson children, also James Robert, could recall 'the careful locking up process at night.'[2] It would be this ingrained fear of intruders that would later lead to tragedy for the family.

Annie Dickson.

Settling in at *Toorak*, Annie advertised for a housemaid and cook to help look after the family. As more children arrived, Chinese servants were employed to assist Annie in caring for the children. Ada Mary was born at Gregory Terrace in 1863 and the next nine children were born at *Toorak*. The large grounds made a happy and healthy playground for the children and the house's strong stone walls made it secure at night.

Toorak was the centre of family life and the setting of many social functions and business meetings. Until 1870, James Robert had immersed himself in his business and the affairs of All Saints Church, Wickham Terrace (of which he was churchwarden) with little thought given to politics. Despite many of his friends, business associates and social connections contesting or holding seats in local and state government he had managed to keep his political opinions neutral.

In February 1870 he stood unsuccessfully for the Valley Ward in the local elections. His still undeclared political leanings were hidden behind pledges to repair dangerous corners and narrow streets in Fortitude Valley, reform cab and wood-carriers' licenses and improve lighting in the city.[3] When the 1873 state election came around, the seat of Enoggera was without a sitting member. In an election speech in October of that year Mr Dickson revealed why he was finally persuaded to stand as a candidate.

> He was requested (not for the first time), by a very great number of men who had known him in business and privately for many years, to stand for one of the electorates. He had always previously declined to do so, as he considered that business requirements claimed his attention, and it was not till after finding that none of the late members was a candidate for Enoggera that he at length consented to stand.[4]

A conservative politician but not a member of a party, he was in favour of 'a thoroughly secular system of education, gratuitously distributed' and 'a continuous and extended system of immigration'. While respecting the contributions of the squatters and Crown tenants to the colony, he believed that when the lands were required for the agricultural settlement of people the occupiers 'must recede before the demands of the people.'[5]

By 1873 Annie Dickson was only 35 and the mother of 11 children. Bustling *Toorak* was now to be included in the round of political functions and meetings that would inevitably accompany election success. Often pregnant and with many small children still demanding her attention, Annie did not appear with her husband at political functions (these were often male-only affairs anyway). Nevertheless she was official hostess and many 'were entertained in a manner befitting the station and character of the family.'[6]

James Robert Dickson won the seat of Enoggera by a margin of 57 votes from Mr. R. A. Kingsford, a fellow Queen Street trader. Beginning his new career by dispensing the charm for which he would later be known, he declared that:

> He had reason to feel proud of his success, opposed as he had been by a colonist and citizen of old standing, who was very deservedly respected.

He went on to add that he would be happy if his opponent found another seat in the Parliament.[7]

In May 1876 Dickson served as the secretary for public works and mines and by the following month he was Colonial Treasurer, a position he held for nearly three years. Family life at *Toorak* continued apace with the arrival of Lillian Grace in 1874, Harold Arthur in 1876, who died aged 11 weeks (just weeks before Dickson's elevation to Colonial Treasurer) and Harold Octavius in 1878. Despite his ministerial workload and the stress of family life, James Dickson continued his auctioneering business, no doubt requiring a healthy income to provide for the education of his children at Grammar Schools, and the upkeep of *Toorak*, which included the substantial cost of numerous servants required to keep the fine home running.

In the early hours of Wednesday, 14 January 1880, Annie Dickson was making her rounds of the house closing up after a long night's social gathering. On the hall table lay a loaded pistol, indicative of the family's long-held fear of intruders and most recently as defence against a spate of burglaries in the area. Checking the pistol, as she may have routinely done every evening, it accidentally discharged into her right hand. The injury, though serious and painful, was at first not expected to cause any long term damage. On the following Sunday her doctors considered her case 'calling for no serious anxiety' but by the afternoon she was experiencing the symptoms of tetanus. After initially appearing to recover, a few days later she succumbed to the illness, aged 40.

Although wishing to secure privacy for the family, James Dickson published a sincere thank you for the sympathy offered the family.

> I am unable to reflect unmoved on the many loving hearts and kind hands which have found employment at this time in endeavoring to solace the woe of a family bereft forever of its purest and best influence. To all and each I tender my heart-felt gratitude, and pray that to none of our many sympathisers may ever be known the bitterness of that draught of which we have had to partake.[8]

James Dickson remained a member of the government but held no ministerial post and continued to run his business. The grieving family was left to the care of servants and friends. Thirteen children between the ages of 22 and 14 months needed a mother. Despite his obvious devotion to Annie, James Robert Dickson began the search for another wife.

Mary MacKinlay arrived in Brisbane in 1878 to take up the position of Principal of the Girls Grammar School. Still a small institution of around 40 pupils, its reputation amongst wealthy Brisbane families was growing. The Dickson children all attended the Grammar Schools. Ada Mary won medals for physiology and history in the Senior Public Exams. Parents, together with the trustees of both the Boy's and Girl's Grammar Schools, took a keen interest in the welfare of the students and were pleased to have secured to services of such a highly respected educator as Mary MacKinlay. Mary held a degree from St Andrew's, Edinburgh and had previously taught at Cheltenham Ladies College and Bath High School in England. She was also noted as having 'more than the usual abilities', 'high culture' and a kind and genial manner.'[9]

Unsurprisingly Mary was not only to win the hearts of her pupils. On Christmas Eve 1881, after just three years in the job, she resigned having doubled the number of students and lifted the school out of debt. No clue was given in the press to her future plans. Regret at her leaving was expressed by the parents and they stated that:

> in no department of the public life of this colony had there been more faithful, energetic, or able service than had been the case in this instance, and they would be very sorry to lose her.[10]

Twelve days later in Carcoar, New South Wales, Mary married James Robert Dickson. Although announced in family notices in the newspaper, no other reports of the wedding emerged and there is no evidence that any of the children attended. To all and sundry Mary seemed a strange choice for such a prominent man as Mr Dickson.

It is one thing to admire and respect your children's headmistress but it's quite another for your father to bring her home as your new mother. For 40-year-old Mary, despite her experience with children, it was a culture shock arriving at *Toorak* in late January 1882. Family stories tell of Mary arriving home to find the windows draped in black as a protest from the children. The three eldest girls, Alice 21, newly-engaged Annie 20, and star pupil Ada Mary 18, were in charge at home and wasted no time exerting their authority upon Mary's arrival. A year later, in March 1883, James went to England on urgent business without Mary. He returned nine months later and, while Mary met him in Sydney and they travelled back to Brisbane together, it was the first of many trips where Mary stayed home. On his return, Dickson was once again elevated to Colonial Treasurer. By 1886 Mary Dickson had dropped from sight and unmarried 20-year-old Agnes Dickson took on the role of official hostess.

Unable to adjust to life without work, management of a large and busy family and friction with the young Misses Dicksons, Mary moved to Toowoomba and returned to her first love – education. She opened *Jeanfield*, a small preparatory school for boys. Although her husband was a prominent public figure, no hint of family disloyalty or scandal emerged in the press. The only clue that anything was amiss was the listing of Miss Agnes Dickson as accompanying her father on many private and public social engagements.

After losing his seat in the 1888 election and turning over the running of the auctioneering business to his eldest son, Dickson had little to keep him occupied. In December 1889, James Dickson, now 57, and daughters, Agnes 23, Lucy 19, Emma 18 and Edith 15 left Australia for a two year holiday to Europe. Mary Dickson was left to run her school in Toowoomba, further cementing the estrangement.

James and his daughters spent six weeks touring the sights of Egypt, wintered in Rome, then travelled through northern Italy to Switzerland, Germany and Belgium. They spent May to September 1890 in London where Agnes enjoyed the social season and was presented to Queen Victoria. Departing London for the Continent once again, they travelled along the Rhine to Austria and back to Italy, spending two months in Venice. After wintering in Florence, they toured the art centres of Italy and visited Greece, finally returning to Australia in November 1891.

In response to toasts drunk to his health on his return, he briefly referred to the economic woes of Queensland and 'the need for all to assist in the government of the country to bring it back to prosperity.'[11] Dickson won the seat of Bulimba in a by-election in April 1892 and in 1897, once again became a minister, securing a minor role as Secretary for the Railways. In 1898 Premier Byrnes died, and Dickson was appointed as his replacement.

Premier Dickson was the first to offer troops to assist Britain in the Boer War and he took up the cause of Federation in Queensland. During his short term as Premier, *The Worker* newspaper (affiliated with the Labor party) continued an unrelenting attack on the policies and actions of the conservative leader bestowing upon him the nickname 'Oily Jimmy' for his abundant possession of the chief characteristics of 'graciousness and affability',[12] and often publishing full-page satirical cartoons depicting the short, bald, bearded leader.

Even when he returned to the position of Chief Secretary, *The Worker* kept up its campaign beginning a diatribe on Dickson's alleged misuse of the Government yacht *Lucinda* with:

> Oily Jimmy, in spite of his sham disposition from the Premiership, appears to be still up to his dirty little tricks. He has practised them too long now that it is almost unreasonable to expect him at this late period of his public life to discontinue the performance.[13]

It was under his ministry that the successful referendum for Federation was held in Queensland. After his term as Premier he joined the delegation to London negotiating Australia's federation and was rewarded in January 1901 with a knighthood and the position of Minister of Defence in Australia's first federal government. *The Worker* chose to view his elevation as a 'political accident', stating:

> Dickson as Minister of Defence – considering that the Home War Office has already appointed a military chief for Australia – can only be looked upon as a joke.[14]

When he travelled to Sydney for the Federation celebrations and the swearing in ceremony he was already ill. Having suffered from diabetes for the previous 18 years, Dickson settled in at the Australian Club in Sydney accompanied not by his wife, but his devoted daughters, Agnes and Lucy. Although encouraged to rest, he was determined to enjoy his, and the country's, success by taking part in the Commonwealth procession and attending the State Banquet in the evening. In addition to diabetes, James had developed a large carbuncle (a large abscess) on his back near his spine. The accompanying bacterial infection and the poor state of his immune system lead to a complete collapse, delirium and finally coma. He passed away peacefully on 10 January 1901, aged 69, with Agnes and Lucy at his bedside. Other family members including Lady Dickson had been summoned from Brisbane but arrived too late.

The Worker was unable to let his death pass without an acerbic comment, this time labelling Dickson's career as 'colourless'. His long-time friend, Mr. E Thorne, however wrote in *The Courier* after his death:

> he had his faults, one of the most apparent of which was an extraordinary facility in the use of long words, and the construction of ambiguous phrases and sentences, which, coupled with a large amount of suaviterin modo (gentle manner) and the milk of human kindness, enabled him to pass through a long public life with less positively negative replies to applicants than fall to the lot of most statesmen.[15]

Within days of Dickson's death in 1901, items appeared in the gossip columns talking about an open secret that Dickson was a non entity in his own household and that Lady Dickson preferred the 'peace and seclusion at Toowoomba to prominence and constant bickering at *Toorak*'.[16] When columnists noted that letters of condolence were addressed to Miss Dickson and not Lady Dickson they asked: 'Is there a Lady Dickson? Yes, she resides at Toowoomba, Queensland'. It was clear that while Dickson had sided with his daughters by his first marriage and progressed successfully up the political ladder, his wife had set up her own life in Toowoomba doing what she herself was best at.

A special train was organised to return the body of Sir James Robert Dickson, his family and friends to Brisbane for the funeral on the following Saturday. Businesses closed and mourners lined the streets as the long procession wove its way from *Toorak* to All Saints Church in Wickham Terrace. He was buried at Nundah cemetery.

> The whole city was in gloom, and on the part of the great mass of people sympathy with the bereaved family was mingled with a realisation of the loss which the State of Queensland has sustained.[17]

In his will, Dickson left everything in trust to his surviving 13 children with no mention of his wife. Lady Dickson continued to live in Toowoomba known only as Mrs Dickson, refusing the title of Lady, where she died in February 1902 after a long illness. Considerable interest was aroused by the sale of her jewellery the following May and in her will she left a £1500 bequest towards a scholarship for the Girls' Grammar School, to be known as the MacKinley Scholarship. Miss Agnes Melanie Dickson, her father's constant companion, witness to his passing and trustee of the estate with her brother Grahame, never married and died in 1944.

Chapter 32

The curious case of Mr Pillow's humpy

Amongst the many wooden structures scattered around the burning street block that could provide fuel for the fire on the Queen Street side was a small unsightly wooden humpy (a rough shelter) sitting on a vacant block in George Street right beside the imposing structure of the Bank of New South Wales building.

Desperate acts of deliberate destruction by firemen throughout the long evening had already reduced many such structures to rubble in the vain hope that a firebreak would be created. Mr. Hampton Pillow's humpy offered one final chance. Its destruction was quick and effective as it was unceremoniously removed with much less regret than other buildings lost that night. Mr Pillow's humpy already had a chequered past with the city administrators and many of its residents and landowners.

The story begins with William Pauley, a cabinetmaker, who lived in a comfortable two-storey stone cottage on the corner of George and Elizabeth Streets. Adjoining the stone cottage was a fenced, neatly-kept allotment leased by Mr. Pauley where, for the past eight years, his chickens had scratched happily alongside horses grazing contentedly awaiting their next task. Even by December 1862 the citizens of Brisbane were amazed that this prime block of land in George Street, nestled between the newly constructed Bank of New South Wales and Mr. Pauley's fine house, was still vacant. (In 1842 at the first public sale of Queensland land – actually held in Sydney – Thomas William Dent, a retired Navy Lieutenant, had purchased the plot in George Street, but had never shown any inclination to develop, utilise or even visit it.)

On 3 December 1862 when William Pauley, contemplating a new addition to his chicken shed, noticed a pile of firewood, three long poles and a untidy heap of canvas in his horse yard. As he strode outside to investigate, he saw a metre-long gap in his neat paling fence. Incensed at this intrusion, he hauled the wood and canvas into the street and immediately repaired the fence, doubtless puzzled by this audacious and unannounced invasion.

Almost before he could return to his workshop, three burly men armed with axes and hammers were demolishing his newly repaired fence. Momentarily Pauley was speechless with rage – possession of land, even though leased, was not something given up easily. Violence was clearly not an option against such force, so arguing, shouting and declaring his right to the land, he warned off the usurpers, but to no avail. Retreating to the safety of his home, he could only watch in horror as the canvas and poles became a tent. The men were soon joined by several ferocious looking dogs followed by women and children laden with small household items.

Shortly afterwards a small, scruffy wood and bark humpy was erected. It didn't take Pauley long to grasp the truth – squatters had arrived right in the centre of Brisbane. Hampton Pillow and his family had taken up residence. Pillow, newly-arrived from the goldfields of Bendigo, Victoria, was a seasoned 'claim jumper'. For reasons then unknown, he believed in his right to occupy the vacant land in Brisbane and defend it. After all, this was how they operated on the rich goldfields in Bendigo Flats.

Pillow and his family, wife Anne, children and niece Mary, arrived in Melbourne from Ireland, among nearly 1,000,000 of his fellow countrymen who fled the Great Famine. They arrived aboard the clipper ship *Marco Polo* in 1852, straight into the largest gold rush in Australia's history. Ten years on, toughened by the daily grind of the goldfields, and well versed in colonial know-how, Hampton Pillow was a formidable opponent.

Pauley complained to everyone he knew. Within days, into the fray came Municipal Councillor Alderman Robert Cribb who was also a member of Parliament and a significant land owner in the Brisbane area. He and his family had arrived on the *Fortitude* in 1849. A veteran of colonial politics and a dedicated Nonconformist, Mr. Cribb was confident that he would be more than a match for Hampton Pillow. It was not unusual that the Council should take an interest in a disturbance in the central business area of the city, but Mr. Cribb arrived at the land with a menacing band of 15 men. By any measure, this was an action above and beyond the duty of an Alderman. Cribb and his men climbed the fence and swarmed onto the block. Obviously expecting a fight, Cribb's plan was to move swiftly and decisively leaving little time for resistance.

Cribb, a wiry man of 57, scrambled onto the flimsy bark roof of Pillow's humpy and proceeded to rip it apart. Within minutes, the invaders had reduced it to a pile of firewood. Having successfully demolished the humpy, Cribb directed his attention to the tent, anticipating an easy victory over the women and children. Mrs. Pillow, as fierce in defence of her claim to the land as her husband, burst from the tent, long finger nails her only weapon. Cribb suffered numerous injuries before fighting her off, giving his men time to remove the tent and belongings. Tired, dusty and battle-weary, Cribb and his crew finally re-possessed the land, and Hampton Pillow and his family were out on the street.

But, for these tough ex-gold miners, it was far from over. A scuffle ensued as Pillow, with his family and friends dragged the timber and tents back onto the block. The ultimate insult came when one of Pillow's mob grabbed Cribb and threw him over a fence. Embarrassed, battered and ex-

Robert Cribb.

hausted, Cribb and his men retreated, joining the 150 or so strong crowd that had gathered for the afternoon's entertainment.

Cribb knew he had lost the battle but planned to use the law and his position to exert his rights, the exact nature of which would remain a mystery to the public for another two years. The bottom line was that Hampton Pillow and his family had regained possession of the land and re-erected their shabby residence. William Pauley, who had lost his spare allotment, was reminded of the insult every time he glimpsed the humpy that Mr Pillow now called home.

During all the argument that was to follow, there was never any mention of police intervention, not during that afternoon in George Street, nor in any further disputes and certainly there never appeared to be any attempt by police to remove the Pillow family. The case of Pauley vs. Pillow found its way into the Magistrates Court just two months later. William Pauley accused Hampton Pillow of entering his leased land without consent. The contentious issue, which remained unresolved for another two years, was the ownership of the land. Who had the right of title and where was the proof?

Although the court found against Hampton Pillow and fined him 20 shillings with six shillings sixpence with costs, the Magistrates made it clear the determination of title was not within their jurisdiction. Consequently, no order was made for the Pillows to vacate the property.

Court cases were expensive, requiring solicitors or barristers to make an appearance. By February 1863 William Pauley, although still in business, was essentially broke. He had lost his house and land through insolvency, being unable to maintain the mortgage on his prime corner block in George Street, and was regularly before the courts for drunkenness, the most recent being just one month before the case against Hampton Pillow.

During one incident, having been held in jail overnight for his own safety, Pauley was bailed for the day to return in the afternoon for his appearance, only to show up that afternoon drunk again. William Pauley could not afford to bring action against Hampton Pillow let alone think straight enough to prepare his case. So when Pauley once again appeared before the Magistrates a month later accusing Hampton Pillow of trespassing on the land, it became apparent that Robert Cribb had decided to become involved.

Since the injured party was actually Cribb, not Pauley, it is possible Cribb funded Pauley's action in an attempt to remove Hampton Pillow without a lot of fuss. During this case, Pauley made no claim to owning the land, stating 'he was merely the occupier' and that he believed the land belonged to Robert Cribb. The court again declared it could not deal with the title of the land, only the occupation, ruling that Pillow had provided no lawful excuse for entering or possessing the land. He was fined him £5.

Further efforts to have the case heard in a higher court were either postponed or denied, mainly due to the inability of the magistrates to determine the court responsible for disputed land title and the confusion and complexities of the current laws surrounding title. It wasn't until March 1864, nearly a year after Pauley's last action, that Robert Cribb decided to have another try. Mr. Pauley had either retired from the fight, or was no longer of any use to Robert Cribb, as he appears to have moved to a block of land at Cleveland which he had purchased in 1854. Without the dozens of hotels formerly available within the city, the remoteness of Cleveland contributed to the recovery of Pauley's health.

This time, rather than try the trespass line again, Cribb went for the action of ejectment which was designed to remove a party occupying real property as a consequence to laying claim to ownership. During this case Cribb mentioned that he had purchased the land in February 1863, about two months after the Pillows had first arrived. Perhaps up until that point he was under some misapprehension that any claim he may have had on Pauley's land transferred to that plot as well. Either way, he quickly set about attaining some lawful title to the property. Much to Cribb's annoyance the case stalled as the Magistrates again refused to rule on a case involving disputation of title.

Obviously keeping his tactics a close secret, Cribb had still not revealed any evidence relating to his claim on the title. Was Robert Cribb really the owner, did he not possess the documents required, or was it a delaying tactic until such proof could be arranged? In any case, it appeared that he would exhaust every avenue open to him, without actually having to present the documents.

With self-interest clearly apparent, Cribb, now the Honorable Member for East Moreton, brazenly took the fight to Parliament in August 1864, seeking to present a bill giving the Magistrates power to decide cases of disputed ownership. The old saying 'Keep your friends close and your enemies closer', was clearly one of Mr Cribb's mantras. Brisbane was also a small town, and many public figures wore more than one hat. Conflict of interest was not uppermost in their minds.

During the Parliamentary debate over Cribb's bill, the Attorney-General, who was to represent Cribb in a later court action, argued that property law and ownership was an intricate matter and it would be unsafe to give magistrates such power. This argument was backed by Mr. Charles Lilley, member for Fortitude Valley (later Premier and Chief Justice of the Supreme Court) who was to act in defence of Pillow later in the same case. Some members were on Cribb's side, notably his brother Benjamin. After much discussion and a good laugh at the expense of Cribb 'wishing to oust every Pillow in the province'[1], the Parliament voted 10 to 6 against the bill.

Hampton Pillow claimed the right to the property on the grounds of prior possession and there being no negotiable title, the only recourse left to Cribb was presenting the documents and proving his title to the land. Once this was achieved he would be able to proceed with the ejectment of Pillow. Curiously, never once in the previous two years having intimated the existence of such evidence, by 3 December 1864, Robert Cribb arrived in court again – this time with documents.

In a remarkable coincidence, just two nights earlier, Pillow's humpy had been demolished during the great Brisbane fire. All Cribb had left to do was prove his case – the fire had done the rest. In his possession were copies of Thomas Dent's original grant of land in 1842, a power of attorney signed by Mr. Dent in favour of a new witness, Mr. William Boyce, allowing disposal of the property to Cribb and a receipt by

Dent for the purchase money. The evidence given by Mr. Boyce to support the validity of the papers was farcical.

William Boyce was a clerk in the Registrar-General's office when he heard about the 'jumping' of the allotment. He wondered if it was his old shipmate, Thomas Dent. Making enquiries he realised that it was indeed his friend at the centre of the dispute. As witness for Cribb he claimed he was familiar with Thomas Dent's handwriting and had acquired a power of attorney from Dent. Cross-examined by Mr. Lilley, Boyce stated that he had resided in Geelong, Victoria for six years, was not a particular acquaintance of Dent's and had last seen him in London in 1838. Any letters sent from Dent to Boyce had been destroyed.

William Boyce last had occasion to note Dent's handwriting 26 years earlier, yet he was willing to swear he recognised Dent's handwriting. Boyce had never seen Thomas Dent in Australia and had not spoken to Pillow about the land. Thomas Dent's whereabouts was not made clear, although William Boyce said he had obtained Dent's address via enquiries to East India House, the London headquarters of the Honorable East India Company for whom Dent and Boyce both once worked. Untangling different versions of the evidence, it appears that Boyce decided, after 26 years, to help his old friend and, for purely altruistic motives, collected the various documents and supplied them to Cribb. Serendipity for Mr Cribb.

Not a man to ever just let fate intervene, it is unlikely Robert Cribb waited for the evidence to fall in his lap. If he truly purchased the land from Thomas Dent, no doubt he had moved heaven and earth to find those documents. Why a wily, experienced trader such as Cribb, would not have such valuable evidence in his possession is the mystery. However, here they were, and Mr. Lilley, for Hampton Pillow, was going to ask the crucial question – where was the evidence that this was Thomas Dent's handwriting other than the words of a man who hadn't seen Dent write for 26 years?

Cribb had dragged the defendant before the court many times and used a series of petty issues to try and remove Pillow from the land. Was this more of the same? Where was Thomas Dent? He could have notified any solicitor in Brisbane in the last 26 years to establish his title. Equally, he could have authorised the same solicitors to convey the land to Cribb. The Attorney-General, appearing on behalf of Cribb, gave no reply and the jury retired. With remarkable haste, the jury returned a verdict, incredibly, in favour of the plaintiff, Robert Cribb, awarding him title to a prime piece of real estate worth in excess of £1000. Having claimed to have paid Dent just £400, this was a good day's work. As Mr Pillow's humpy had been cast into history by the great fire, Robert Cribb finally had vacant possession.

However, at the completion of the trial in December 1864, Mr. Lilley applied for leave for a new trial which was granted. In March 1865, Mr. Lilley appeared again for Mr. Pillow to make an application for a new trial on the grounds that the power of attorney supplied by William Boyce, although being attested by the Lord Mayor of London, was not attested by a Justice of the Peace and that it had been improperly submitted as evidence. The Attorney-General opposed the application and the court ruled against the motion.

With legal costs mounting, Pillow appears to have withdrawn from the fight and in April 1865 he applied for a certificate of insolvency claiming debts of £55 which he was unable to meet. A court date of 10 July 1865 was set to hear

> the Proof of Debts against the said Estate, and for such other matters connected with the Estate as may be required to be brought before the Court.[2]

In a final twist Cribb, unable to let the matter rest, took the above quote to heart and appeared against the application for insolvency claiming that on 23rd December, Pillow had declared to him that he had more than enough money to pay the £55 as well all his just and lawful debts. Cribb was like a terrier with a rat and tried one last time to cause Pillow lasting embarrassment in an attempt to drive him to bankruptcy. He appeared at a further insolvency sitting, declaring that Pillow should not be allowed a certificate of insolvency as he had brought this financial situation upon himself by pursuing an unjustifiable action against Cribb. This final insult was ignored, the certificate granted, and a repayment plan set up enabling Pillow to repay his debts.

Chapter 33

Taken at the top end of Queen Street, looking across George Street, this photograph of the morning after the December fire clearly shows the burnt stumps of both the Victoria and Sovereign Hotels with the badly damaged bank building sitting between them. The tall pole to the front left of the picture with ropes running to the opposite side of the street is part of the crane system still being used to complete the new Town Hall. As in the previous fire, the street is choked with stock, fittings, belongings and debris pulled from the path of the fire.

Dawn Breaks

As dawn broke over the once thriving town centre of Brisbane, the only sound was the occasional dull, hollow thud of a falling wall or the crackling snap of a still smouldering rafter as it fell into the ashes. The early morning light revealed a street on one side black and smoking, and on the other an immense tangle of items. Scattered, crumpled boxes of delicate lace gloves sat alongside barrels of wine and sacks of spilled grain. Huge sides of beef were mixed with cartons of cotton shirts and woollen socks. Pots and pans and broken tables and chairs lay where they had been hurled from windows.

> If the circumstances were not of such a depressing character, some mirth might have been extracted from the strange manner in which the goods of the various sufferers had been thrown together. Kid gloves, oysters, lavender water and polonies [a type of sausage], were the absurdly miscellaneous contents of one basket whilst salt beef, champagne, and crinolines filled a large barrel.[1]

Fifty houses and businesses had been destroyed in one long night, including two banks, three hotels and four drapery establishments. Four men and a boy were taken to hospital. The only other serious casualty, Mr. Cutbush, after having his wound attended to, made a speedy recovery. The Volunteer Fire Brigade headed by Edmund McDonnell had carried out its task to the limits of the equipment available but without piped water to fight the blaze, it was a battle lost before it began.

As the day wore on the sounds of bustling activity slowly returned to the streets. Tired, dusty, smoke-blackened faces that had caught a few hours fractured rest returned to the scene to sort through the immense mess under the watchful eyes of those members of the 12th Regiment who had remained awake and sober. In their desire to quench their thirst the previous evening, and with the obvious lack of water, the men of the 12th had resorted to liquor.

> To say they were drunk would be a base libel, but they might be described as suffering from weakness in their knees caused by their excessive exertions during the night, and also a bronchial affection, which rendered their articulation somewhat obscure a misfortune doubtless to be assigned to a similar cause.[2]

Some members of the regiment were dozing on abandoned couches and beds or sheltering under the elegant arched portico of the new Town Hall with other weary fire-fighters. The firearms and bayonets that had flashed so brilliantly the previous night seemed less threatening to the gathering crowd.

> Here a grimy fireman might be seen sitting on an old barrel, with his feet on a quantity of haberdashery, fraternising with a clean

policeman, whilst some distance away several dirty-looking guardians of the night mingled with anything but cleanly red-coats.[3]

Drays arrived, arguments ensued, and goods and chattels were retrieved. Many business owners stood amongst the rubble and stared, stunned into silence by the enormity of their loss. Others just continued trading amongst the debris including butcher George Edmondstone who had watched his shop burn to the ground. Some of his meat had been saved, so he set up his butcher's block in the street and proceeded to dress, chop and sell meat which otherwise would have quickly spoiled in the summer heat.

As in the face of such disasters anywhere, the citizens of Brisbane rallied once more to help in the recovery, offering safe storages for the piles of belongings, donating furniture and loaning vehicles. By sunset of the day after the fire, all the merchandise and furniture had been removed from the street and many businesses were already setting up in temporary premises. Underfoot was a treacherous carpet of still smouldering ash, spilled feed, shattered wine and beer bottles, and the rubble of smashed furniture, shop fittings, crockery and household belongings.

As the darkness gathered on Queen Street, where once bright lights, music, and laughter had emanated all that was left was darkness, punctuated by dull glowing patches of still burning embers. Occasional flaring sparks produced brief but bright glaring torches from within the rubble over the entire city block as the evening breeze stirred across the shattered landscape. At the sunken burnt out corner cellar of Hemmant's drapery shop where it had all started the glow seemed particularly strong.

It would be several days before the remnants of the fire died enough for the rubble to begin to be cleared and the rebuilding to commence. For the citizens of Brisbane it was enough to impress upon them their vulnerability and the immediate need for enhanced fire services, an adequate water supply and improved building regulations.

Indeed a scant two weeks later *The Brisbane Courier* noted that the buildings constructed after the April fire, along with the architectural plans they had viewed already for the replacement of buildings from the December fire, were 'an infinite improvement to the property and to the city generally' and would ensure that the city's business centre, Queen Street 'will ere long be scarcely inferior, as regards its architecture, to any street in the Australian colonies.'[4]

Out of disaster a modern city would emerge.

Postscript

Thinking Like A Surveyor: How Brisbane CBD Got Its Shape

Robert Dixon and Henry Wade

The detailed survey drawing of Brisbane made by Henry Wade in 1843[1] has made it easy to locate key buildings in the story of Brisbane's great fires and allowed the construction of the map on page ix at the front of this book. The survey became Brisbane's first useful town plan and created the Queen Street centred central business district we know today. Although Wade's map is to scale, it has no dimensions. That leaves an interesting puzzle — what size were the original city blocks?

The first survey and attempt at a future plan of Brisbane was created by Robert Dixon in 1840[2]. At the time Brisbane was a simple penal colony with just a handful of public buildings supporting the jails. Surrounding these were small vegetable plots, some operated by the military and others privately owned, and large areas of crops.

Dixon clearly envisaged a rapidly-growing settlement as he mapped out large square blocks in a perfect grid laid over the gentle slopes of Gardens Point. While Dixon was an experienced surveyor — albeit with a somewhat chequered past including nearly perishing while surveying west of Sydney and being charged with attempting to incite mutiny – he was clearly not a town planner. Just three years later when Henry Wade was tasked with modifying the plan, the shortcomings would have already been clear.

The problem with Dixon's plan was that his very large (about 200 m square) city blocks were unsuitable for urban development. Houses and stores only needed lots 30-40 m deep, which would have left the centre of each square block wasted space. The long distances would also have caused development of the city centre to spread out, making access inconvenient and reducing the ease with which the city's citizens could walk between establishments.

This left Henry Wade with an interesting challenge. The roads of Dixon's huge blocks would already have been marked out and new buildings were lining some streets. How could he modernise the plan without disrupting the existing lots? Instead of an awkward combination of alleys, 'little streets' and boulevards like those used in Melbourne's CBD Hoddle Grid, Wade's solution was simple: an extra full-width NE/SW street running through the centre of each block (becoming Adelaide, Elizabeth, Mary and Alice Streets), mostly cutting into what was still empty space. This left long rectangular blocks much more suited to rows of houses and shops, and a design which is still effective for today's office towers.

Just like modern surveyors, it's safe to assume Henry Wade used simple round numbers wherever possible. It was not only convenient but also made it easier for untrained (or even illiterate) townsfolk to mark out their land titles with standardised measures. In his time, surveyors used units of *chains* (66 feet) and *links* (100 links to a chain). Dixon had laid out blocks 10 chains square, with roads 1 chain wide (except Queen St at 1.2 chains). This made Wade's blocks 10 x 4.5 chains once the space for the extra road was removed. While the standard Sydney and Melbourne width for such lots was 1 chain, individual Brisbane lots became an awkward-sounding 1 x 2.25 chains. However, also in common use at the time were units of *rods* (with 4 rods to a chain). A square rod equals a *perch*. So the new Brisbane lots could be advertised as a simple 4 x 9 rods, or 36 perches, deviating from the normal 4 x 8 rod (32 perch) lots used in southern cities and later development. Today the 36-perch standard can even be found in Brisbane's outer suburbs such Gaythorne, Clayfield and Coorparoo; presumably influenced by Robert Wade's original CBD survey.

Wade's genius extended to the corner lots, rotated to face their cross street. This prevented the cross streets being made into ugly alleyways lined with blank walls and loading docks. He adjusted the sizes of these corner plots to a neat 8 x 4.5 rods, which is still 36 perches.

The difference between the Dixon and Wade plan is best seen on a walk through the streets of Brisbane's CBD. Where Dixon applied a crude square grid best suited to farming areas and with little respect for the city's natural contours, Wade managed to adapt the existing streets to a shape still in use today. Shops along Elizabeth Street are still 66 feet (1 chain) wide; tall, modern office towers on George Street sit on adjoining titles of 36 perch blocks; and the parks Henry Wade imagined in his distant future became part of the City Botanic Gardens and Roma Street Parklands[3]. Without his input at a crucial time in Brisbane's history the city was heading towards a town planning disaster. Henry Wade could never have envisaged that 150 years on his legacy would be a towering cosmopolitan city, friendly to both pedestrians and vehicles – and yet still measured precisely to his plan for a small, remote penal colony.

Brisbane Burns

Endnotes

Chapter 2

1 *The Brisbane Courier*, 12 April 1864, p. 2
2 *The Brisbane Courier*, 15 April 1864, p. 2
3 *Empire*, 11 November 1856, p. 7

Chapter 3

1 *The North Australian*, 12 April 1864, p. 2
2 *Queensland Times, Ipswich Herald and General Advertiser*, 14 April 1864, p. 3
3 *Pugh's Almanac*, 1863
4 *The Moreton Bay Courier*, 14 February 1860, p. 3
5 *The Brisbane Courier*, 29 April 1864, p. 1
6 *Pugh's Almanac*, 1863
7 *The Brisbane Courier*, 19 November 1881, p. 2
8 *The Central Queensland Herald*, 19 July 1934, p. 27

Chapter 4

1 *The Brisbane Courier*, 12 April 1864, p. 2
2 *The Moreton Bay Courier*, 31 March 1855, p. 3
3 *The Moreton Bay Courier*, 21 September 1859, p. 1
4 *The Brisbane Courier*, 27 August 1873, p.1
5 *The Brisbane Courier*, 21 May 1875, p. 3
6 *Morning Post (Cairns)*, 7 January 1902, p. 2

Chapter 5

1 *The Brisbane Courier*, 11 May 1868, p. 3
2 *The Queensland*, 7 January 1932, p. 35
3 *The Queensland*, 7 January 1932, p. 35
4 *The Brisbane Courier*, 21 January 1889, p. 4
5 *The Brisbane Courier*, 27 September 1910, p. 5.

Chapter 6

1 *The North Australian*, 12 April 1864, p.2
2 *The Brisbane Courier*, 14 April 1923, p. 17
3 *The Courier*, 22 June, 1861, p. 3
4 *The Brisbane Courier*, 17 December 1868, p. 2

Chapter 7

1 *The Brisbane Courier,* 12 April 1864, p. 2
2 *The Courier,* 31 March 1863, p. 2
3 *The Courier,* 1 April 1863, p. 3
4 *The Courier,* 1 April 1863, p. 3
5 *The Courier,* 17 June 1863, p. 2
6 *The Brisbane Courier,* 17 June 1863, p. 2
7 *The Brisbane Courier,* 15 April 1864, p. 2

Chapter 8

1 *The Moreton Bay Courier,* 7 January 1860, p. 2
2 12th Regiment of Foot (East Suffolk), Ken Larbalestier, 2010, p. 145
3 12th Regiment of Foot (East Suffolk), Ken Larbalestier, 2010, p. 146
4 *The Courier,* 22 April 1862
5 12th Regiment of Foot (East Suffolk), Ken Larbalestier, 2010, p. 185
6 *The Courier,* 7 January 1864
7 *The Courier,* 7 January 1864
8 *The Brisbane Courier,* 17 October 1866

Chapter 9

1 *The North Australian,* 12 April 1864, p. 2
2 *The Moreton Bay Courier,* 7 January, 1860, page 2.
3 *The Courier,* 16 December 1863, page 2.
4 T*he Brisbane Courier,* 26 April 1864, page 2.
5 *The Brisbane Courier*, 9 August 1870, page 3.
6 Friendship is Life: A History of Tattersall's Club, Brisbane, Longhurst, 1993, page 51, 52.
7 *Queensland Figaro,* 6 September 1884, p. 7

Chapter 10

1 *The Brisbane Courier*, 12 April 1864, p. 2
2 *The Brisbane Courier*, 21 January 1908, p. 7
3 *The Worker*, 12 December 1918, p. 5
4 *The Worker*, 14 December 1895, p. 5
5 *The Queenslander*, 14 March 1896, p. 501
6 *The Queenslander*, 14 March 1896, p. 501
7 *The Queenslander*, 14 March 1896, p. 501

Chapter 11

1 *The Moreton Bay Courier*, 20 August 1859, page 1.

2 *The Courier*, 13 June 1862, page 1.
3 The Brisbane Courier, 2 May 1864, page 2.
4 Queensland State Archives Item ID1057597, Insolvency file

Chapter 12

1 *The North Australian*, 12 April 1864, p. 2
2 *The Moreton Bay Courier*, 5 March 1851, p. 1.
3 *The Moreton Bay Courier*, 20 January 1855, p. 1
4 *The Moreton Bay Courier*, 17 October 1857, p. 3
5 *The Brisbane Courier*, 15 October 1868, p. 2.
6 *The Brisbane Courier*, 7 December 1870, p. 3
7 *The Queenslander*, 23 August 1873, p. 7.
8 *Queensland Times, Ipswich Herald and General Advertiser*, p. 3

Chapter 13

1 *The Courier*, 27 April, 1863, p. 2
2 *The Brisbane Courier*, 19 April 1882, p. 2

Chapter 14

1 *The Brisbane Courier*, 13 April 1864, p. 1
2 *The Brisbane Courier*, 13 April 1864, p. 1
3 *The Brisbane Courier*, 13 April 1864, p. 2

Chapter 15

1 *Brisbane Courier*, 5 September 1864, p. 2
2 *Brisbane Courier*, 22 October 1870, p. 3
3 *The Queenslander*, 31 March 1877, p. 18
4 *The Queenslander*, 16 October 1875, p. 15
5 *The Week*, 31 March 1877, p. 21
6 *The Week*, 31 March 1877, p. 21
7 *Queensland Times, Ipswich Herald and General Advertiser*, 28 July 1877, p. 3

Chapter 16

1 *The Brisbane Courier*, 30 November 1864.

Chapter 17

1 *The Brisbane Courier*, 14 December 1864, p. 2
2 *The Moreton Bay Courier*, 16 June 1860, p. 3

3 *The Moreton Bay Courier*, 12 July 1860, p. 3
4 *The Queenslander*, 24 April, 1930, p. 50
5 *The Brisbane Courier*, 14 August 1918, p. 15

Chapter 18

1 *The Brisbane Courier*, 17 December 1864, p. 6
2 *The Brisbane Courier*, 28 January 1865, p. 5
3 *Queen of the Colonies*, Thorne E., 1876, p. 16

Chapter 19

1 *The Brisbane Courier*, 17 May 1862, p. 5
2 *The Brisbane Courier*, 24 December, 1864, p. 2
3 *The Brisbane Courier*, 3 July, 1865, p. 5
4 *The Brisbane Courier*, 8 February 1873, p. 6
5 *The Brisbane Courier*, December 16 1870, p. 3
6 *The Brisbane Courier*, July 10 1875, p. 5

Chapter 20

1 *The Brisbane Courier*, 30 June 1864, p. 2
2 *The Brisbane Courier*, 4 July 1864, p. 2
3 *Queensland Figaro*, 28 April 1910, p. 11

Chapter 21

1 Queensland State Archives Item ID 348608, Inquest file 81
2 Queensland State Archives Item ID 348608, Inquest file 81
3 Queensland State Archives Item ID 348616, Inquest file 228
4 Queensland State Archives Item ID 348616, Inquest file 228

Chapter 22

1 *The Moreton Bay Courier*, 14 July 1855, p. 3
2 *The Moreton Bay Courier*, 2 October 1858, p.1
3 *The Moreton Bay Courier*, 4 February 1860, p. 2
4 *The Brisbane Courier*, 21 June 1864, p. 2
5 *The Brisbane Courier*, 25 May 1865, p. 2
6 *The Brisbane Courier*, 21 October 1865, p. 4

Chapter 23

1 *The Courier*, 15 March 1864, p. 1
2 *The Brisbane Courier*, 8 September 1865, p. 1
3 *The Brisbane Courier*, 7 October 1865, p. 2

4 *The Brisbane Courier*, 23 February 1877, p. 1
5 *Western Star and Roma Advertiser*, 20 December 1882, p. 4
6 *The Brisbane Courier*, 22 December 1886, p. 7
7 *The Brisbane Courier*, 17 August 1886, p. 5
8 *The Brisbane Courier*, 17 August 1886, p. 5

Chapter 24

1 *The Courier*, 21 May 1861, p. 2
2 *The Moreton Bay Courier*, 5 May 1849, p. 1
3 *The Moreton Bay Courier*, 17 February 1851, p. 2
4 *The Moreton Bay Courier*, 9 July 1859, p. 2
5 *The Brisbane Courier*, 3 March 1888, p. 7

Chapter 25

1 *The North Australian*, 15 September 1863, p. 2
2 *The Brisbane Courier*, 7 December 1864, p. 1

Chapter 26

1 *The Brisbane Courier*, 12 May 1865, p. 2
2 *The Brisbane Courier*, 12 May 1865, p. 2
3 *The Courier*, 5 December 1863, p. 3
4 The *Moreton Bay Courier*, 3 January 1860, p. 3
5 *The Courier*, 5 November 1861, p. 2
6 An early jeweller in Queensland: the life and career of Augustus Kosvitz, Timothy Roberts in *Australiana* Vol 31 No 3 August 2009
7 *The Brisbane Courier*, 28 August 1871, p. 3
8 *The Brisbane Courier*, 5 December 5 1871, p. 3
9 *The Brisbane Courier*, 22 December 1871. p. 4
10 *The Brisbane Courier*, 21 November 1873, p. 2
11 *The Brisbane Courier*, 21 November 1873, p. 2
12 *The Brisbane Courier*, 9 December 1873, p. 3
13 *The Brisbane Courier*, 9 December 1873, p. 3
14 *The Brisbane Courier*, 20 November 1873, p. 2
15 *The Brisbane Courier*, 21 November 1873, p. 2
16 *The Brisbane Courier*, 21 November 1873, p. 2
17 *The Brisbane Courier*, 21 November 1873, p. 2
18 *Sydney Morning Herald*, 10 May 1876, p. 7

Chapter 27

1 *Brisbane: Squatters, Settlers and Surveyors*, BHG, 2000, p. 27

2 *Brisbane: Squatters, Settlers and Surveyors*, BHG, 2000, p. 27
3 *The Genesis of Queensland*, Henry Stuart Russell, 1888, p. 355
4 *Brisbane: Squatters, Settlers and Surveyors*, BHG, 2000, p. 27
5 *The Genesis of Queensland*, Henry Stuart Russell, 1888, p. 356
6 *The Genesis of Queensland*, Henry Stuart Russell, 1888, p. 357
7 *Brisbane: Squatters, Settlers and Surveyors*, BHG, 2000, p. 27
8 *The Courier*, 11 March 1933, p. 19
9 *Moreton Bay Courier*, 3 Jun 1848, p. 2
10 *Moreton Bay Courier*, 3 June 1848, p. 2
11 *Moreton Bay Courier*, 3 June 1848, p. 2
12 *Brisbane Courier*, 18 Oct 1865, p. 2
13 *The Queenslander*, 10 Jan 1874, p. 9

Chapter 28

1 Brisbane: Squatters, Settlers & Surveyors, BHG, 2000, p. 27
2 *Moreton Bay Courier*, 17 Nov 1849, p. 1
3 *Queensland Figaro and Punch*, 2 July 1887, p. 9
4 *The Brisbane Courier,* 23 April 1864, p. 3

Chapter 29

1 *Queensland Times, Ipswich Herald and General Advertiser*, 15 May 1894, p. 2
2 *The Northern Herald*, 5 May 1924, p. 30
3 .*The Brisbane Courier*, 21 April 1870, p. 4
4 Gateway to a Golden Land, Townsville to 1884, Dorothy M Gibson-Wilde, p. 109
5 *Queensland Figaro and Punch*, 11 September 1886, p. 11
6 *The Northern Herald,*5 Mar 1924, p. 30
7 *Queensland Figaro*, 11 September 1886, p. 11
8 *Queensland Figaro and Punch,* 23 June 1888, p. 7
9 Queensland State Archives Item ID 1961638, Insolvency file
10 *The Northern Miner*, 2 August 1892, p. 2

Chapter 30

1 *The Courier*, 8 May 1863, p. 4
2 *The Brisbane Courier*, 11 February 1868, p. 2
3 *The Queenslander*, 16 May 1874, p. 11
4 *The Brisbane Courier*, 3 March 1888, p. 4
5 *Brisbane in the 1890s*, Ronald Lawson, 1973, p. 39
6 *The Brisbane Courier*, 19 March 1901, p. 2

Chapter 31

1 *The Queenslander*, 26 June, 1930, p. 7
2 *The Queenslander*, 26 June, 1930, p. 7
3 *The Brisbane Courier*, 5 February 1870, p. 4
4 *The Queenslander*, 11 October 1873, p. 3
5 *The Queenslander*, 11 October 1873, p. 3
6 *The Queenslander*, 26 June, 1930, p. 7
7 *The Brisbane Courier*, 29 November 1873, p. 5
8 *The Brisbane Courier*, 28 January 1880, p. 1
9 *The Brisbane Courier*, 16 October 1878, p. 2
10 *The Queenslander*, 24 December 1881, p. 820
11 *Warwick Argus*, 14 November, 1891, p. 2
12 *Worker*, 2 April 1898, p. 2
13 *The Worker*, 6 January 1900, p. 3
14 *The Worker*, 5 January 1901, p. 3
15 *The Brisbane Courier*,18 January 1901, p. 3
16 *The Worker*, 12 January, 1901, p. 8
17 *The Brisbane Courier*, 14 January 1901, p. 5

Chapter 32

1 *Queensland Times, Ipswich Herald and General Advertiser*, 11 August 1864, p. 4
2 *The Brisbane Courier*, 22 April 1865, p. 3

Chapter 33

1 *The Brisbane Courier*, 3 December 1864, p. 4
2 *The Brisbane Courier*, 3 December 1864, p. 4
3 *The Brisbane Courier*, 3 December 1864, p. 4
4 *The Brisbane Courier*, 17 December 1864, p. 5

Postscript

1 https://www.qld.gov.au/recreation/arts/heritage/museum-of-lands/first-survey
2 https://c1.staticflickr.com/8/7078/7173003438_80c7fe0dec_b.jpg
3 http://www.visitbrisbane.com.au/roma-street-parkland-and-spring-hill/news-and-features/parkland-history?sc_lang=en-au

Brisbane Burns

Cast of Characters

                                        Chapter Number

ALLISON, Joseph Donald   25
   B. 15 Jan 1829 (Bap. 18 Feb 1829), Cumberland
   M. Elizabeth Edmondstone, 28 April 1857, Brisbane
   D. 1 June 1866, Callao, Peru

BUCKLAND, John Francis   5
   B. 1825, Runnymede, Wraysbury, Surrey
   M. Ellen Gertrude Ashton, 1862, Victoria
   D. 21 September 1910, Brisbane
   Buried: Nundah Cemetery, Brisbane

BULCOCK, Robert   10
   B. 21 May 1832, Lancashire
   M. Elizabeth Grandidge, 1853, Clitheroe, Lancashire, England
   D. 10 May 1900
   Buried: Toowong Cemetery, Brisbane

COLLINS, James   16, 22
   B. ~1829
   M. Hannah Willis, 26 June 1848, Brisbane
   D. 4 February 1896, Brisbane
   Buried: Toowong Cemetery, Brisbane

CRIBB, Robert   32
   B. 7 January 1805, Poole, Dorset, England
   M. (1) Sarah Sanson 18 November 1827, London, England
   M. (2) Sarah Walton, 1 August 1860, Brisbane
   D. 16 April 1893, Brisbane
   Arrival: *Fortitude*, 1849

CUTBUSH, George   20
   B. 1839, Hawkhurst, Kent, England (bap 31 May 1840 aged 13 mths)
   M. Annie Murphy, 23 September 1866, Brisbane
   D. 25 December 1913, Redcliffe, Queensland
   Buried: Nudgee Cemetery, Brisbane

DALLAS, Donald 21
   B. 19 Jan 1826, Caithness, Scotland
   M. Ann King, 26 Apr 1858, Glasgow, Scotland
   D. 16 December 1867, Brisbane

DICKINS, George 6
   B. 13 Dec 1820, Marylebone, London, England
   M. Jane Lockington, 7 Feb 1843, Northampton, England
   D. 8 September 1886, Benevolent Asylum, North Stradbroke Island, Queensland
   Arrival: *Chasely*, 1849

DICKSON, James Robert 31
   B. 30 November 1832 (Bap. 13 Jan 1819), Plymouth, Devon, England
   M. (1) Annie Ely, 8 November 1855, Collingwood, Melbourne, Victoria
   M. (2) Mary McKinlay, 5 January 1882, Carcoar, New South Wales
   D. 10 January 1901, Sydney, New South Wales
   Buried: Nundah Cemetery, Brisbane

DIX, Robert Edmund 28
   B. 1818 (Bap. 13 Jan 1819), Bermondsey, London, England
   M. (1) Annie Maria Elliot, 9 July 1844, Sydney, New South Wales
   M. (2) Ellen Scott, 7 November 1861, Ipswich, Queensland
   D. 10 August 1865, Brisbane

EDMONDSTONE, Elizabeth 12, 25
   B. 25 Sep 1839, West Maitland, New South Wales
   M. Joseph Donald Allison, 28 April 1857, Brisbane
   D. 22 March 1924, Brisbane
   Buried: Toowong Cemetery, Brisbane

EDMONDSTONE, George 12, 25
   B. 4 May 1809, Edinburgh, Scotland
   M. Alexandra Tillery (Telleray), 10 July 1837, New South Wales
   D. 23 February 1883, Brisbane
   Buried: Toowong Cemetery, Brisbane

EDMONDSTONE, Georgina 12
   B. 17 Jun 1837, New South Wales (Edmonston)
   M. John Markwell, 8 December 1853, Brisbane (Edmondston)
   D. 4 October 1870, Brisbane

Cast of Characters

FEGAN, Edward William 2
    B. ~1829
    M. Marie Claire Meillon, 6 November 1855, Bathurst, New South Wales
    D. 9 January 1881, Redfern, Sydney, New South Wales

FRASER, Simon 5
    B. 1824 Inverness, Scotland
    M. Lucy Ann Simpson, 5 Sep 1856, London, England
    D. 8 January 1889, Brisbane
    Buried: South Brisbane Cemetery, Brisbane

GAUJARD, Emile 19
    B. 1826, Orleans, France
    M. Sarah Curtis, Victoria
    D. 7 October 1890, Brisbane
    Buried: South Brisbane Cemetery, Brisbane

HEMMANT, William 17, 18
    B. 24 November 1837, Yorkshire, England
    M. Lucy Ground, 20 September 1866, Cambridgeshire, England
    D. 20 September 1916, Kent, England
    Arrival: *Yorkshire*, 1859

HOCKINGS, Albert John 24
    B. 21 February 1826, London, England
    M. Elizabeth Bailey, 17 August 1851, Brisbane
    D. 11 November 1890, Brisbane
    Buried: South Brisbane Cemetery, Brisbane
    Arrival: *William Jardine*, 1841

HOCKINGS, Henry 24
    B. 23 May 1829, London, England
    M. Eliza Emmes, 10 Dec 1853, Sydney, New South Wales
    D. 19 October 1912, Sydney, New South Wales
    Buried: Rookwood, Sydney, New South Wales
    Arrival: *William Jardine*, 1841

ILLIDGE, Rowland 3
    B. 3 January 1826, London, England
    M. Lucy Miller, 6 November 1850, Camberwell, London, England
    D. 16 January 1907, Brisbane
    Buried: Toowong Cemetery, Brisbane

JONES, John   6
    B. ~1841, Wales
    M. (1) Sarah Hitchings, 9 May 1867, Brisbane
    M. (2) Harriet Grant, 2 January, 1868, Brisbane
    D. 7 December 1868, Brisbane

JOST, John Phillip   9
    B. 7 November 1835, Darmstadt, Germany
    M. Catherine Leahey, 1 February 1859, Brisbane
    D. 4 July 1921, Oakey, Queensland
    Buried: Oakey Cemetery, Queensland
    Arrival: *Cesar Godeffroy*, 1856

KEITH, William McKenzie   11
    B. 11 May 1825, Olrig, Caithness, Scotland
    M. Mary Low, 23 November 1849, Old Machar, Aberdeen, Scotland
    D. 25 April 1885, Brisbane
    Buried: Toowong Cemetery, Brisbane
    Arrival: *Glentanner*, 1859

KINGSFORD, John   4
    B. 30 March 1818, Canterbury, Kent, England
    M. (1) Kitty Banks, 27 September 1842, Kent, England
    M. (2) Clara Grimes, 19 July 1905, Brisbane
    D. 4 August 1905, Brisbane
    Buried: Toowong Cemetery, Brisbane

KINGSFORD, Richard Ash   4
    B. 2 October 1821, Kent, England
    M. Sarah Southerden, 2 October 1851, Kent, England
    M. Emma Jane Dexter, 31 Aug 1892, Launceston, Tasmania
    D. 2 January, 1902, Cairns, Queensland

KOSVITZ, Augustus John   26
    B. 1831, Yauer, Prussia
    M. Elizabeth Mary Josephine Doyle, 20 October 1868, Brisbane (Rosvitz)
    D. 12 July 1894, Brisbane
    Buried: South Brisbane Cemetery, Brisbane, (Rosvitz)
    Arrival: *William Oswald*, 1855, Sydney, New South Wales

Cast of Characters

LADE, Nathaniel   30
    B. 20 March 1835, Kent, England
    M. Elizabeth Helen Bridges, 1859, Victoria
    D. 17 July 1895, Brisbane
    Buried: Toowong Cemetery, Brisbane

LENNEBERG, Isaac   23
    B. 10 August 1819 Lenhausen, Westphalia, Prussia
    M. (1) Sara Rosenberg
    M. (2) Amalia Simon
    D. 27 January 1910, Sydney, New South Wales
    Buried: Rookwood Cemetery, New South Wales
    Arrival: *Belle Creole*, Melbourne

MARKWELL, John   12, 25
    B. 10 August 1822, Horncastle, Lincolnshire, England
    M. (1) Mary Izard, 8 June 1841, Bloomsbury, England
    M. (2) Georgina Edmondstone, 8 August 1853, Brisbane
    M. (3) Harriet Hunt Beal, 13 June 1872, Brisbane
    D. 26 October 1881, Brisbane
    Buried: Toowong Cemetery, Brisbane
    Arrival: *Fortitude*, 1849

MASON, George Birbeck   27
    B. 29 Oct 1828, London, England
    M. Margaret Tomlins, 17 July 1852, Gosford New South Wales
    D. 2 October 1899, Thargomindah, Queensland

McADAM, George   22, 28
    B. 1826, Aberdeen, Scotland
    M. Mary McDonald, 14 February 1848, Sydney, New South Wales
    D. 13 December, Warwick, Queensland

MacDONALD, John   13
    B. ~1836, Nairn, Scotland
    M. (1) Alice Malcolm, 13 December 1860, Collingwood, Melbourne, Victoria
    M. (2) Louisa Elizabeth McPherson, Nairn, Scotland
    D. 18 June 1895, Brisbane
    Buried: Toowong Cemetery, Brisbane

PALMER, Benjamin Henry 29
  B. ~1834
  M. Mary Burke, 2 March 1861, Sydney, new South Wales
  D. 1894, Perth, Western Australia

SEYMOUR, David Thompson 8, 22
  B. 15 Nov 1832, Ballymore Castle, Galway, Ireland
  M. (1) Caroline Matilda Brown, 28 January 1864, Brisbane
  M. (2) Sara Stevenson, 6 June 1888, Melbourne, Victoria
  D. 1916 Chelsea, London, England

STEWART, Alexander 17, 18
  B. 4 August 1835, Caputh, Perthshire, Scotland
  M. (1) Maria Vine, 13 March 1862, Brisbane
  M. (2) Annie Killough, 27 February 1866, Brisbane
  M. (3) Edith Annie Best, 15 January 1907, Melbourne, Victoria
  D. 12 August 1918, Brisbane
  Buried: Toowong Cemetery, Brisbane

STEWART, Matthew 6
  B. 1809, Londonderry, Northern Ireland
  M. Honora Minogue, 29 January 1846, Brisbane
  D. 2 Dec 1873, Brisbane
  Arrival: *Waverly*, 1839, Sydney, *Curlew*, 1839, Brisbane

WALKER, Matthew 6
  B. 24 June 1809, Beith, Ayrshire, Scotland
  M. Jane Holliday, 17 Jul 1837, St Andrew's Presbyterian, Sydney, New South Wales
  D. 18 August 1882, Liverpool, New South Wales

Bibliography

Bartley, Nehemiah and Knight, J. J., *Australian Pioneers and Reminiscences: Together with portraits of some of the founders of Australia*, Ebook, Brisbane, Gordon and Gotch, 1986.
http://www.textqueensland.com.au/item/book/47a2c6b5172104e50ae1d25ea425ac3b

Barton, E. J. T. ed., *Jubilee History of Queensland: a record of political, industrial and social development from the landing of the first explorers to the close of 1909*, Ebook, Brisbane, Diddams, 1910.
http://www.textqueensland.com.au/item/book/7cbc3b9ff645a650586f93419c6ee34f

Brisbane History - A History of Old Brisbane to 1900, http://www.brisbane-history.com/

Brisbane History Group, *Brisbane by 1888: The Public Image*, Chelmer, Brisbane History Group, 1988

Calthorpe, K.D. & Capell, K., *Brisbane on Fire*, Moorooka, Ken Capell, 1997.

De Vries, Susanna and Jake, *Historic Brisbane, Convict Settlement to River City*, Chapel Hill, Qld, Pandanus Press, 2003.

Finger, Jarvis, *The St Helena Story*, Brisbane, Fernfawn Publications & Boolarong press, 2010.

Fisher, Rod, *The Best of Colonial Brisbane*, Moorooka, Boolarong Press, 2012.

Fisher, Rod, *Boosting Brisbane Imprinting the Colonial Capital of Queensland*, Moorooka, Boolarong Press, 2009.

Fisher, Rod and Harrison, Jennifer, *Brisbane: Squatters, Settlers & Surveyors*, Kelvin Grove, Brisbane History Group, 2000

Fox, Matthew J., *The History of Queensland: its people and industries*, Ebook, Brisbane, States Publishing Company, 1923.
http://www.textqueensland.com.au/item/book/26fad461fe61b9d3d31e147fca5c82e9

Gibson-Wilde, Dorothy M., *Gateway to a Holden Land: Townsville to 1884*, Townsville, James Cook University, 1985.

Greenwood, Gordon and Laverty, John, *Brisbane 1859 – 1958*, Brisbane, Brisbane City Council, 1959.

Hall, Thomas, *The Early History of Warwick District and Pioneers of the Darling Downs*, Ebook, Toowoomba, Robertson & Proven Ltd, 1925. http://www.textqueensland.com.au/item/book/83641e15c48af9bf76918134bcdf123a

Harrison, George, *A Jubilee History of Ipswich: a record of municipal, industrial and social progress*, Ebook, Brisbane, Diddams, 1910. http://www.textqueensland.com.au/item/book/18374483b66ed33be1a5914b7f8bcc5b

Hockings, Albert John, *The Flower Garden in Queensland*, Brisbane, Geo. Slater & Co., 1875

Hockings, Albert John, *Queensland Garden Manual*, Brisbane, Muir & Morcom, 1888

Hogan, Janet, *Historic Homes of Brisbane*, Brisbane, National Trust of Queensland, 1979.

Hopkins-Weise, Jeff and Pratt, Rod, 'The Scarlet legacy: the British Army's forgotten presence in Moreton Bay, 1860 – 69', *Sabretache : the journal of the Military Collectors Society of Australia.*, Vol 42, Issue 2, 2001, p3 – 39.

Horton, David and Raymond, Kerry, http://www.chapelhill.homeip.net/

Johnson, Beth, *Robert Cribb: from an Iceberg to Brisbane Town*, Auchenflower, Qld, Longleat House Publishing, 2005.

Johnson, Beth ,'Robert Cribb of Brisbane: His many faceted life', *Royal Historical Society of Queensland* Vol. 19, Issue 8, 2006.

Johnston, W Ross, *Brisbane The First 30 Years*, Bowen Hills, Boolarong Press, 1988.

Knight, J. J., *In the Early Days: History and Incident of Pioneer Queensland: with dictionary of dates in chronological order*, Ebook, Brisbane, Sapsford, 1895. http://www.textqueensland.com.au/item/book/0935f34247e5d647bab29c7d84bf367e

Knight, J. J., *Brisbane: a historical sketch of the capital of Queensland, giving an outline of old-time events, with a description of Brisbane of the present day, and a municipal retrospect*, Ebook, Brisbane, Biggs & Morcom, 1897. http://www.textqueensland.com.au/item/book/0136505eaa51dbcc3c0c68770bef1ef4

Larbelestier, Ken, *12th Regiment of Foot (East Suffolk)*, Ebook, 2010. http://twelfthregiment.info/wp/wp-content/uploads/Australian_Introduction.pdf

Laverty, John R, *The Making of a Metropolis: Brisbane 1823-1925*, Kelvin Grove, Brisbane History Group, 2009.

MacKenzie Smith, John, *Moreton Bay Scots 1841-59*, Nudgee, Church Archivists Press, 2000.

Morrison, W. Frederic, *The Aldine History of Queensland*, Ebook, Sydney, Aldine Pub. Co., 1888. http://www.textqueensland.com.au/item/book/de239c7c475e278f21e1545000094f2a

Norris, Merle, *Brisbane Hotels & Publicans Index 1842-1900*, Brisbane, Brisbane History Group, 1993.

Pugh, Theophilus P., *Pugh's Almanac 1863*, Brisbane, Theophilus Pugh, 1863.

Pugh, Theophilus P., *Pugh's Almanac 1864*, Brisbane, Theophilus Pugh, 1864.

Pugh, Theophilus P., *Pugh's Almanac 1865*, Brisbane, Theophilus Pugh, 1865.

Queensland Family History Society Inc., *Queensland Founding Families*, Indooroopilly, Queensland Family History Society Inc., 2009.

Roberts, Beryl, *He Made His Mark Joshua Jeays*, Brisbane, Boolarong Press, 2009.

Roberts, Timothy, 'An early jeweller in Queensland: the life and career of Augustus Kosvitz', *Australiana*, Vol.31, Issue 3, 2009, pp.4-8.

Russell, Henry Stuart, *A Genesis of Queensland*, Ebook, Sydney, Turner & Henderson, 1888. http://www.textqueensland.com.au/item/book/b86c5755be236c74a8fc29e7ae220cb6

Shaw, Barry, *Brisbane: People and Places of Ashgrove*, Brisbane, Brisbane History Group, 2010.

Siemon, Rosamund, *The Mayne Inheritance*, Brisbane, University of Queensland Press, 2000.

Smout, Arthur H., *Queensland Centenary The First 100 Years 1859 – 1959*, Brisbane, Penrod Publishers, 1959.

Steele, J. G., *Brisbane Town in Convict Days 1824 – 1842*, Brisbane, University of Queensland Press, 1987.

The Queensland Water Police, http://www.qldwaterpolice.com/history.html

Watson, Donald and McKay, Judith, *Brisbane Architects of the 19th Century, Brisbane*, Queensland Museum, 1994.

Webb ,E. A. H., *History of the 12th Regiment 1685-1913*, London, Spottiswoode & Co, 1914

Wendt, W. H., *Queensland, 1900: a narrative of her past, together with biographies of her leading men*, Ebook, Brisbane, Alcazar, 1900. http://www.textqueensland.com.au/item/book/a79ed4b0ea0e5169f68ca40626d3079a

www.ingramcontent.com/pod-product-compliance
Lightning Source LLC
Chambersburg PA
CBHW081847170426
43199CB00018B/2834